PRAIRIE HOME BREADS

PRAIRIE HOME BREADS

150 Splendid Recipes from America's Breadbasket

JUDITH M. FERTIG

THE HARVARD COMMON PRESS
BOSTON, MASSACHUSETTS

THE HARVARD COMMON PRESS
535 Albany Street
Boston, Massachusetts 02118

.... ⁂ ....

Printed in the United States of America

Printed on acid-free paper

Library of Congress Cataloging-in-Publication Data

Fertig, Judith M.
    Prairie home breads : 150 splendid recipes from America's breadbasket / Judith M. Fertig ;
illustrations by John MacDonald.
        p. cm.
    Includes index.
    ISBN 1-55832-172-1 (hc : alk. paper)
    1. Cookery (Bread) I. Title.

TX769.F477 2001
641.8'15—dc21   00-057510

Special bulk-order discounts are available on this and other Harvard Common Press books. Companies
and organizations may purchase books for premiums or resale, or may arrange a custom edition, by
contacting the Marketing Director at the address above.

Cover illustration by John MacDonald

Cover and interior design by Kathy Herlihy-Paoli, Inkstone Design

10 9 8 7 6 5 4 3 2 1

For my family,
the latest in a long line of bread bakers.

CONTENTS

ACKNOWLEDGMENTS

First of all, I wish to thank everyone who generously gave of their time and talents to help create this book, including my agent and friend Karen Adler, editors Dan Rosenberg and Judith Sutton, and everyone at The Harvard Common Press.

Thanks also to my mother and father, Jean and Jack Merkle, for researching our own family's bread-baking past and introducing me to schnecken on a visit to Cincinnati. My children, Sarah and Nick Fertig, for bravely suffering through an ongoing blizzard of flour and bowls of starter gurgling all over the house. My former sister-in-law Bev Fertig for making family gatherings so delicious with her homemade bread and rolls. All the great bakers I have met, and all the people who have helped me with wheat and bread stories for newspapers and national magazines, including: Lisa Grossman, Alvin Brensing, Jane Pigue, Susan Welling, Donna Grosko, Ted and Helen Walters, Don Coldsmith, everyone at Wheat-Fields Bakery, Jean Keneipp, Janice Cole, Colman Andrews and Christopher Hirsheimer, Linda Hodges, Bonnie Knauss, Debbie Givhan-Pointer, Gerry Kimmel-Carr, Bill Penzey, the Wenger family, Herb and Susan White, Emogene Harp, and Judy Pilewski.

When you want to make sure that every bread recipe is clear, concise, and ultimately successful, you need the help of a lot of people. My sincere thanks to Mary Pfeifer, Kim Fosbre, and the test kitchens of *Cooking Pleasures* and *Saveur* magazines for helping me test recipes formally. And to Dee Barwick, Karen Adler, Jean Merkle, and Julie Fox for helping me test recipes informally.

INTRODUCTION

I live and work in a part of the country that takes the phrase "daily bread" very seriously. Although I live in a suburb of Kansas City, wheat fields are only five minutes from my house. We are witness to the cycle of wheat, as much a part of our daily commute as the traffic report on the radio.

As we drive by the wheat fields in the fall, we see the seeds being drilled into the ground. (Winter wheat seeds are planted deep to survive the cold and stay moist.) By early November, the emerald-green wheat grass has sprouted after a chilly rainfall. During January and February, the dormant wheat grass stays green when every other grass has turned brown and sere. As the weather warms up in April, we know spring is here when the wheat starts to grow again. By early June, we're blessed to see a knee-high field of chartreuse-green wheat rustling in the breeze against a brilliant blue sky—one of my favorite sights. By late June, the wheat fields have turned golden, bordered with purple wildflowers and native sunflowers that are starting to reach toward the sky. Under the brilliant sunlight, I have to remind myself that this is Kansas, not the South of France. By early July, the harvest is complete, and the fields lie fallow.

That's when the business side of "daily bread" takes over. In rural communities, the journey from wheat field to grain elevator and flour mill is often a matter of minutes for the family farmers whose lives revolve around wheat, and whose dinner tables revolve around homemade bread.

In Kansas City, the wheat-growing cycle has become an integral part of other cycles. The milling and baking industry estimates that it takes approximately twelve people, from beginning to end, to produce one ten-pound bag of flour. Besides the farmer, production involves the trader, the writer, the grain elevator employees, the miller, and the grocer—before you scoop out the flour to make bread.

At the Kansas City Board of Trade, traders speculate on the quantity and quality of the grain harvest as wheat futures are bought and sold daily. The leading baking industry journal, *Milling and Baking News,* is headquartered nearby, where Sosland Publishing Company writers and editors can keep their fingers on the pulse of the business. Towering grain elevators, like prairie cathedrals, anchor the landscape along Southwest Boulevard and where the Missouri River flows under the concrete tangle of highways.

After storage, the wheat berries are milled into flour at mills owned by Archer Daniels Midland, General Mills, ConAgra, and Cereal Food Processors. Other local companies make vital wheat gluten from the kernels. The flour makes its way onto grocery store shelves or to huge commercial enterprises like Interstate Bakeries. And every day in Kansas City, traditional, ethnic, and artisanal bakeries turn out countless loaves of bread, feeding us with a true taste of home.

Symbolic of hearth and home, stability, and freedom from want, a good loaf of bread still speaks to us even in an age of relative affluence. The indescribable aroma of bread baking in the oven says "home" like nothing else. Its aroma triggers that primitive part of our brains that tells us that all is well. We're settled, safe, and secure—even when it's harder than ever to keep up with the ever-quickening pace of change. We know that we're never *really* settled anymore. But when we enjoy the sensual pleasure of bread warm from the oven, we *feel* settled. That's the power of good bread.

For the home baker, there is also the sense of accomplishment that comes from combining inert ingredients—water and flour—with a leavening agent to make something that changes so dramatically in texture, taste, and appearance. Nurturing a starter or levain over the course of several days and baking your first incredible loaf of Rustic French Bread (page 64) or Wheat-Fields Olive Bread (page 68) is a revelation. Recreating an antique loaf like Ozarks Salt-Rising Bread (page 78) or Sourdough Graham Bread (page 61) of the type that Abraham Lincoln and Mark Twain probably enjoyed connects you in a vital (and delicious) way with the past. Bringing a basket of warm homemade Herbed Squash Rolls (page 118) or Iowa Corn Clovers (page 119) to the table marks a celebration of friends and family. Baking, then eating a loaf of whole-grain Northern Prairie Barley Sunflower Bread (page 102) or Minnesota Wild Rice Bread (page 105) makes you feel virtuous and healthy. Serving a Biscuit-Topped Pheasant, Morel, and Corn Potpie (page 168) on a cold winter night warms you body and soul. Welcoming weekend guests with an Apple Custard Kuchen (page 199), Summery Lemon Coffee Cake with Fresh Berries (page 181), or a platter of flaky, rich Danish Pastry (page 182) on a Saturday morning turns a simple get-together into a memorable event. We all understand the language of bread.

In the course of developing and testing the recipes in this book, I also came to understand how flour, bread, and baking became essential ingredients in my family's recipe for happiness and well-being. During the late nineteenth century, my great-grandfather George Willenborg left northwestern Germany to settle in Cincinnati, Ohio. As a flour salesman, he called on a small grocery store and met a pretty young girl who did the meat cutting. Gertrude Rotherm was also a German immigrant, who had come from the same area as George. The two struck up a conversation each time he called on the store. After many more visits than flour sales actually warranted, the two-time widower and the feisty meat cutter were married. She raised his children by his two former wives, and they had three children of their own. George passed away when his daughter Gertrude, my grandmother, was a teenager.

Great-grandma, like other widows of her time left in similar circumstances, began to take boarders into her three-story Victorian home in Arlington Heights, Ohio. She baked—as well as cleaned, cooked, and laundered—for a houseful of people. When my grandmother married Raymond Vanderhorst—the boy across the street—she took her mother's recipe for Cloverleaf Rolls to her new household. She later passed the recipe on to my mother, my sister, and me.

My other great-grandfather, Benjamin Vanderhorst, was a second-generation Dutch immigrant who left Minster, Ohio, for Cincinnati in the early 1900s. During the Depression, out of work when the local shingle factory closed, he made a bold move. He took out a mortgage on the family home, bought two ovens, bags of flour, yeast, lard, and sugar, and started up a bakery in his house. Every week, he produced loaves of white bread and coffee cakes and sold them. He also made and sold delicious cloverleaf rolls, from my great-grandmother's recipe. When the Depression ended, Benjamin closed his in-home bakery, sold the house, and moved to Maineville, Ohio, to start a restaurant.

During the 1950s and '60s, my grandmother and mother rarely baked bread at home. They bought their bread, rolls, and coffee cakes from local Cincinnati bakeries like Servatii's, Osterhues, Wyoming, and Busken. The lunch boxes my sister and I carried contained peanut butter sandwiches made with butter-top bakery bread. On weekends we enjoyed kuchen-style coffee cake with a cherry filling and a crunchy, meringue-like topping. Sunday dinner at Grandma's always included buttery Parker House rolls. My first job in high school was working for the Wyoming Bakery after school and very early on Saturday mornings. But I didn't bake bread, either—I sliced it and wrapped it up for customers.

Our family's bread-baking history echoes much of America's. According to the King Arthur Flour Company, more than 90 percent of all-purpose flour produced at the time my great-grandfather was selling it was for baking bread at home. Today, only 8 percent is sold to home bakers. If this trend continues, could it mean that a simple bag of flour is destined for the specialty foods section of the gourmet shop?

I don't think so. Gradually, our family has come back to its roots and is baking bread again, although not always the same kinds our forebears made. My mother, Jean Vanderhorst Merkle, loves to make sourdough and Amish Pinwheel Bread (page 28), and she has a fondness for WheatFields Olive Bread (page 68). My sister, Julie Merkle Fox, enjoys making savory breads like Sun-Dried Tomato Bread (page 11) and Summertime Basil and Garlic Bread (page 9). My children's aunt, Bev Fertig, has made a version of Fly-off-the-Plate Rolls (page 122) for over twenty years, a "must-have"

at family gatherings. My daughter, Sarah, now in law school, loves using her automatic bread machine to mix yeast doughs when she needs a respite from the law library. In fact, mixing doughs in the bread machine has helped all of us bake bread from scratch even when our schedules are harried.

As my children leave home and our families are more spread out than ever, I find I place more emphasis on making bread, coffee cakes, and rolls from scratch. When we gather for meals now, it's a special occasion for all of us, deserving of the magical chemistry of yeast, flour, and water. There's just something about homemade bread, warm from the oven, that says, "You're home."

No matter where you live in North America, whenever you buy a bag of all-purpose or bread flour, you're getting a taste of my home—a taste of the prairie. A 150-million-acre inland sea of grass, the prairie once stretched from central Ohio westward to the Rockies and from the southernmost tip of Texas northward through the Prairie Provinces of Canada. Today, the prairie is essentially confined to the areas known as the American Midwest—Ohio, Indiana, Illinois, Michigan, Wisconsin, Minnesota, North Dakota, South Dakota, Iowa, Nebraska, Missouri, and Kansas—and the Canadian Prairie Provinces of Saskatchewan, Alberta, and Manitoba. Some of the original prairie is now city and town, ranch and industrial complex. But most of it is farmland.

More than 90 percent of the all-purpose and bread flour produced in the United States and Canada originates in the wheat fields of the prairie, the Breadbasket of North America. Besides wheat grown in Kansas, the Midwest contributes cornmeal, barley, rye, oats, soy, durum wheat, and wild rice, to create unique and truly delicious breads. Cheddar from Wisconsin, Maytag Blue cheese from Iowa, hand-crafted beers from Heartland micro-breweries, native pecans and black walnuts from Missouri and Kansas groves, and dried tart cherries from Michigan add their own wonderful flavors.

In the pages of *Prairie Home Breads*, you'll find more than 150 recipes that celebrate the wonderful bounty that is the Heartland's claim to fame. From artisanal and small-town bakeries, the best home bread bakers, and my own family's kitchen, these coffee cakes, yeast rolls, doughnuts, pastries, quick breads, muffins, biscuits, flatbreads, crackers, and naturally leavened and yeast breads of all kinds display the stunning diversity America's Breadbasket offers. Drawing on the bread-baking traditions of many ethnic groups, *Prairie Home Breads* translates the language of bread into one we all can understand, with easy-to-follow step-by-step instructions. *Prairie Home Breads* also allows you to savor every last crumb and crust with recipes that transform

leftover bread into wonderful appetizers, salads, bread puddings, and desserts. And it offers accompaniments such as jams and jellies, chutney, fondue, and savory spreads as well.

As you might have discovered in *Prairie Home Cooking*, there are always more stories to tell in our shared kitchen. So I welcome you back with *Prairie Home Breads*, this time for a slice of homemade bread or fragrant coffee cake still warm from the oven.

BREAD-BAKING TIPS AND TECHNIQUES

BREAD-BAKING MAGIC

Whenever I bake bread, I marvel at how basic ingredients mixed in the right way can produce something so delicious. Flour, water, and yeast combine to make a soft dough that rises—sometimes dramatically. You can form that mass of dough into any number of shapes. And once it's baked, the spongy dough is transformed into a loaf with crust and crumb and even more culinary possibilities. That's kitchen magic at its best.

Bread-baking magic, like the pulling-a-rabbit-out-of-a-hat kind, relies on a few fundamentals. The recipes in *Prairie Home Breads* reflect a wide variety of these techniques. Once you've understood and mastered them, you can make any bread, coffee cake, quick bread, biscuit, or roll recipe.

Certain combinations of ingredients will produce unique flavor and texture characteristics in your bread or rolls. Temperature is crucial, for proofing the yeast, for letting the dough rise, and for knowing when your bread is done. The culinary magician has just the tool to make checking the temperature look easy—an instant-read thermometer. Likewise, kneading is essential to getting bread with the right texture. Each recipe has a suggested kneading time, but you'll know that you've reached the right stage when the dough is elastic and not sticky anymore. Most bread recipes call for two rising times: one for the dough after it has been kneaded, and the second and shorter time for after the loaf has been formed. How the loaf is baked—in a loaf pan or on a baking stone, misted with water or not, at a high or medium temperature—also helps create a signature bread.

As in *The Wizard of Oz*, here's a glimpse of the "man behind the curtain"—the techniques that produce the magic.

CHECKING THE TEMPERATURE At the beginning of the bread-baking process, use an instant-read thermometer to check the temperature of the liquid used for proofing the yeast. The liquid should be lukewarm or warm—usually 110 degrees—no hotter than 130 degrees, or the yeast will die. At the end of the bread-baking process, use an instant-read thermometer to check the doneness of the bread. An internal temperature of 190 to 200 degrees usually guarantees that the bread is done.

PROOFING The first step in making bread is proofing the yeast to make sure the yeast is active. When you combine active dry (not instant) yeast with a warm liquid, it should start to bubble and turn an opaque beige after 5 minutes. If this does not happen, start again, using a fresh package or jar of yeast.

MIXING Usually the liquid ingredients in a dough are mixed together first, along with the proofed yeast. Then the dry ingredients are added, a little at a time, using just enough flour to make a dough that will hold together. You may need to use more or less flour than a bread recipe calls for, depending on variables like the moisture content of the flour or the dryness/humidity of your kitchen.

KNEADING Sprinkle a work surface with flour. Place the dough on the surface, pat it into a ball, and dust it with flour. Flatten the dough into a rough oval and fold it in half. With the heel of your hand, press and push the dough away from you. Turn the dough a quarter turn and repeat the folding, pressing, and pushing motions; continue until the dough is smooth and elastic.

RISING When you place dough in an oiled or greased bowl, turn it over once to coat the top as well as the bottom with a little oil. This will prevent the top of the dough from cracking as it rises. Cover the bowl with plastic wrap or a moistened clean tea towel (or use a plastic container with an airtight lid). If you can't tell by looking if the dough has doubled in size, check by quickly poking your fingers 1/2 inch into the dough. If the dents stay, the dough has risen enough. The gluten is strong and elastic, and yeast fermentation has produced air pockets in the dough.

PUNCHING DOWN With your fist, punch the center of the dough down so it deflates. Then turn the dough over and cover again for another rise, or proceed as directed in the recipe. This step is necessary in some recipes to rid the dough of excess carbon dioxide.

SHAPING To form a loaf, pat the dough into a flat oval. Fold the long right and left sides over to meet in the middle. Starting from the top, roll up the dough like a jelly roll, using your thumbs to keep the roll tight. Then use your hands to shape the cylinder of dough to fit the loaf pan. Press the long seam together and pinch the ends closed. Place seam side down in the loaf pan.

To form a round loaf, pat the dough into a round, turning any rough edges under.

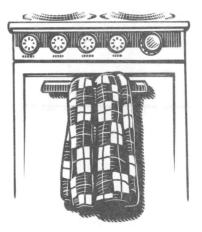

BAKING Always allow enough time for the oven and baking stones or tiles to preheat. Darker baking pans will produce a darker-colored crust; lighter pans a lighter-colored crust. For best results, place baking pans in the middle of the oven. Placing loaf pans or the dough itself on a preheated baking stone or tiles will produce an evenly baked loaf with an evenly colored crust. Misting the dough with water or placing a pan of boiling water on the lower oven rack while the bread is baking helps promote a shiny, crisp, attractively blistered crust. Brushing the top of the loaf with an egg glaze lends glossiness to the crust. Brushing the top of the loaf with melted butter after it is removed from the oven produces a softer, buttery crust.

FREEZING AND REHEATING BREAD, COFFEE CAKES, AND ROLLS After your baked goods are out of the oven and have cooled, you can freeze them by wrapping them well in aluminum foil and then placing them in zippered plastic freezer bags. With a marker, write the type of bread and the date on the outside of the freezer bag. Bread, rolls, and coffee cakes are best frozen for up to three months.

Baked goods taste best when reheated from frozen. When you want to reheat, first preheat the oven to 350 degrees. Remove the still-frozen bread, coffee cake, or rolls from the plastic bag, but keep them in the foil. Place the foil packet on a baking sheet to thaw and warm in the oven for at least 20 to 30 minutes.

YEAST OF THE NEW EDEN

Yeast is the essence of traditional homemade bread, what makes it aromatic and delicious. Each package of yeast contains thousands of tiny microorganisms. When nurtured by warm liquid and sugar and starch, yeast cells begin to bubble, releasing carbon dioxide gas. This process is what makes bread rise—and beer foam.

Before there were packaged yeasts, homemakers had to make a leavening of flour mixed with water and left to ferment naturally. Austrian-Hungarian immigrants to Missouri changed all of that. In 1868, brothers Charles and Maximilian Fleischmann transformed their yearning for the softer-textured breads of their family into a new yeast technology. Charles had been trained in commercial yeast production in Europe, and he helped introduce the technology in America. Along with American businessman Charles Graff, the Fleischmanns developed and patented a way to make cakes of compressed fresh yeast and built a plant in Cincinnati to produce this revolutionary new way to leaven bread reliably. During World War II, the company developed a way to dry yeast for the armed forces. Because fresh compressed yeast cakes require refrigeration, packets of dry yeast were much better suited to wartime conditions. A living organism, yeast goes into a dormant phase but is not killed when it is dried. Each yeast manufacturer uses a different strain of yeast with varying characteristics, so baking recipes usually specify a certain kind of yeast for best results.

INSTANT YEAST—a newer type of yeast with finer granules blended with ascorbic acid, or Vitamin C, to provide the ideal conditions for yeast to grow. No need to proof this yeast with water first: just add it to the recipe. It's also called rapid-rise or quick-rising yeast.

ACTIVE DRY YEAST—a yeast dried at higher temperatures, and with larger granules, than instant yeast. Active dry yeast requires an initial blending with lukewarm water to proof, or activate.

BREAD MACHINE YEAST—finer-grained instant yeast that does not need to be proofed. It is usually the last ingredient added to the automatic bread machine.

FRESH YEAST—professional bakers sometimes use moist, fresh cakes of compressed yeast, which must be kept refrigerated.

DOUGH ENHANCERS

Dough enhancers do more than just help dough rise higher. They can also help produce a moister loaf with a browner crust, give the bread a finer texture and flavor, and extend the shelf life of homemade bread. By adding certain ingredients to a basic flour-leavening-and-water dough, you can create the characteristics you want in the resulting loaf. Commercially available powdered dough enhancers (see Source Guide, page 215) usually contain lecithin, ascorbic acid, and vital wheat gluten.

LECITHIN—derived from soybeans, helps bread stay fresh longer.

ASCORBIC ACID (vitamin C)—helps yeast work efficiently.

VITAL WHEAT GLUTEN—a concentrated protein derived from wheat flour (not the same as wheat gluten, which is a combination of flour and vital wheat gluten), improves the rise and texture of bread.

NONDIASTATIC MALT—derived from barley, contributes to a softer, more tender crumb.

DRIED GINGER—helps boost the activity of yeast.

FATS—contribute to taste and texture.

DAIRY PRODUCTS

MILK—contributes to a browner crust, a moist texture, and the flavor of the bread.

DRIED WHEY—derived from buttermilk, helps yeast work efficiently and helps bread stay fresh longer.

BUTTERMILK—helps yeast work quickly and vigorously.

EGGS—contribute to the rise, taste, color, and texture of the bread.

SCALDING

Many sweet yeast bread or roll recipes using fresh milk call for scalding, which means to heat milk almost to the simmering point. The reason for doing this is to deactivate a protease enzyme in milk that inhibits yeast activity. Pasteurization does not render protease inactive, but scalding does. Sweet doughs are often rich with butter and eggs, which also slow down yeast activity. Scalded milk, with its disabled protease, helps yeast to do its work a little more easily. Often butter or lard and sugar are added to the scalded milk. When it has cooled to lukewarm, the milk, or the milk mix-

ture, is combined with yeast, eggs, and flour to make light and airy sweet bread or rolls.

HOW HOT IS LUKEWARM?

Experienced bakers can tell by feel when a liquid is lukewarm. Since yeast is killed by temperatures higher than 130 degrees, beginning bread bakers would be wise to use an instant-read thermometer for recipes that call for starting yeast in lukewarm water. Liquid that is tepid (80 degrees) or lukewarm (90 to just below 110 degrees) is considered safe for yeast to proof.

HAS THE DOUGH RISEN ENOUGH?

Most recipes call for allowing the dough to rise until doubled in bulk. How can you know for sure when this has occurred? The time it takes for the dough to double in bulk can depend on the temperature as well as the amount and type of ingredients in the recipe. Rather than just relying on how the dough looks, press two fingers about 1/2 inch into the top of the dough. If it feels light and spongy and the depressions remain in the dough, then the dough has risen sufficiently.

ADAPTING RECIPES FOR THE AUTOMATIC BREAD MACHINE

Make sure that the bread pan (1-pound, 1 1/2-pound, or 2-pound capacity) in your bread machine will accommodate the volume of the bread recipe. As a general rule, recipes that call for 2 cups of flour will make a 1-pound loaf; for 3 cups, a 1 1/2-pound loaf; for 4 cups, a 2-pound loaf. Make sure there is enough room in the bread pan for the dough to double in volume.

The automatic bread machine can be used just to mix and knead a dough, using the Dough cycle. The dough will go through the first rise in the bread machine. Then you can turn the dough out onto a floured surface, form it into a loaf by hand, let it rise a second time, and bake it in the oven. I find that using the bread machine to mix and knead the dough produces a superior loaf in the bread recipes that I have indicated with the symbol ▢ . It's best to use a sturdy electric stand mixer to mix heavier whole-grain doughs.

• Add the ingredients to the bread pan of the bread machine in the order indicated in the manufacturer's instruction manual. Usually, that sequence is liquids first (water, milk, honey, eggs, etc.), then dry ingredients such as sugar and flour, and last, instant or bread machine yeast.

• Substitute instant or bread machine yeast for the active dry yeast called for in your recipe, because instant or bread machine yeast does not need to be dissolved in a liquid first to start its action.

• Check the dough in the bread machine after about 5 minutes into the Knead cycle. If it is too dry, add liquid—about 1 tablespoon at a time. If it is too wet, add flour—1 tablespoon at a time. By about 10 minutes into the Knead cycle, the dough should have formed a ball that leaves the sides of the bread pan.

YEAST BREADS

SHAKER DAILY BREAD

In the Shaker community of North Union Village, Ohio, established in 1822 in what is now Cleveland, the kitchen sisters rose at four during the summer and five in winter to begin baking bread. First the ovens had to be fired up, then the dough that had been set out to rise overnight in large dough trays had to be formed into thirty or more loaves, baked, and allowed to cool before the noontime meal. More dough was made in the afternoon, and the whole process repeated.

The virtues of this bread, adapted from a recipe in Amy Bess Miller and Persis Fuller's *The Best of Shaker Cooking*, are much like those of the Shakers who made it. The dough will not be rushed, as the yeast is used sparingly. It rises slowly but reliably, at its own pace, patient and persistent. In a cool place, it could be covered and allowed to rise even more slowly overnight, true to the original Shaker practice. The dough is easy to work with and produces a crusty, finely textured loaf. Although the Shakers believed that eating bread hot out of the oven was an unhealthy practice, I have often succumbed to temptation and eaten a slice of the warm bread with a little homemade butter and Old-Fashioned Quince Preserves (page 12).

MAKES 2 LOAVES

HOME

It is the place of renewal and of safety, where for a little while there will be no harm nor attack and, while every sense is nourished, the soul rests.
—MAY SARTON

---

1 (1/4-ounce) package (2 1/2 teaspoons)
   active dry yeast
1/4 cup warm (110 degrees) water
1 3/4 cups milk
3 tablespoons unsalted butter, cut into
   3 pieces
2 tablespoons sugar
2 teaspoons salt
5 to 5 1/2 cups unbleached all-purpose flour
Melted butter, for brushing

1. IN A LARGE BOWL, sprinkle the yeast over the warm water; set aside to proof until foamy, about 5 minutes. Scald the milk (heat it until small bubbles form around the edges) in a small saucepan, then add the butter and sugar and stir until the butter melts. Remove from the heat and set aside to cool to lukewarm (80 to 90 degrees).

2. ADD THE MILK MIXTURE to the yeast mixture. With a wooden spoon or a Danish dough whisk, beat in 5 cups of the flour, 1 cup at a time, until you have a smooth dough, adding more flour if necessary.

3. TURN THE DOUGH OUT onto a floured surface and knead for 10 minutes, or until smooth and elastic. Place the dough in a large oiled bowl and brush the top with a little melted butter. Cover with plastic wrap and let rise in a warm place until doubled in bulk, 1 1/2 to 2 hours.

4. GREASE TWO 9-BY-5-BY-3-INCH LOAF PANS and set aside. Punch down the dough and transfer it to a floured surface. Cut it in half with a serrated knife and form it into two loaves. Place the dough in the prepared loaf pans and brush the tops with a little melted butter. Cover with plastic wrap and let rise in a warm place until doubled in bulk, 1 1/2 to 2 hours.

5. PREHEAT THE OVEN to 400 degrees. Bake the bread for 30 minutes, or until the loaves are browned on top and sound hollow when lightly tapped on the bottom; an instant-read thermometer inserted into the center should register 190 to 200 degrees. Cool in the pans or on a wire rack.

 The automatic bread machine symbol indicates that the dough for this recipe can be made in an automatic bread machine. Add the ingredients to the bread pan following the manufacturer's directions. Make the dough using the Dough Cycle, including the first rise. Then, remove the dough from the bread pan and proceed with the recipe. This symbol is repeated throughout the book wherever this procedure may be followed.

QUICKSILVER BREAD

In Mark Twain's Huckleberry Finn, *the townsfolk have launched several fine loaves of bread embedded with mercury into the river in the belief that the loaves will locate a drowning victim—supposedly, Huck himself. When Huck spots the floating loaves coming toward him on the other side of the river, he recognizes his chance to eat something good for a change: "A big double loaf come along, and I most got it with a long stick, but my foot slipped and she floated out further....But by and by along comes another one, and this time I won. I took out the plug and shook out this little dab of quicksilver, and set my teeth in. It was 'baker's bread'—what the quality eat; none of your low-down cornpone."*

SUMMER GARDEN MOLDED BREAD SALAD WITH GARLIC AND LEMON VINAIGRETTE

When I was working at the Shelburne Museum in Vermont one summer, I got to know a remarkable Frenchwoman who always made a version of this molded bread salad for her lunch. Every day it was delicious and different, depending on what was at its peak in her garden. It's important to assemble this early in the day, then weight it down so all the flavors have several hours to mingle, like a savory summer pudding. Let your summer garden inspire even more variations.

SERVES 6 TO 8

FOR THE SALAD:
1 loaf Shaker Daily Bread (page 3), Nonna's Italian Bread (page 15), Italian Bread Imperiale (page 16), Old-Fashioned Buttermilk Bread (page 41), or a good bakery loaf
1 sprig arugula or fresh tarragon
1/2 cup extra virgin olive oil
1 cup small yellow pear tomatoes, cut in half lengthwise
2 tablespoons fresh tarragon leaves
Salt and freshly ground black pepper to taste
1 lemon, halved
1 small cucumber, peeled, halved, seeded, and thinly sliced
4 sprigs fresh dill

1 large ripe red tomato, thickly sliced, or
   1 cup canned plum tomatoes, chopped
6 fresh basil leaves

FOR THE GARLIC AND LEMON
   VINAIGRETTE:
1 large garlic clove, minced
1 teaspoon fine sea salt
3 tablespoons extra virgin olive oil
1 tablespoon fresh lemon juice

Baby lettuces, for garnish

1. LINE A 9-BY-5-BY-3-INCH LOAF PAN with plastic wrap so that the plastic wrap hangs over at least 6 inches on both long sides. Slice off the rounded top of the bread (reserve for another use, if desired). Slice the bread horizontally into 4 equal slices. Place the sprig of arugula or tarragon in the bottom of the loaf pan (it will be on top of the salad when it is unmolded).

2. BRUSH THE TOP SLICE of bread on both sides with olive oil and place in the pan. Arrange the yellow tomatoes and tarragon on top of the bread. Season to taste with salt and pepper and a squeeze of lemon juice. Brush a second slice of bread on both sides with olive oil and place on top of the tomatoes. Arrange the cucumber and dill on top of the bread. Season to taste with salt and pepper and another squeeze of lemon juice. Brush a third slice of bread on both sides with olive oil and place on top of the cucumber. Arrange the tomatoes and basil leaves on top of the bread. Season to taste with salt and pepper and a squeeze of lemon juice. Brush the cut side of the last slice of bread with olive oil and place cut side down on top of the tomatoes and basil. Wrap the pan well with plastic wrap and place a heavy can or a brick on top to weight the salad down. Let sit at room temperature

HOME

They say Home . . . is where when you go . . . they have to take you in. I rather prefer Home . . . when you could go anywhere . . . is the place you prefer to be.
—NIKKI GIOVANNI, SACRED COWS . . . AND OTHER EDIBLES

for 4 hours, or until the juices have risen to the top.

3. MAKE THE GARLIC AND LEMON VINAIGRETTE: Mash the garlic and salt to a fine paste in a mortar with pestle. Using the pestle, blend in the olive oil and lemon juice. (This also makes enough to dress a green salad to serve 6 to 8.)

4. UNWRAP THE PAN and invert the bread salad onto a cutting board. Slice into 6 or 8 portions. Arrange on salad plates, garnished with baby lettuces. Drizzle about 1 1/2 teaspoons of the vinaigrette over each salad, and serve.

CHALLAH

In September, Rosh Hashanah, the Day of Judgment, begins the New Year in the Jewish religious calendar. The ten-day observance, revolving around the themes of judgment, repentance, and renewal, ends with a fast day on Yom Kippur, the Day of Atonement. Throughout this time, the faithful examine their hearts to see if they need to make amends to another person or to God. As families gather to feast on Rosh Hashanah or after the Yom

Kippur fast is broken, they share foods made with honey to signify sweetness in the New Year, and foods that are round to signify a year with no endings.

When this airy, tender egg bread with a sweet touch of honey is baked as a round loaf instead of the traditional braided one, it can start the year—or the day—off right. Challah is delicious toasted, or made into bread pudding.

MAKES 1 LOAF

1 cup warm (110 degrees) water
1/2 cup honey
2 (1/4-ounce) packages (1 1/2 tablespoons)
    active dry yeast
2 tablespoons vegetable oil
1 large egg
1 teaspoon salt
3 1/2 to 4 cups bread flour
1/2 cup raisins, optional
1 large egg, beaten, for egg glaze
Sesame seeds or poppy seeds, optional,
    for sprinkling

1. IN THE BOWL OF AN ELECTRIC MIXER or another large bowl, stir the warm water and honey together. Sprinkle the yeast over the top and set aside to proof until foamy, about 5 minutes.

2. USING THE PADDLE ATTACHMENT or a wooden spoon, beat the vegetable oil, egg, and salt into the yeast mixture. Gradually beat in the flour, 1/2 cup at a time, until you have a soft dough.

3. USING THE DOUGH HOOK, knead the dough for several minutes, until smooth and shiny, adding more flour if necessary. Or transfer the dough to a floured surface and knead by hand. Knead in the optional raisins.

4. GREASE A BAKING SHEET. Form the dough into a round loaf and place it on the baking sheet. Cover with plastic wrap and let rise in a warm place until doubled in bulk, 1 to 1 1/2 hours.

5. PREHEAT THE OVEN to 350 degrees. Brush the dough with the egg glaze and sprinkle with sesame seeds or poppy seeds, if desired. Bake for 30 to 35 minutes, until the loaf sounds hollow when tapped on the bottom; an instant-read thermometer inserted into the center should register 190 to 200 degrees. Transfer to a wire rack to cool.

VARIATION: For Braided Challah, in Step 4, divide the dough into 3 pieces. With your hands, roll each portion into a 16-inch-long rope. Lay the ropes out side by side on a floured surface so that they are very close, but not touching. Braid the 3 ropes together snugly. Tuck the ends under to form an oblong loaf about 12 inches long. Place the dough on the greased baking sheet and proceed as directed.

THE TOASTS OF THE TOWN

Good homemade or bakery bread can be the basis of many delicious appetizers or light snacks. Whether you call them bruschetta, panini, or just plain "toasts," there's a taste for everyone and every season.

Rye bread toasts with acorn squash and fried sage

Semolina bread toasts with Maytag Blue cheese and ground cherry preserves

Smoked whitefish on Danish pumpernickel rye toast

Toasted Wisconsin onion and dill bread with aged Cheddar and butter

Rye bread toasts with grilled brats, homemade sauerkraut, and fresh horseradish

Creamed fresh morels and asparagus on buttered buttermilk bread toast

Toasts with roasted pheasant breast and cranberry-chokecherry conserve

Cinnamon toast challah with mascarpone and fresh pear slices

HEIRLOOM APPLE CHARLOTTE

When making homemade bread was a time-consuming art, Midwestern cookbooks were full of ways to make sure not a crumb was wasted. This country recipe, a cousin of summer pudding with French and English roots, made its way first to New England and then westward to the prairie. It's delicious made with Challah (page 5), The Miller's Cinnamon and Raisin Bread (page 20), Pecan Brioche (page 33), or Shaker Daily Bread (page 3). The buttery apple scent of the charlotte as it bakes is a tantalizing forecast of the wonderful taste to come.

SERVES 6 TO 8

12 tablespoons (1 1/2 sticks) plus
  1 tablespoon unsalted butter
6 to 8 slices stale bread, crusts removed
1/4 to 1/2 cup (to taste) plus 1 tablespoon
  sugar
1 1/2 pounds Golden Delicious apples,
  peeled, cored, and diced
1/4 cup water
1 teaspoon instant tapioca
Whipped cream, optional, for garnish

1. PREHEAT THE OVEN to 400 degrees. Melt 12 tablespoons (1 1/2 sticks) of the butter in a small saucepan. Line a sieve with dampened cheesecloth and strain the clarified butter into a bowl.

2. TRIM THE BREAD AS NECESSARY to line the bottom and sides of a charlotte mold or 1-quart ovenproof bowl; cut enough of the remaining bread to make a "lid" for the filled mold. Brush the inside of the mold or bowl with the clarified butter and sprinkle with 1 tablespoon of the sugar. Line the bottom and sides of the mold with the bread, brushing the slices on both sides with the clarified butter. Set aside.

3. MELT THE REMAINING 1 TABLESPOON BUTTER in a large saucepan over low heat. Add the apples, 1/4 cup of the remaining sugar, the water, and tapioca and cook until the apples are soft and pulpy, but not watery, about 10 minutes. Taste and add more sugar if necessary, stirring until it dissolves. Remove from the heat.

4. POUR THE APPLE FILLING into the bread-lined mold. Put the bread "lid" on top and bake for 20 minutes or until the top is golden brown. Let cool for several minutes.

5. TO SERVE, invert the charlotte onto a serving platter. Slice into wedges and serve with dollops of whipped cream, if desired.

CHEDDAR CHIVE BREAD

Whether you get your herbs from the garden or from the grocery, this no-knead bread is a good excuse to use them. Use an aged Cheddar for its depth of flavor. If you're new to baking yeast bread, this is a good recipe to start with—and the results will have you hooked.

MAKES 2 LOAVES

2 (1/4-ounce) packages (11/2 tablespoons) active dry yeast
2 tablespoons sugar
2 cups lukewarm (90 degrees) water
2 teaspoons salt
2 tablespoons unsalted butter, softened
11/2 cups plus 2 tablespoons finely grated aged Cheddar cheese, preferably from Wisconsin
1/2 cup snipped fresh chives
41/2 cups all-purpose flour

1. IN A LARGE BOWL, sprinkle the yeast and sugar over the water; set aside to proof until foamy, about 5 minutes.

2. WITH A WOODEN SPOON, beat the salt, butter, 11/2 cups of the Cheddar, and the chives into the yeast mixture until very smooth. Beat in the flour, 1/2 cup at a time, until you have a soft and somewhat sticky dough. Cover the bowl with plastic wrap and let rise in a warm place until doubled in bulk, about 1 hour.

3. GREASE TWO 9-BY-5-BY-3-INCH LOAF PANS and set aside. Stir down the dough and beat well for 1 minute. Transfer the dough to a floured surface and cut it in half. Place each half in a prepared loaf pan and smooth the top. Sprinkle the tops of the loaves with the remaining 2 tablespoons Cheddar. Cover with plastic wrap and let rise in a warm place until doubled in bulk, about 45 minutes.

4. PREHEAT THE OVEN to 375 degrees. Bake the bread for 30 minutes, or until the loaves are golden brown on top and sound hollow when tapped on the bottom; an instant-read thermometer inserted into the center should register 190 to 200 degrees. Cool in the pans on a wire rack.

.... ✤✤✤ ....

SUMMERTIME BASIL AND GARLIC BREAD

✤✤✤

When the garden is full of fresh basil, make Basil and Garlic Oil, the secret of this herb-flecked bread. The flavored oil can be made ahead and kept in the refrigerator for up to a day or frozen indefinitely—a great way to capture the essence of summer for wintertime use. The aroma of this bread as it rises and then bakes is absolutely wonderful.

MAKES 1 LOAF

FOR THE BASIL AND GARLIC OIL:
1 cup packed fresh basil leaves
6 garlic cloves, peeled

¹/₄ cup olive oil

1¹/₄ cups warm (110 degrees) water
2 teaspoons sugar
1 (¹/₄-ounce) package (2¹/₄ teaspoons)
    active dry yeast
1 teaspoon salt
3¹/₂ cups all-purpose flour

1. MAKE THE OIL: Place the basil and garlic in the bowl of a food processor and process for 30 seconds, or until the basil is very finely chopped but not pureed. With the machine running, slowly drizzle in the oil. Transfer to a bowl, cover, and set aside. (The oil is best made at least an hour before baking to allow the flavors to blend.)

2. IN THE BOWL OF AN ELECTRIC MIXER or another large bowl, combine the warm water and sugar. Sprinkle the yeast over the top and set aside to proof until foamy, about 5 minutes. With the paddle attachment or a wooden spoon, beat the basil oil and salt into the yeast mixture, then beat in the flour, 1 cup at a time, until you have a soft dough.

3. TURN THE DOUGH OUT onto a floured surface and knead for 8 to 10 minutes, until smooth and elastic. Place the dough in a large oiled bowl and turn to coat. Cover with plastic wrap and let rise in a warm place until doubled in bulk, 1 to 1¹/₂ hours.

4. GREASE A 9-BY-5-BY-3-INCH LOAF PAN. Punch down the dough and turn it out onto a floured surface. Form the dough into a loaf and place it in the prepared pan. Cover with plastic wrap and let rise in a warm place for 30 minutes, or until almost doubled in bulk.

5. PREHEAT THE OVEN to 350 degrees. Bake the bread for 30 to 35 minutes, or until it is golden brown on top and sounds hollow when tapped on the bottom; an instant read thermometer inserted into the center should register 190 to 200 degrees. Let cool in the pan on a rack.

VARIATION: For Summertime Basil and Garlic Rolls, in Step 4, grease a 12-cup muffin tin. With a serrated knife, cut the dough into 12 portions. Form into rolls and place in the prepared muffin tin. Cover with plastic wrap and let rise for 30 minutes, or until almost doubled in bulk. Bake the rolls for 15 to 20 minutes, or until risen and lightly browned on top. Transfer to a wire rack to cool.

ROASTED SWEET PEPPER BREAD

In Lou Jane Temple's culinary mystery *Bread on Arrival*, Midwestern chef and reluctant sleuth Heaven Lee decides to enter a bread-baking contest. You just know that before you turn too many pages, someone will end up dead in the dough. This bread, delicious with a creamy goat cheese spread slathered on it, was adapted from one served at Temple's fictional Café Heaven.

If you have a stoneware bowl, use it to simulate an artisanal bakery oven for this recipe. After you slide the dough onto the pre-heated baking stone, carefully cover the dough with the inverted bowl. Baking the loaf covered gives it a wonderfully crisp, blistered crust.

MAKES 1 LOAF

1 red bell pepper
1 yellow bell pepper
1/4 cup olive oil
1 teaspoon kosher salt
2 teaspoons active dry yeast
1 1/4 cups warm (110 degrees) water
4 cups bread flour
2 teaspoons salt
Yellow cornmeal, for dusting

1. TO ROAST THE PEPPERS, preheat the oven to 350 degrees. Place the peppers in a shallow baking dish, drizzle with 2 tablespoons of the olive oil, and sprinkle with the kosher salt. Cover the pan with foil and bake for 40 to 50 minutes, or until the peppers are soft. Let cool, then remove the cores, seeds, and skins. Finely chop the peppers and set aside.

2. IN A LARGE BOWL, sprinkle the yeast over the warm water and set aside to proof until foamy, about 5 minutes. With a wooden spoon or a Danish dough whisk, stir in the peppers and oil, then stir in the flour, 1 cup at a time, and salt.

3. TURN THE DOUGH OUT onto a floured surface and knead for about 5 minutes, until smooth and elastic. Place the dough in a large oiled bowl and turn to coat. Cover with plastic wrap and let rise in a warm place until doubled in bulk, about 1 hour.

4. SPRINKLE A COOKIE SHEET (without sides) generously with cornmeal. Punch down the dough and form it into a round loaf. Place on

the prepared baking sheet, cover with plastic wrap, and let rise in a warm place until doubled in bulk, about 1 hour.

5. ABOUT 30 MINUTES BEFORE BAKING, place a baking stone or tiles on the middle rack of the oven and preheat the oven to 450 degrees. Just before baking, place a pan of boiling water on the bottom oven rack.

6. CAREFULLY PULL OUT THE MIDDLE OVEN RACK and, using a wooden peel, or with a quick jerk of your arms, slide the loaf off the baking sheet onto the stone. With a plastic spray bottle, mist the dough. Close the oven door and immediately turn the heat down to 400 degrees. Bake, misting the bread twice more, for 35 minutes, or until the loaf is lightly browned and sounds hollow when tapped on the bottom; an instant-read thermometer inserted into the center should register 190 to 200 degrees. Transfer the loaf to a wire rack to cool.

SAVORY SUN-DRIED TOMATO BREAD

On a gray February weekend, when August seems far away, open a jar of sun-dried tomatoes preserved in oil to make this bread tasting of hot sun, ripe tomatoes, and summer herbs. Then brush the snow off the grill and cook a steak over the coals—along with the first early-season asparagus—to cast a culinary spell for warmer weather to come. My version of this bread was adapted from a recipe from Heart of the Prairie Bakery in West Des Moines, Iowa.

MAKES 2 ROUND LOAVES

1 ($^{1}/_{4}$-ounce) package (2$^{1}/_{4}$ teaspoons)
   active dry yeast
$^{1}/_{4}$ cup warm (110 degrees) water
1 cup water
$^{1}/_{2}$ cup coarsely chopped oil-packed
   sun-dried tomatoes, drained;
   reserve 1 tablespoon of the oil
1 teaspoon salt
3 to 3$^{1}/_{2}$ cups unbleached all-purpose flour
1 large egg, beaten
2 tablespoons finely chopped green onion
2 garlic cloves, minced
2 tablespoons finely chopped fresh Italian
   parsley
1 large egg white, beaten, for egg glaze

1. IN A LARGE BOWL, sprinkle the yeast over the warm water; set aside to proof until foamy, about 5 minutes. In a small saucepan, heat the 1 cup water, the reserved sun-dried tomato oil, and the salt until very warm (about 120 degrees). Remove from the heat.

2. WITH A HAND-HELD ELECTRIC MIXER, beat 1¹/2 cups of the flour and the warm water mixture into the yeast mixture until smooth. With a wooden spoon, stir in the tomatoes, egg, green onion, garlic, and parsley.

3. TRANSFER THE DOUGH to a floured surface and gently knead for 6 to 8 minutes, adding enough of the remaining flour to make a stiff dough. Shape the dough into a ball, place it in a large oiled bowl, and turn to coat. Cover with plastic wrap and let rise in a warm place until doubled in bulk, about 1 to 1¹/2 hours.

4. PUNCH DOWN THE DOUGH, cover, and let rise again until doubled in bulk, about 45 minutes.

5. PUNCH DOWN THE DOUGH and turn it out onto a floured surface. Cut it in half with a serrated knife, cover with plastic wrap, and let rest for 10 minutes.

6. GREASE A LARGE BAKING SHEET and set aside. Shape the dough into 2 round loaves, about 6 inches in diameter. Place about 2 inches apart on the baking sheet, cover with plastic wrap, and let rise until almost doubled in bulk, about 40 minutes.

7. PREHEAT THE OVEN to 375 degrees. Brush the egg glaze over the loaves. Bake for 40 to 45 minutes, or until the bread is golden brown and sounds hollow when tapped on the bottom; an instant-read thermometer inserted into the center should register 190 to 200 degrees. Transfer to a wire rack to cool.

OLD-FASHIONED QUINCE PRESERVES

Vibrantly colored ruby-red quince preserves have a taste somewhere between apple and pineapple. These preserves are delicious on homemade bread, but they can also crown a homemade cheesecake or become a substitute filling for Latticed Rhubarb Sheets (page 201). In this Ohio recipe, inspired by one in *Buckeye Cookery and Practical Housekeeping* (1877), equal weights of fruit and sugar are used, so you can adapt it if necessary to the amount of quinces you're able to get.

Because quinces must be cooked to be edible and they're not the easiest fruits to pare and cut up, it's nice to get two delicious results from all your work. First make these preserves with the cut-up fruit, saving the quince parings and trimmings, seeds and all. After you've prepared the preserves, make Quince Jelly (page 14) from the trimmings.

MAKES 6 TO 7
HALF-PINT JARS

Juice of 1 lemon
4 large firm quinces
6³/4 cups sugar

1. POUR 2 CUPS OF WATER into a large saucepan and add the lemon juice. Peel, core, and dice the quinces. (If you wish, reserve the parings, trimmings, and seeds for Quince Jelly.) As you work, add the diced quinces to the saucepan of lemon water. Stir the fruit occasionally to keep it from discoloring. You should have about 6 cups of diced quinces.

QUINCES

On an unusually mild sunny day in early November, I took the rolling back lanes of north-central Ohio through college towns like Gambier and canal towns like Cochocton. As I drove along, I kept noticing some especially striking trees, most often around abandoned farmsteads, with what looked like golden apples dangling from their dark, leafless branches. Finally, I stopped the car and got out to look. On closer inspection, the fruits weren't golden apples at all, but quinces, heirlooms once prized for their keeping qualities and the fine jellies and preserves they make. A bowl of golden quinces can perfume a winter room.

Old quince varieties like Smyrna, Champion, and Orange traveled westward with New England settlers to the northeast region of frontier Ohio. From there, quinces spread to settlements such as Norwalk around Lake Erie, then south to central Ohio and westward to Indiana and Illinois. Today, in the area around Wooster, Ohio, in the north-central part of the state, quince jelly and quince pies are still prepared and appreciated.

Hardy fruits, quinces endure the extremes of prairie weather very well. Some varieties have a fuzzy exterior, like the down on a peach. Hard and astringent when raw, quinces are usually cut up and cooked in a sugar syrup, baked like apples, or stewed. Cooked, they take on a beautiful rosy color and have a flavor somewhat like pineapple. And when you taste the combination of quince preserves and fresh butter on toasted homemade bread, or crostini spread with quince preserves over a thin slice of an aged Wisconsin pecorino, you'll wonder where this fruit has been all your life.

2. ADD ENOUGH WATER to the saucepan to barely cover the quinces and bring to a boil over medium-high heat. Boil for 30 minutes, or until the quinces are tender.

3. WITH A SLOTTED SPOON, transfer the quinces to a bowl. Stir the sugar into the liquid remaining in the saucepan, return the quinces to the pan, and bring to a boil once again. Turn the heat down to a simmer and cook for about 2 hours, or until the quinces are translucent and a deep ruby red.

4. MEANWHILE, sterilize 7 half-pint jars and lids; keep the jars warm.

5. SPOON THE FRUIT INTO THE STERILIZED JARS, then add the juice, leaving a 1/4-inch headspace. Cool, then seal the jars. The preserves will keep in the refrigerator indefinitely.

QUINCE JELLY

"Waste not, want not," says that invisible person over your shoulder when you make beautiful rosy red quince jelly from the trimmings you might have thrown out. Toast slices of Life-in-the-Slow-Lane Baguettes (page 47) and top each with shavings of aged Wisconsin pecorino and a dollop of the jelly for a delicious appetizer.

MAKES ABOUT 3 HALF-PINT JARS

Parings, trimmings, cores, and seeds from 4 quinces (reserved from making Quince Preserves, page 12)
2 cups sugar

1. PLACE THE PARINGS, trimmings, cores, and seeds in a medium saucepan with just enough water to barely cover. Bring to a boil over medium heat and cook for 30 minutes, or until the fruit is soft. Remove from the heat.

2. TRANSFER THE QUINCE MIXTURE to a jelly bag or a strainer lined with a tea towel set over a large bowl and let drain slowly. You should have about 2 cups of liquid; discard the solids.

3. PLACE THE LIQUID in a medium saucepan and stir in the sugar. Bring to a boil over medium-high heat and cook for 15 to 20 minutes, or until the jelly reaches 235 degrees on a candy thermometer. Or test for gelling by placing a spoonful of the liquid on a chilled plate; if it keeps its shape, without running, it is done.

4. MEANWHILE, sterilize 3 half-pint jars and lids; keep the jars warm.

5. POUR THE JELLY through a funnel into the hot jars, leaving a 1/4-inch headspace. Let cool, then seal. The jelly will keep indefinitely in the refrigerator.

SWEDISH RYE BREAD

Tekla Erikson emigrated to the wheat country of Lindsborg, Kansas, from Vastmanland, Sweden, in 1907, bringing with her a heritage of family recipes. Those recipes include this rye bread that Tekla's granddaughter, Judy Pilewski, still makes today. "I have such wonderful memories of growing up in Lindsborg," Judy says. "My mother made this bread every Saturday." It needs three risings to get the authentic texture and taste, so it takes some time, but the loaves can be wrapped well and frozen for up to 3 months. This farm bread recipe uses the "autolyse" method of letting the dough rest briefly after mixing, which allows the dough to relax and become easier to work, so less flour is required during kneading.

MAKES 2 LOAVES

1 (1/4-ounce) package (2 1/4 teaspoons) active dry yeast
2 cups warm (110 degrees) water
2 tablespoons vegetable oil
6 tablespoons molasses
6 tablespoons sorghum (available in larger grocery stores) or dark corn syrup
5 to 6 cups unbleached all-purpose flour
1 tablespoon packed brown sugar
1 1/2 teaspoons anise seeds
1 1/2 teaspoons salt
1 cup rye flour
1 tablespoon unsalted butter, melted

1. IN THE BOWL OF AN ELECTRIC MIXER or another large bowl, sprinkle the yeast over the warm water; set aside to proof until foamy, about 5 minutes. With a wooden spoon, stir in the oil, molasses, and sorghum. Beat in 2 cups of the all-purpose flour and blend well. Cover this sponge with plastic wrap and set aside to rest in a warm place for 45 minutes.

2. WITH THE PADDLE ATTACHMENT or a wooden spoon, beat the brown sugar, anise seeds, salt, rye flour, and 1¹/₂ more cups all-purpose flour into the sponge. Let rest for 10 minutes.

3. SWITCH TO THE DOUGH HOOK and knead the dough for several minutes, until smooth and elastic, adding more all-purpose flour as needed. Or turn the dough out onto a floured surface and knead by hand. Place the dough in a large oiled bowl and turn to coat. Cover with plastic wrap and let rise in a warm place until doubled in bulk, about 45 minutes.

4. PUNCH DOWN THE DOUGH, cover, and let rise again until doubled in bulk, about 45 minutes.

5. GREASE TWO 9-BY-5-BY-3-INCH LOAF PANS and set aside. Punch down the dough. Turn it out onto a floured surface and cut it in half with a serrated knife. Shape it into 2 loaves and place in the prepared loaf pans. Cover with plastic wrap and let rise in a warm place until doubled again, about 45 minutes.

6. PREHEAT THE OVEN to 375 degrees. Bake the loaves for 35 to 40 minutes, until they are browned on top and sound hollow when tapped on the bottom; an instant-read thermometer inserted into the center should register 190 to 200 degrees. Brush the tops of the loaves with the melted butter. Place the loaf pans on their sides (so that the tops of the loaves stay high) on a wire rack and let cool.

NONNA'S ITALIAN BREAD

In traditional Italian families throughout the Heartland, the keeper of the culinary flame was *nonna*, or grandmother. Every few days, she would bake loaves of this easy, basic, crusty bread meant to mop up every last bit of her own unique simmered-for-hours pasta sauce. Today, when you want to make panini, bruschetta, or crostini, use this bread or Italian Slipper Bread (page 70).

Placing a pan of water in the bottom of the oven while the bread is baking creates steam that helps form a good crust.

MAKES 2 LOAVES

1 (¹/₄-ounce package) (2¹/₄ teaspoons) active dry yeast
2 cups warm (110 degrees) water
2 tablespoons olive oil
2 teaspoons fine sea salt
1 large egg, beaten
5 to 6 cups bread flour, sifted
2 tablespoons milk
2 tablespoons sesame seeds

1. IN A LARGE BOWL, sprinkle the yeast over the water; set aside to proof until foamy, about 5 minutes. With a wooden spoon, stir in the olive oil, salt, and egg. Stir in about 5 cups of the flour, a little at a time, until you have a firm dough.

2. TURN THE DOUGH OUT onto a floured surface and knead for 5 minutes, adding more flour if necessary. Put the dough into a large oiled bowl and turn to coat. Cover with plastic wrap and let rise in a warm place until doubled in bulk, about 1 hour.

3. GREASE A LARGE BAKING SHEET and set aside. Turn the dough out onto a floured surface and cut it in half. Form each half into an 12-inch-long oblong loaf and place about 2 inches apart on the prepared baking sheet. Cover with plastic wrap and let rise in a warm place until doubled in bulk, about 45 minutes to 1 hour.

4. PREHEAT THE OVEN to 350 degrees. Just before baking, place a baking pan of boiling water on the bottom rack of the oven.

5. BRUSH THE LOAVES WITH THE MILK, then sprinkle with the sesame seeds. Bake for 35 to 40 minutes, or until the loaves are browned on top and sound hollow when tapped on the bottom; an instant-read thermometer inserted into the center should register 190 to 200 degrees. Cool in the pans or on a wire rack.

VARIATION: Jake Imperiale loves to bake Italian Bread Imperiale, his prairie version of Italian

THE BREAD OF LIFE

············· ⁂ ·············

The Northeast neighborhood in Minneapolis runs on the fuel of home and family. It's a place where mom-and-pop businesses and third-generation restaurants still welcome customers by name, church bells chime on the hour, and residents are proud of their old-fashioned food. If you're hungry—and it's hard not to be, with the combined force of the melting-pot aromas—you have a smorgasbord of choices. Head for the tall spire of Our Lady of Lourdes for a take-out hand-crimped French *tourtière*, a homemade meat pie that is their specialty. Or make your way to St. Constantine Ukrainian Catholic church for *pyrohy* or St. Mary's Orthodox Cathedral for *piroghi*—different spellings, but the same delicious homemade noodle dumplings stuffed with potato, sauerkraut, or prune filling. Amble over to Dusty's Bar for one of their famous burgers, an Italian sausage patty topped with grilled pepper strips. At Kramarczuk's, you can get a huge Polish sausage sandwich, a side of kraut, and a cold Polish beer. If you're a dainty eater, you can nibble half a garlic roast beef sandwich at Mayslack's Polka Lounge; big appetites polish off a whole one.

So it's no surprise that Blackey's Bakery, Polish-owned for eighty years, produces bread that everyone loves. Now owned by Svea Ernst, a Danish woman, Blackey's specializes in her native night-dark *rugbrod*, Danish pumpernickel rye, but it also makes sesame seed–crusted Italian, cinnamon-and-raisin-swirled American white, French baguettes, and light Polish onion rye. In a melting-pot neighborhood, everyone reaches a hand into the breadbasket.

bread. His grandmother was born in the north of Italy, his mother in the south, and Jake in the wheat country of the Great Plains, so it's no wonder his recipe uses three kinds of flour. The bread has a moist, feathery crumb and a little more texture than Nonna's Italian Bread. To make his bread, use 2 to 3 cups bread flour, 2 cups "00" Italian flour, and 1 cup semolina for pasta instead of the 5 to 6 cups bread flour in the recipe above.

..........✦✦✦..........

PRAIRIE PANZANELLA

✦✦✦

In metropolitan areas of the Heartland where artisanal bakeries have sprung up, you'll find this Tuscan salad at cafés and restaurants. At Honeymom's in Kansas City, I had a delicious version with small crumbles of Maytag Blue cheese and bites of sweet orange. It was so good I tried to duplicate it at home, and I came up with this recipe. When you bake your own naturally leavened or slow-rising breads, save some to make this dish, the perfect salad for a light summer meal on the porch.

SERVES 4

¹/2 loaf Italian Bread Imperiale (page 16), Rustic French Bread (page 64), Spring Wheat Semolina Bread (page 49), Italian Slipper Bread (page 70), WheatFields Olive Bread (page 68), or a similar-textured rustic loaf, crust removed and cut into ¹/2-inch cubes

2 ripe tomatoes, peeled and chopped
¹/2 cup orange segments, chopped
6 green onions (including part of the green), sliced
¹/2 cup crumbled blue cheese, preferably Maytag Blue
2 tablespoons chopped fresh Italian parsley, plus a few sprigs for garnish
¹/4 teaspoon salt
¹/4 cup extra virgin olive oil

1. PREHEAT THE OVEN to 300 degrees. Place the bread cubes on a baking sheet and toast in the oven for 10 minutes, or until lightly browned.

2. TRANSFER THE BREAD CUBES to a large bowl. Add the tomatoes, oranges, green onions, blue cheese, parsley, salt, and olive oil and toss well. Let the salad stand for about 30 minutes before serving.

3. SERVE ON INDIVIDUAL SALAD PLATES, garnished with parsley sprigs.

THE MILLER'S TALE

··········· ❦ ···········

Once wheat is harvested and goes into storage at the co-op, then what? That's when the miller's tale begins. "Wheat that's harvested in June won't even be processed until September," says Alvin Brensing, the octogenarian "miller emeritus" of the Stafford County Flour Mill in Stafford, Kansas. Dressed in his standard gear of plaid shirt, jeans, Western-style belt and buckle, and cowboy hat, Brensing still comes into work most days. The milling business, after all, has been his life.

"Wheat has to age a little before we can mill it," he says. And that process begins with tempering the wheat—first washing, then cleaning and tempering the wheat berries with a little water to boost the moisture content up to about 16 percent. This makes for easier removal of the outer bran layer from the inner germ at the bottom of the kernel and endosperm at the top. Because the germ contains fat, it can cause the flour to go rancid quickly if left in, as it is in whole wheat flour. Most of the flour comes from the starchy endosperm.

Brensing buys the local red winter wheat to first store, and then mill into Hudson Cream Flour, which is so finely sifted that one hundred pounds of wheat kernels translate into only sixty-two pounds of this top-grade all-purpose flour. Because wheat varies in protein content from field to field, blending wheats to get the right protein content also takes place before milling. In flour, protein means the presence of tough, elastic gluten. Bread flour has a higher protein level, with the gluten working with yeast to raise bread dough. Cake flour has a low protein level, because cakes need a finer texture and so rely on eggs to raise the batter. All-purpose flour, like Hudson Cream, has a medium protein level and can be used with either additional gluten and yeast to make bread or with eggs to make soft yeast rolls, cookies, and cakes. To arrive at Hudson Cream's 11 percent protein content or the $11^{1}/_{2}$ to 12 percent protein for the slightly lower grade Diamond H flour, Brensing has to start with batches of wheat with $12^{1}/_{2}$ to 13 percent protein.

Once they are tempered and blended, the wheat kernels travel through corrugated rollers to be cracked and separated. The bran and germ are removed, and the flour from the endosperm goes through several sifting processes, the flour blown through silky woven netting so fine that if you poured water into it, the water would bead up, not drain out. Out of that original one hundred pounds of wheat kernels, twenty-eight pounds are sifted out to become animal feed, while another ten pounds sift into "clear flour," a low-grade flour often added to spice blends or Jewish rye bread doughs. The sifting process is what separates Hudson Cream from other commercial millers like Pillsbury, Continental, and Archer Daniels Midland, who don't sift their flour as fine.

Along the way, a tiny proportion of malted barley flour is added, which, according to Brensing, helps the rising quality of the flour by converting some of the starch particles into malt sugar. Some Hudson Cream Flour is chemically bleached, the rest remaining unbleached—but all flour bleaches naturally if left to age for eight to twelve weeks, he says. Then the flour is bagged and each bag marked with the time and date.

The activity is nonstop, and there's a constant hum, as well as a fine fog of flour dust in the air. The mill machinery goes twenty-four hours a day. Trucks drive in with deliveries and out with shipments. Millers from all over the world may stop by for a visit, perhaps as part of a milling and baking seminar at Kansas State University in Manhattan, to the north. Occasionally a rabbi from nearby Great Bend comes down to approve the kosher flour that goes in green and orange packages to the East Coast. And then there are the McDonald's folks, who buy Brensing's flour for their hamburger buns. "We do the same things every day, but it's always different," Brensing says with a chuckle.

THE MILLER'S CINNAMON AND RAISIN BREAD

"People love my cinnamon and raisin bread because it's got a very soft, tender crumb," says Alvin Brensing, the octogenarian miller in charge of producing Hudson Cream Flour in Stafford County, Kansas. He gives his home economist daughter full marks for helping him perfect this recipe. Although he makes this bread in a bread machine, you can also make it by hand. If you wish, you can substitute bread flour and omit the vital wheat gluten, but the loaf will not be as tender.

MAKES 1 LOAF

1 cup plus 2 tablespoons milk
2 1/2 tablespoons unsalted butter
3 to 3 1/2 cups unbleached all-purpose flour
3 tablespoons packed brown sugar
2 tablespoons vital wheat gluten (available at larger grocery stores and through mail-order)
2 tablespoons ground cinnamon
1 1/2 teaspoons salt
2 teaspoons dry instant, rapid-rise, or quick yeast
2/3 to 3/4 cup raisins, plumped in hot water and drained
2 large eggs, beaten

1. IN A SMALL SAUCEPAN, heat the milk until warm (100 degrees). Remove from the heat and add the butter so it melts.

2. IN THE BOWL OF AN ELECTRIC MIXER or another large bowl, combine 3 cups of the flour, the brown sugar, gluten, cinnamon, salt, and yeast. Using the paddle attachment or a wooden spoon, beat in the raisins, then beat in the eggs and warm milk until you have a soft dough.

3. SWITCH TO THE DOUGH HOOK and knead the dough for 3 to 4 minutes, until smooth and elastic, adding more flour if necessary. Or turn the dough out onto a floured surface and knead by hand. Place the dough in a large oiled bowl and turn to coat. Cover with plastic wrap and let rise at room temperature until doubled in bulk, about 1 hour.

4. GREASE A 9-BY-5-BY-3-INCH LOAF PAN and set aside. Punch down the dough and turn it out onto a floured surface. Shape the dough into a loaf and place in the prepared pan. Cover with plastic wrap and let rise at room temperature until doubled in bulk, about 30 minutes.

5. PREHEAT THE OVEN to 350 degrees. Bake the bread for 30 minutes, or until it is golden brown on top and sounds hollow when lightly tapped on the bottom; an instant-read thermometer inserted into the center should register 190 to 200 degrees. Cool in the pan or on a wire rack.

VOLGA GERMAN PEPPERNUT BREAD

There's nothing new about fusion cooking: it's been going on for centuries. A good example is this recipe, adapted from one in Norma Jost Voth's *Mennonite Foods and Folkways from South Russia*. Voth attributes the recipe to the Volga Germans, Catholic Germans who went to Russia at the invitation of Catherine the Great in the eighteenth century to live near Russian Mennonite settlements along the Volga River. The Mennonites had come to Russia by way of the Netherlands, and then Germany, where they had fled religious persecution for their pacifist views. Then, in the late nineteenth century, when Russia required military service from every man, groups of Russian Mennonites and the neighboring Volga Germans resettled on the Kansas prairie. Russian Mennonites made peppernuts as a Christmas spice cookie, not a bread, but Volga German *Pfeffernusse Brot* uses allspice and ground star anise as flavorings, the same as in many peppernut cookie recipes.

MAKES 1 LARGE LOAF

1 tablespoon active dry yeast
1/4 cup warm (110 degrees) water
1/4 cup reserved potato water (see Note)
1/2 cup milk
1/4 cup mashed potatoes (see Note)
1/4 cup shortening, lard, or unsalted butter, softened
1/2 cup sugar
1/3 cup molasses
1 large egg
1/2 teaspoon salt
1/2 teaspoon ground allspice
1/2 teaspoon ground star anise (see Note, page 22)
1/8 teaspoon freshly ground black pepper
3 1/2 to 4 cups bread flour

1. IN THE BOWL OF AN ELECTRIC MIXER or another large bowl, sprinkle the yeast over the warm water and set aside to proof until foamy, about 5 minutes. In a small saucepan, heat the reserved potato water with the milk until just warm (110 degrees); remove from the heat.

2. WITH THE PADDLE ATTACHMENT or a wooden spoon, beat the potato water mixture, potatoes, shortening, lard, or butter, sugar, molasses, egg, salt, and spices into the yeast mixture. Beat in enough of the flour, 1 cup at a time, to make a stiff dough.

3. SWITCH TO THE DOUGH HOOK and knead the dough gently for 5 to 6 minutes, adding more flour if necessary, until smooth and elastic. Or turn the dough out onto a floured surface and knead by hand. Place the dough in a large oiled bowl and turn to coat. Cover with plastic wrap and let rise in a warm place until doubled in bulk, about 1 hour.

4. GREASE TWO 9-BY-5-BY-3-INCH LOAF PANS and set aside. Punch down the dough, and turn it out onto a floured surface. Cut the dough in half and form it into 2 loaves. Place in the prepared loaf pans, cover with plastic wrap, and let rise in a warm place until doubled in bulk, about 45 minutes.

5. PREHEAT THE OVEN to 350 degrees. Bake the loaves for 35 to 40 minutes, or until they are browned on the top and sound hollow when tapped on the bottom; an instant-read thermometer inserted into the center should register 190 to 200 degrees. Transfer to a wire rack to cool.

NOTE: One medium potato will make enough mashed potatoes for this recipe; reserve ¼ cup of the potato water.

Grind the star anise in a spice grinder or clean coffee grinder.

·········· 🌿🌿 ··········

CARAWAY-RYE FLATBREAD WITH SAUSAGE AND SAUERKRAUT

🌿🌿

All types of meat pies, from the French Canadian *tourtière* to the Spanish *empanada*, have become part of the rich cultural heritage of prairie cooking. In this recipe with Eastern European roots, a caraway-rye crust takes on a savory topping of sauerkraut, Italian sausage, and Gruyère cheese. A combination of Dijon mustard, smoked turkey or ham, and a good Wisconsin Cheddar would also work well. This is a wonderful Sunday night supper, when you can invite friends over to enjoy a casual meal in front of the fire. A dark, full-bodied beer from a Midwestern microbrewery or a glass of crisp German Riesling or Midwestern Vignoles would be just the thing to wash down every delicious bite.

SERVES 6 TO 8

FOR THE DOUGH:
1 cup water
½ cup milk
1½ tablespoons unsalted butter
1 tablespoon plus 2 teaspoons sugar
1 (¼-ounce) package (2¼ teaspoons) active dry yeast
¼ cup warm (110 degrees) water
3 cups unbleached all-purpose flour
1 cup rye flour
2 teaspoons salt
3 tablespoons caraway seeds

FOR THE FILLING:
2 tablespoons unsalted butter
1 large onion, thinly sliced
½ pound bulk Italian sausage (hot or sweet)
3 cups sauerkraut, rinsed several times and drained
2 large eggs, beaten
1 cup heavy cream
½ cup grated Gruyère cheese
½ teaspoon freshly grated nutmeg
½ teaspoon white pepper

1. MAKE THE DOUGH: In a medium saucepan, combine the water, milk, butter, and 1 tablespoon of the sugar and bring to a boil. Remove from the heat and set aside to cool to lukewarm (80 to 90 degrees).

2. IN A SMALL BOWL, sprinkle the yeast over the warm water and set aside to proof until foamy, about 5 minutes. Add the yeast mixture to the lukewarm milk mixture and blend well.

3. SIFT THE FLOURS, salt, and the remaining 2 teaspoons sugar into a large bowl. Stir in the caraway seeds. Pour in the yeast mixture and knead until the dough forms a ball. Cover with

plastic wrap and let rise in a warm place until doubled in bulk, 1¹/2 to 2 hours.

4. WHILE THE DOUGH IS RISING, make the filling: In a large skillet, melt the butter. Add the onion and sauté until translucent, about 5 minutes. Add the sausage, breaking up any lumps, and cook, stirring, until browned, about 5 minutes. Add the sauerkraut and simmer for about 15 minutes. Remove from the heat and set aside.

5. PREHEAT THE OVEN to 350 degrees. Oil a 12-inch pizza pan and set aside. Punch down the dough and transfer it to a floured surface. Roll it out into a 16-inch circle. Transfer the dough to the pizza pan and roll the edges of the dough over to form a 2-inch-high rim.

6. IN A BOWL, whisk together the eggs, cream, Gruyère, nutmeg, and white pepper. Spoon the sauerkraut mixture over the dough and pour the egg mixture over the top.

7. BAKE FOR 35 TO 40 MINUTES, or until the filling is set and browned and a knife inserted in the center comes out clean. Cut into wedges and serve warm.

CHICAGO DEEP-DISH PIZZA DOUGH

The Midwest has its own unique style of pizza, created in Chicago in 1943. Two rivals claim the honor—Rudy Malnati, the scion of Lou Malnati's Pizzeria, and Ike Sewell, who founded Pizzeria Uno. Chicago-style deep-dish pizza is typically eaten with a knife and fork. Although there is a lot of dough involved, the crust is relatively thin, patted out by hand and pulled up high against the sides of a deep-dish pan to encase the delicious ingredients. According to Rudy's grandson Rick, "Only Chicago's finest Lake Michigan water can produce a truly delicious Chicago-style deep-dish pizza crust!"

For Malnati's deep-dish pizza, the ingredients are placed on the dough in reverse order from a regular pizza. The mozzarella cheese is sprinkled over the dough, ingredients like mushrooms, onions, and sausage are scattered on top of the cheese, and the sauce is slathered on top, with a few sprinklings of cheese and herbs to top it off before the pizza goes in the oven. At Pizzeria Uno restaurants across the country, a variety of toppings—including potatoes—will tempt you to dream up your own version of this Chicago specialty.

This dough also makes delicious grilled or traditional round pizzas (see page 25). Leftover dough can be frozen for later use; simply thaw it and then roll out.

MAKES 2 (8-INCH-SQUARE) DEEP-DISH PIZZAS

3¹/4 cups unbleached all-purpose flour
¹/4 cup semolina for pasta
2 tablespoons instant yeast
1 cup water
1 tablespoon honey
5 tablespoons olive oil
¹/2 teaspoon salt

1. COMBINE THE FLOUR, semolina, and yeast in the bowl of a food processor or an electric mixer. Combine the water, honey, 3 tablespoons of the olive oil, and the salt in a cup and stir to blend. With the food processor or mixer on, add the liquid mixture in a steady stream and process or mix until the dough forms a mass and cleans the sides of the bowl.

2. TURN THE DOUGH OUT onto a floured surface and knead for 5 minutes, or until smooth and elastic. Place in a large oiled bowl and turn to coat. Cover with plastic wrap and let rise in a warm place until doubled in bulk, 1 to 1¹/2 hours.

3. GREASE TWO 8-INCH SQUARE BAKING PANS and set aside. Punch down the dough and turn it out onto a floured surface. Cut the dough in half with a serrated knife. Roll each half out into a 10-inch square and fit into the prepared baking pans, pressing it over the bottom and up the sides of the pans. Brush the dough with the remaining 2 tablespoons olive oil and top with the ingredients of your choice.

GARLIC-HERB PIZZA DOUGH: Heat 2 tablespoons olive oil in a small skillet. Add 1 tablespoon minced garlic, ¹/4 teaspoon dried oregano, ¹/4 teaspoon dried basil, and 1 teaspoon freshly ground black pepper. Cook, stirring, for 2 minutes, or until the garlic softens. Remove from the heat and let cool. Add the garlic oil along with the honey mixture in Step 1 and proceed as directed.

USING BAKING STONES

Baking stones or tiles placed in a modern gas or electric oven help replicate the special qualities of a wood-burning or tile-lined bake oven. The stone or tiles absorb and hold the oven's heat in a constant, steady manner, resulting in more even browning and a better crust for baked goods.

Most baking stones need to be seasoned before using. For off-white stoneware, the seasoning process usually involves placing the stone on the middle rack of a cold oven, then turning the oven temperature to 200 degrees and letting the stone season for several hours. These baking stones are porous and should never be greased or oiled. Follow the individual manufacturer's specific instructions for seasoning.

Some bakers prefer to line the oven rack with unglazed tiles or even 12-inch terra-cotta flowerpot saucers. To season these, first wash and dry them. Grease the tops of the tiles or the insides of the saucers with shortening and place in a cold oven. Turn the oven temperature to 250 degrees; after 20 minutes, turn the temperature up to 350 degrees. Then, after 20 minutes more, turn the temperature up to 450 degrees. Heat for 20 minutes more, then turn off the oven and leave the tiles or saucers inside to cool completely, about 2 hours. Remove from the oven and rinse under hot running water. After your tiles or saucers have been seasoned this way, do not grease them again or use soap to clean them, as this would damage their porosity.

To use a stone or tiles, place in the middle rack of a cold oven and preheat.

PIZZA POLLOTATE

Chicago is not the only Midwestern city with distinctive pizza. A wood-burning oven with an oak fire that reaches temperatures of over 600 degrees makes the Ricci family's Wood-Roasted Pizza restaurant a hit in the Kansas City area. Their delicious Pizza Pollotate is based on grandmother Julia Leofanti's recipe from her birthplace of Lucca in Tuscany. Use a seasoned pizza or baking stone to get a crisp crust like theirs. This pizza is a delicious way to recycle leftovers—in this case, grilled chicken and baked potatoes.

MAKES 4 (8-INCH) PIZZAS

Yellow cornmeal, for sprinkling
1 recipe Chicago Deep-Dish Pizza Dough
    (page 23), prepared through Step 2
1/4 cup extra virgin olive oil
1/2 teaspoon red pepper flakes
1/2 teaspoon dried basil
4 grilled chicken breasts, thinly sliced
4 small baked potatoes, sliced
1 large red onion, thinly sliced
2 cups shredded mozzarella cheese
    (about 8 ounces)
2 cups shredded provolone cheese
    (about 8 ounces)
1 cup shredded Asiago cheese
    (about 4 ounces)
1 tablespoon chopped fresh rosemary

1. PLACE A BAKING STONE or tiles on the middle rack of the oven to preheat. Preheat the oven to 500 degrees. Sprinkle two cookie sheets (without sides), a board, or a baker's peel with cornmeal and set aside.

2. PUNCH DOWN THE DOUGH and turn it out onto a floured surface. Divide it into 4 portions. Roll out 2 pieces of the dough to 8-inch rounds and place on a prepared cookie sheet or the board or peel. Brush each round with 1 tablespoon of the olive oil and sprinkle with 1/8 teaspoon each of the red pepper flakes and basil. Arrange one-quarter of the chicken, potatoes, and onion on each pizza and top with 1/2 cup of the mozzarella, 1/2 cup of the provolone, and 1/4 cup of the Asiago. Sprinkle each pizza with one-quarter of the rosemary.

3. CAREFULLY PULL OUT THE MIDDLE RACK of the oven and, using the peel, or with a quick jerk of your arms, carefully slide the pizzas onto the stone. Bake for 8 to 10 minutes, or until the cheese is bubbly and the crust is golden brown. Meanwhile, assemble the remaining 2 pizzas. When the first pizzas come out of the oven, bake the remaining pizzas. Serve hot.

RUSTIC GRILLED PIZZA WITH FRESH CORN, TOMATOES, AND BASIL

In late July and early August, the first tomatoes are ripening in the garden and farm stands showcase the season's first sweet corn—Purdue Super Sweet and Silver Queen in the more humid eastern Midwest, Peaches and Cream in the drier western prairie. When it's too hot to contemplate heating the oven, make this smoky-flavored pizza. Although you get a better wood smoke flavor by using hardwood charcoal in a kettle grill, the recipe also works in a gas grill. The technique is to grill one side of the dough over direct heat, flip it over onto a baking sheet and add the toppings, and then carefully slide the pizza back onto the grill, over indirect heat, to finish cooking. With a frosty glass of wheat beer enlivened with a wedge of lemon, and a fresh fruit dessert, you can beat the heat in style. This method also works well with the Flatbread with Caramelized Onions and Brie (page 27).

MAKES 4 (10- TO 12-INCH) PIZZAS

3 cups sweet corn kernels or thawed frozen
    shoepeg corn
1 recipe Chicago Deep-Dish Pizza Dough
    (page 23), prepared through Step 2
Extra virgin olive oil, for brushing
1 teaspoon red pepper flakes
1 1/3 cups finely chopped fresh tomatoes
1/2 cup chopped fresh basil or 1/4 cup pesto
2 cups shredded Fontina cheese
    (about 8 ounces)

1. BUILD AN INDIRECT hardwood charcoal fire on one side of a kettle grill or start a medium fire on one side of a gas grill. Set the grill rack about 3 to 4 inches above the coals. The fire is ready when white ash begins to appear on the coals.

2. MEANWHILE, blanch the corn kernels in a large saucepan of boiling water for 2 minutes. Drain and pat dry.

3. GREASE TWO BAKING SHEETS. Punch down the dough and turn it out onto a floured surface. Divide the dough into 4 pieces. One at a time, pat and press or roll 2 of the pieces out on one of the greased baking sheets to a very thin circle 10 to 12 inches in diameter. Don't worry if the pizzas aren't perfectly round: that adds to their charm.

4. SET THE SECOND BAKING SHEET by the grill. Carefully lift up each round of dough with your fingers and drape it over the grill rack over direct heat. Grill for 1 minute, or until the dough begins to puff up and grill marks appear on the bottom. Using tongs, transfer the partially cooked pizzas to the second baking sheet, grilled side up. Brush the grilled surface with olive oil, then sprinkle 1/4 teaspoon of the red pepper flakes over each pizza. Top each with 1/3 cup of the chopped tomatoes, 3/4 cup of the corn, 2 tablespoons of the chopped basil or 1 tablespoon of the pesto, and 1/4 cup of the shredded Fontina. Carefully slide the pizzas onto the grill rack over indirect heat, away from the hottest part of the fire. Grill until the cheese begins to melt and the other ingredients are heated through, about 4 minutes. While the first pizzas are baking, prepare the remaining two, and slide them onto the grill to finish cooking as soon as you remove the first ones. Serve immediately.

FLATBREAD WITH CARAMELIZED ONIONS AND BRIE

VARIATION: You can also make the pizzas in the oven. Place a pizza stone or tiles on the middle oven rack and preheat the oven to 500 degrees. Assemble the pizzas 2 at a time and place them on a cookie sheet (without sides) or a peel sprinkled with cornmeal. Carefully pull out the middle oven rack and, using the peel, or with a quick jerk of your arms, slide the pizzas off the baking sheet or peel and onto the stone. Bake for 8 to 10 minutes, or until the cheese is bubbly and the crust is golden brown. While the first pizzas are baking, prepare the remaining two. As soon as you remove the first pizzas, slide the remaining pizzas into the oven to bake. Serve hot.

At a distinguished gathering of Les Dames d'Escoffier members at Rose Kallas's home in suburban Chicago, Karen Adler and I served a grilled version of this recipe on pizza dough to rave reviews. Made with a Midwestern Brie from Minnesota or Illinois, this luscious flatbread can be served in wedges as an appetizer or an accompaniment to soup or a salad. Hot roll mix, made according to the package instructions, or fresh pizza dough from an Italian grocer are viable shortcuts to making the dough. Once baked or grilled, this flatbread freezes well; to reheat, cover the frozen bread with foil and warm in a 350-degree oven for about 15 minutes.

SERVES 6 TO 8 AS PART OF A LIGHT MEAL, 24 AS AN APPETIZER

2 tablespoons unsalted butter
2 large onions, thinly sliced
1/2 teaspoon sugar
2 tablespoons port
1 recipe Chicago Deep-Dish Pizza Dough (page 23) or Nonna's Italian Bread dough (page 15), prepared through Step 2
8 ounces Brie cheese, preferably from the Midwest, rind removed and cut into small cubes

1. MELT THE BUTTER in a large skillet over medium-low heat and sauté the onions for 15 minutes, or until translucent and very soft.

Sprinkle the onions with the sugar and drizzle with the port. Turn the heat to medium-high and cook, stirring, until the onions are golden brown. Remove from the heat and set aside to cool.

2. PREHEAT THE OVEN to 375 degrees. Grease a large baking sheet. Turn the dough out onto the prepared baking sheet and pat or roll into a 13-by-9-inch rectangle or a 12-inch circle. Spread the caramelized onions over the dough. Scatter the Brie over the onions.

3. BAKE FOR 15 TO 18 MINUTES, or until the crust is golden brown. Serve warm or at room temperature.

.... ✿✿✿ ....

AMISH PINWHEEL BREAD

From the Amish community in northern Ohio, this bread looks as good as it tastes, with a swirl of white and whole wheat. The molasses gives a rich color and a hint of sweetness to the whole wheat dough.

MAKES 3 LOAVES

> 2 ($^1/_4$-ounce) packages ($1^1/_2$ tablespoons) active dry yeast
> 2 cups warm (110 degrees) water
> 2 cups milk
> $^1/_2$ cup sugar
> $^1/_2$ cup shortening, lard, or unsalted butter
> $1^1/_2$ to 2 tablespoons salt
> About $8^1/_2$ cups bread flour
> Melted butter, for brushing
> $^1/_4$ cup molasses
> 4 to $4^1/_2$ cups whole wheat flour

1. IN THE BOWL OF AN ELECTRIC MIXER or another large bowl, sprinkle the yeast over the water; set aside to proof until foamy, about 5 minutes. Meanwhile, in a medium saucepan, heat the milk, sugar, shortening, lard, or butter, and salt until just warm (110 degrees), stirring until the shortening melts. Remove from the heat and pour over the proofed yeast.

2. STIR IN 4 CUPS of the bread flour and beat until a smooth batter forms. Brush this sponge with melted butter, cover with plastic wrap, and let rise in a warm place until doubled in bulk, about 45 minutes to 1 hour.

3. PUNCH DOWN THE SPONGE. Transfer half of it to a large oiled bowl and set aside. Using the paddle attachment or a wooden spoon or Danish dough whisk, beat 4 more cups of the bread flour into the remaining sponge, then beat in enough additional bread flour to make a stiff dough. Switch to the dough hook and knead the dough for 6 to 8 minutes, until smooth and elastic. Or turn the dough out onto a floured surface and knead by hand. Return the dough to the oiled bowl and turn to coat. Cover with plastic wrap and let rise in a warm place until doubled in bulk, 45 minutes to 1 hour.

4. MEANWHILE, using the paddle attachment or a wooden spoon or Danish dough whisk, beat the molasses into the reserved sponge, then beat in enough whole wheat flour to make a somewhat stiff dough. Switch to the dough hook and knead the dough for 5 to 8 minutes, until smooth and elastic. Or turn it out onto a floured surface and knead by hand. Place the dough in the second oiled bowl and turn to coat. Cover with plastic wrap and let rise in a warm place until doubled in bulk, 45 minutes to 1 hour.

5. PUNCH DOWN BOTH DOUGHS and let rest for 10 minutes.

6. GREASE THREE 9-BY-5-BY-3-INCH LOAF PANS and set aside. Divide each dough into thirds. On a floured surface, roll out one-third of the lighter-colored dough to a 12-by-8-inch rectangle. Roll out one-third of the darker-colored dough to a rectangle of the same size. Place one rectangle on top of the other, aligning the edges. Starting with an 8-inch side, roll up the dough jelly-roll fashion and place seam side down in one of the prepared loaf pans. Repeat with the remaining dough. Cover the loaves with plastic wrap and let rise in a warm

place until doubled in bulk, about 45 minutes to 1 hour.

7. PREHEAT THE OVEN to 375 degrees. Loosely cover the top of each loaf with aluminum foil and bake for 20 minutes. Remove the foil and bake for 10 to 15 minutes longer, or until the loaves are browned on top and sound hollow when tapped lightly on the bottom; an instant-read thermometer inserted into the center should register 190 to 200 degrees. Transfer to wire racks to cool.

SPICY PEAR BREAD

On a recent road trip through southern Wisconsin, my son and I stopped for a visit at the tiny Swiss town of New Glarus, nestled near the Little Sugar River in rolling dairy country. When we walked into the town drugstore/soda fountain/Swiss emporium, cuckoo clocks cuckooed, someone began to yodel, polka music blared, and a tourist rang a Swiss cow bell. It was too much for my teenage son, whose taste in music includes neither polkas nor yodeling. Thankfully, the usual quiet of a sleepy prairie town was just a few steps away, and we headed toward the bakery. Served at the New Glarus Bakery and Tea Room and enjoyed in nearby homes, Swiss specialties like this pear bread, known as *bierenbrot*, are passed down from generation to generation. This recipe is adapted from one in *Swiss Cookery* (1992), a book of recipes collected by descendants of Marianne Rothlesberg Strahm, who came to

Wisconsin from Switzerland in 1892. Using both fresh and dried pears gives the bread a deeper flavor.

MAKES 1 LOAF

1 cup dried pears (see Note)
1/3 cup plus 2 tablespoons sugar
1 1/2 cups pear nectar
1 teaspoon salt
1 tablespoon lard or shortening
1 (1/4-ounce) package (2 1/4 teaspoons)
    active dry yeast
1/4 cup lukewarm (80 to 90 degrees) water
1 cup cored and finely chopped ripe pears
1 teaspoon ground ginger
1/2 teaspoon crushed anise seeds
3 to 3 1/2 cups all-purpose flour

1. PUT THE DRIED PEARS and 2 tablespoons of the sugar in a medium saucepan. Pour the pear nectar over the pears, and bring to a boil. Reduce the heat to a simmer, cover, and cook until the pears have softened but are still firm, about 15 minutes. Remove from the heat and set aside to cool.

2. DRAIN THE PEARS, reserving the cooking liquid. Chop the pears into small pieces; set aside. Measure the cooking liquid and, if necessary, add enough water to make 1 cup. Bring to a boil in a small saucepan, then remove from the heat and add the remaining 1/3 cup sugar, the salt, and lard or shortening. Let cool to lukewarm (90 degrees).

3. IN THE BOWL OF AN ELECTRIC MIXER or another large bowl, sprinkle the yeast over the lukewarm water and set aside to proof until foamy, about 5 minutes. With the paddle attachment or a wooden spoon or Danish dough whisk, beat in the pear cooking liquid mixture, the cooked pears, fresh pears, ginger, and anise seeds. Beat in 3 cups of the flour, 1 cup at a time, until you have a stiff, slightly sticky dough. Place the dough in a large oiled bowl and turn to coat. Cover with plastic wrap and let rise in a warm place until doubled in bulk, 2 1/2 to 3 hours.

4. LINE THE BOTTOM of a 9-by-5-by-3-inch loaf pan with waxed paper and set aside. Turn the dough out onto a floured surface and shape it into a loaf, sprinkling it with enough of the remaining 1/2 cup flour so that it is no longer too sticky to handle. Place the dough in the prepared pan, cover with plastic wrap, and let rise in a warm place until doubled in bulk, about 2 hours.

5. PREHEAT THE OVEN to 325 degrees. Bake the bread for 1 hour, or until it has browned on top and pulled away from the sides of the pan; an instant-read thermometer inserted into the center should register 200 degrees. Transfer to a wire rack to cool.

NOTE: You can find dried pears (4 ounces is equal to 1 cup) at health food stores.

DECADENT CHOCOLATE CHERRY BREAD

When I make this rich, brioche-like bread— a prairie version of panettone—I buy the best dark chocolate I can find, such as Lindt, Valrhona, or Maillard, or I go to one of our local boutique chocolatiers. In a pinch, I've also used semisweet chocolate chips, and the bread tastes almost as good. If there's any bread left the next day, I toast it and spread it with creamy mascarpone cheese, or use it as the base for decadent French toast.

MAKES 1 LARGE ROUND LOAF

1/3 cup hazelnuts or slivered almonds
1/2 cup heavy cream
1 (1/4-ounce) package (2 1/4 teaspoons) active dry yeast
5 tablespoons plus 1 teaspoon granulated sugar
8 tablespoons (1 stick) unsalted butter, softened
2 large eggs, beaten
1/2 teaspoon salt
Finely grated zest of 1 orange
2 1/2 to 3 cups all-purpose flour
1/3 cup dried cherries
1/4 cup brandy, Cognac, or rum
6 ounces bittersweet or semisweet chocolate, cut into chunks, or 1 cup semisweet chocolate chips
1 tablespoon unsalted butter, melted
Confectioners' sugar, for dusting

1. PREHEAT THE OVEN to 350 degrees. Spread the hazelnuts or almonds on a baking sheet and toast in the oven for 10 to 15 minutes, or until lightly browned. Set aside to cool.

2. IN A SMALL SAUCEPAN, heat the cream until warm (110 degrees). Transfer to the bowl of an electric mixer or another large bowl. Sprinkle the yeast and 1 teaspoon of the granulated sugar over the cream; set aside to proof until foamy, about 5 minutes.

3. WITH THE PADDLE ATTACHMENT or a wooden spoon, beat the remaining 5 tablespoons granulated sugar, the butter, and eggs into the yeast mixture until smooth. Add the salt and orange zest, then beat in 2 1/2 cups of the flour, 1 cup at a time, until you have a smooth dough.

4. TURN THE DOUGH OUT onto a floured surface and knead for 4 to 6 minutes, adding additional flour if necessary, until smooth and elastic. Place the dough in a large oiled bowl and turn to coat. Cover with plastic wrap and let rise in a warm place until doubled in bulk, about 1 hour.

5. MEANWHILE, place the dried cherries in a small bowl. In a small saucepan, heat the brandy, Cognac, or rum until just warm (100 degrees). Pour over the cherries and set aside to plump.

6. GENEROUSLY BUTTER a 1-quart fluted brioche mold or scalloped round baking dish and set aside. Turn the dough out onto a floured surface and flatten it under your palms. Drain the cherries, reserving the liquor. Place one-quarter each of the chocolate chunks, cherries, and nuts on the top half of the dough. Fold the bottom half of the dough over them and knead gently, then give the dough a quarter turn. Repeat until all of the chocolate, cherries, and nuts have been kneaded into the dough. Place the dough in the prepared mold or dish, cover with plastic wrap, and let rise in a warm place until doubled in bulk, 45 minutes to 1 hour.

7. PREHEAT THE OVEN to 400 degrees. Press any exposed chocolate back into the dough to prevent it from scorching. Cover the loaf loosely with aluminum foil and bake for 15 minutes. Turn the heat down to 375 degrees and bake for 20 to 25 minutes more, or until the loaf has risen, browned, and pulled away from the sides of the mold; an instant-read thermometer inserted into the center should register 190 to 200 degrees. Transfer to a wire rack.

8. MEANWHILE, mix the reserved liquor with the melted butter. While the loaf is still hot, brush it with the melted butter mixture and dust with confectioners' sugar. Let cool.

A WHOLE LOT OF SHAKIN' GOIN' ON

It's a frosty day in mid-November and the four-hundred-acre Wilson farm near Horton, Missouri, is in the midst of the pecan harvest. The pecan trees look as if they've got a terrible case of the shivers. A vise-like device attached to a tractor grabs the trunk of each 60-to-80-foot tree and shakes. . .and shakes. . .and shakes. Nuts rain and rattle down, along with any leaves not taken already by the autumn winds and frost. A tractor-drawn sweeper moves in to scoop the nuts that have fallen, then both machines move on to the next tree. This process does not damage the trees; in fact, it helps by aerating the roots a little bit, and is much kinder to the farmer than the way the nuts used to be harvested.

Gone are the days when someone had to climb up each pecan tree and beat the limbs with a stick to dislodge the nuts; a man down below would have to stoop to pick up one hundred pounds or so of nuts each day of the harvest. And someone was always getting hurt falling from a tree. The modern method is less folksy, but a lot more efficient. And the harvest is loaded with special effects thrills for people who come out to watch the goings-on. The harvest technique "always leaves people with their mouths open," Jim Wilson says. "Kids love it. Ask them later and they say one thing—Wow!"

Wilson's pecan groves produce one hundred thousand pounds of nuts in a good year. The term "grove" indicates nuts that grew naturally. The term "orchard" refers to pecan trees that were planted. The indigenous or native pecans in groves have a much better flavor, with more concentrated oils. "I won't touch pecans you get in the store," says Bill Reid, a county extension specialist from Chetopa, Kansas, part of prairie pecan country. "Ours just taste better."

PECAN BRIOCHE BREAD

❧

Early one winter, I bought two bags of native pecans from a farm in Missouri. Smaller and thinner-shelled than Southern pecans, these pecans have a higher percentage of essential oils and a more pronounced pecan flavor. At the same time, I came across this recipe for a light brioche-style dough with a double-swirled nut filling baked in a loaf pan, a nutty relative of the decadent Schnecken (page 192) so beloved of Cincinnatians. The third stroke of fate was receiving a gourmet food catalog in the mail that praised indulgence, breakfast in bed, *"il dolce far niente,"* or the sweetness of doing nothing. What could I do but vow to take a lazy weekend morning, sip my French-press coffee, and savor this warm, fragrant bread? The sad truth is, however, that this kind of laziness requires planning and work. Make the soft dough a day ahead of time, so it has time to rest. Bake the bread the next day—and freeze at least one loaf to reheat for a sybaritic weekend.

MAKES 2 LOAVES

FOR THE DOUGH:
1/2 cup warm (110 degrees) water
1 (1/4-ounce) package (2 1/4 teaspoons) active dry yeast
1/4 cup granulated sugar
1 teaspoon salt
1/2 pound (2 sticks) unsalted butter, softened
6 large eggs
4 1/2 cups all-purpose flour

FOR THE FILLING:
3 tablespoons unsalted butter, softened
2/3 cup packed light brown sugar
2 large egg yolks
2 tablespoons milk
1 teaspoon ground cinnamon
1 teaspoon vanilla extract
2 cups finely ground pecans or walnuts (about 8 ounces)

4 tablespoons (1/2 stick) unsalted butter
Confectioners' sugar, for dusting

1. THE DAY BEFORE BAKING, make the dough: In the bowl of an electric mixer, sprinkle the yeast over the warm water and set aside to proof until foamy, about 5 minutes. With the paddle attachment, beat in the granulated sugar, salt, butter, and eggs until well blended.

2. ON MEDIUM SPEED, beat in 3 cups of the flour, 1 cup at a time, until you have a soft dough, then beat the dough for 4 to 5 minutes. Reduce the speed to low, add the remaining 1 1/2 cups flour, and beat until smooth, about 2 minutes. Cover the bowl with plastic wrap and then a warm damp tea towel. Let rise in a warm place until doubled in bulk, 1 1/2 to 2 hours. Refrigerate overnight.

3. THE NEXT DAY, make the filling: In a medium bowl, beat the butter, brown sugar, and egg yolks together with a wooden spoon. Stir in the milk, cinnamon, and vanilla extract, then the nuts. Set aside.

4. GREASE TWO 9-BY-5-BY-3-INCH LOAF PANS and set aside. Melt 3 tablespoons of the butter; set aside. Remove the dough from the refrigerator and stir it down with a wooden spoon. Turn it out onto a lightly floured surface and cut it in half. Return half of the dough to the bowl, cover, and return to the refrigerator.

5. ON THE FLOURED SURFACE, roll the other half of the dough out to a 14-by-9-inch rectangle. Brush the dough with about 1 tablespoon of the melted butter. Spread half of the filling over the dough, leaving a 1/2-inch margin all around. Starting from one short end, carefully roll up the dough jelly-roll fashion, stopping at the center. Starting from the other short end, carefully roll up the dough jelly-roll fashion, stopping at the center. Place seam side down in one of the prepared loaf pans and lightly brush with melted butter. Repeat with the remaining dough and filling. Cover the loaves with plastic wrap and let rise in a warm place until doubled in bulk, 1 to 1 1/2 hours.

6. PREHEAT THE OVEN to 350 degrees. Bake the bread for 35 minutes, or until the loaves are golden brown; an instant-read thermometer inserted into the center should register 190 degrees. Transfer the loaves to a wire rack.

7. MEANWHILE, melt the remaining 1 tablespoon butter. Brush the tops of the hot loaves with the melted butter and dust with confectioners' sugar. Let cool.

PAN DE LOS MUERTOS

Although this fragrant bread is usually a part of the Mexican Day of the Dead, you don't have to wait until November 2 to enjoy it. It's delicious on its own as part of a festive brunch buffet or even for an elegant tea.

MAKES 1 ROUND LOAF

FOR THE DOUGH:
1/4 cup milk
4 tablespoons (1/2 stick) unsalted butter
1/4 cup water
1 1/4 teaspoons instant or bread machine yeast
1/4 cup granulated sugar
2 teaspoons anise seeds
1/2 teaspoon salt
2 large eggs, beaten
1 tablespoon grated orange zest
2 1/2 to 3 cups all-purpose flour

FOR THE GLAZE:
1/4 cup granulated sugar
1 tablespoon grated orange zest
1/4 cup fresh orange juice

Pearl or decorating sugar, for sprinkling

1. HEAT THE MILK AND BUTTER in a medium saucepan until the butter melts. Remove from the heat and stir in the water. Set aside to cool to lukewarm (90 degrees).

2. IN A LARGE BOWL, combine the yeast, granulated sugar, anise seeds, and salt. Beat in the warm milk mixture, then add the eggs and orange zest and beat until well combined. Beat in 2½ cups of the flour, 1 cup at a time, then beat in additional flour if needed until you have a soft dough.

3. TURN THE DOUGH OUT onto a floured surface and knead until smooth and elastic, about 5 minutes. Place the dough in a large oiled bowl and turn to coat. Cover with plastic wrap and let rise in a warm place until doubled in bulk, 1½ to 2 hours.

4. GREASE A BAKING SHEET and set aside. Punch down the dough and turn it out onto a floured surface. Twist off about ¼ cup of the dough and set it aside. Form the remaining dough into a large round loaf and place on the prepared baking sheet. Shape the reserved dough into a ball and place it in the center of the loaf. Loosely cover with plastic wrap and let rise in a warm place until almost doubled in bulk, about 1 hour

5. PREHEAT THE OVEN to 350 degrees. Bake the bread for 35 to 40 minutes, or until it is golden brown; an instant-read thermometer inserted into the center should register 190 to 200 degrees.

6. WHILE THE BREAD IS BAKING, make the glaze: In a small saucepan, combine the granulated sugar, orange zest, and orange juice. Bring to a boil over medium heat and boil for 2 minutes. Remove from the heat and set aside to cool.

7. WHEN THE BREAD IS DONE, transfer it to a wire rack to cool for several minutes. Lightly brush the loaf with the glaze and sprinkle with pearl sugar. Let cool.

PAN DE LOS MUERTOS

Mexican immigrants to the Heartland followed the railroad and meatpacking industries to settle in places like Chicago, Illinois; Topeka, Kansas; and Kansas City, Missouri. Although home cooks still make corn-based dishes like tamales, Mexican bakeries feature wheat-based traditional breads brought to Mexico during the period of French rule in the nineteenth century. This orange-and-anise-scented bread is a distant relative of the Provençal fougasse, *a sweet bread flavored with fennel seeds and orange, and the plainer anise seed bread known as* pain à l'anis. *It is usually made for the Mexican* Dio de los Muertos *(Day of the Dead) celebration on November 2, a day set aside to honor friends and family members who have died. After all, to many of Mexican ancestry, life on earth is but a dream state; only in dying do humans fully awaken. And those who have departed this world still remain as important connections between those on earth and those in the heavens. As with the St. Joseph Table tradition in Italian households, traditional Mexican homes feature food displayed on elaborate altars, and* Pan de los Muertos *is usually included. Sometimes Mexican bakeries feature* Pan de los Muertos *molded into different shapes like angels and animals, or with a crossed-bones design on top instead of the brioche-like topknot in this version.*

FESTIVE BREADS FROM THE HEARTLAND

BABKA *A tall, rich yeast bread with Polish and Russian roots.*

BISHOP'S BREAD *A rich yeast bread studded with dried fruit and almonds and baked in a large coffee can. This bread is made in such diverse communities as Enemy Swim Lake in Waubay, South Dakota, and Cedar Rapids, Iowa.*

DOPPBROD *On Christmas Eve, traditional Swedish-American households make "Dip-in-the-Pot Soup," for which this "Dip-in-the-Pot Bread" is named. Hungry members of the family can furtively dip pieces of the fennel-and-anise-flavored rye bread, made with buttermilk, into the brothy soup while the lady of the house attends to the finishing touches on the smorgasbord.*

HOUSKA *A braided rich Czech loaf studded with almonds and golden raisins. Patrons of Vesecky's in Berwyn, Illinois, take a number and count themselves lucky if there's a loaf of houska left.*

PANETTONE *An Italian Christmas bread resembling a giant brioche, made in special paper molds. The best are made with a* biga, *or starter, saved from a previous batch. The rich yeast dough is flavored with lemon and orange zest, dried fruits, and nuts.*

PASKA *An Easter bread of Russian* (pascha) *and Russian Mennonite roots, often baked in a mold. In rural prairie communities, this usually meant a tall coffee or tomato juice can. Rich with cream, butter, and eggs, paska may have lemon zest in the dough, but little else. The top is sometimes drizzled with confectioners' sugar icing and decorated with colored sprinkles.*

POVITICA *A Serbian/Croatian bread composed of a thin strudel-like dough spread with a walnut or cream cheese filling, rolled up into a long cylinder, folded over itself, and baked in a loaf.*

STOLLEN *A half moon–shaped Christmas bread that is a hallmark of German and Swiss holidays. Dried fruits, citrus peel, nut filling, and spices flavor the rich yeast dough. The Swiss Christmas stollen from the tiny New Glarus Bakery in New Glarus, Wisconsin, is studded with nuggets of rich marzipan; Zingerman's Bakehouse Stollen, from Ann Arbor, Michigan, is flavored with white rum, glacéed fruits, golden and Red Flame raisins, vanilla, and cinnamon. (See Prairie Bakeries, page 219.)*

TSOUREKI *A fine-textured Greek Easter bread subtly flavored with anise seeds, cinnamon, and honey. Formed into a braided ring, the golden bread is often studded with red-dyed Easter eggs for a colorful Sunday morning centerpiece. Some home cooks use this same dough to make a New Year's bread known as* vasilopita, *in which a lucky coin is hidden; whoever gets the piece with the coin will have good fortune for the rest of the year.*

YULEKAGE *Festive with candied fruit, scented with cardamom, and glazed with confectioners' sugar icing, this Christmas loaf bread flies off the shelves of Midwestern Danish, Swedish, and Norwegian bakeries, such as Lehmann's in Racine, Wisconsin.*

ICED ALMOND
AND CHERRY BABKA

Polish and Russian immigrants to the prairie gloried in their Easter babkas, enriched yeast breads studded with dried fruit and nuts. Russian Mennonites in wheat-farming communities still make a plainer babka, baked in a coffee can and drizzled with confectioners' sugar icing. This traditional bread—which looks like a rounded, glistening, snow-capped hill—is great for showing off on the holiday table.

MAKES 1 LARGE ROUND LOAF

FOR THE BABKA:
1 cup dried sour cherries or cranberries
1 tablespoon amaretto or other almond-
*   flavored liqueur*
1 cup milk
8 tablespoons (1 stick) unsalted butter
1 (¹/4-ounce) package (2¹/4 teaspoons)
*   active dry yeast*
¹/4 cup warm (110 degrees) water
2 large eggs
2 large egg yolks
¹/2 cup plus 1 tablespoon granulated sugar
¹/2 teaspoon salt

2 teaspoons almond extract
5 to 5¹/2 cups all-purpose flour
¹/2 cup slivered almonds
1¹/2 cups candied cherries, cut in half

FOR THE ICING:
¹/4 cup heavy cream
1¹/2 cups confectioners' sugar
1¹/2 teaspoons almond extract

Sanding sugar, for dusting, optional

1. PLACE THE DRIED CHERRIES or cranberries in a small bowl and pour the liqueur over them; set aside to soften. In a small saucepan, heat the milk to a simmer. Add 6 tablespoons (³/4 stick) of the butter and remove from the heat; let stand until the butter has melted and the mixture has cooled to lukewarm (90 degrees). In a small bowl, sprinkle the yeast over the warm water and set aside to proof until foamy, about 5 minutes.

2. IN THE BOWL OF AN ELECTRIC MIXER or another large bowl, beat the eggs, egg yolks, and ¹/2 cup of the granulated sugar until thick and pale lemon colored, about 5 minutes. Beat in the salt, almond extract, and the milk and yeast mixtures. Using the dough hook or a wooden spoon, beat in 5 cups of the flour, 1 cup at a time, until you have a stiff dough, adding additional flour if necessary.

3. GREASE A LARGE BOWL with 1 tablespoon of the butter and set aside. With the dough hook, knead the dough for 5 minutes, or until elastic. Or turn the dough out onto a floured surface and knead by hand. Place the dough in the prepared bowl and turn to coat. Cover with plastic wrap and let rise in a warm place until doubled in bulk, about 1 hour.

4. GREASE A 3-QUART KUGELHOPF, babka, or brioche mold with the remaining 1 tablespoon butter and sprinkle with the remaining 1 tablespoon granulated sugar; set aside. Transfer the dough to a floured surface and pat out into a large oval. Place one-quarter of the dried cherries or cranberries, candied cherries, and almonds on the bottom half of the dough. Fold the upper half of the dough over the cherries and almonds and knead gently. Turn the dough a quarter turn, pat it out to a large oval again, and place another quarter of the fruit and almonds on the bottom half of the dough. Fold over the upper half of the dough, knead gently, and turn the dough.

Repeat the process until all the cherries and almonds have been incorporated. Place the dough in the prepared pan, cover with plastic wrap, and let rise in a warm place until doubled in bulk, 45 minutes to 1 hour.

5. PREHEAT THE OVEN to 350 degrees. Bake the babka for 45 minutes, or until it is golden brown; an instant-read thermometer inserted into the center should register 190 degrees. Let cool in the pan on a rack for 5 minutes.

6. MEANWHILE, make the icing: In a small bowl, whisk the cream, confectioners' sugar, and almond extract together until smooth. Turn the babka out of the pan onto a sheet of aluminum foil, then turn it right side up. Pour, spread, or drizzle the icing over the babka so that the top is coated and the icing drips down the sides. Dust with sanding sugar, if desired. Let cool.

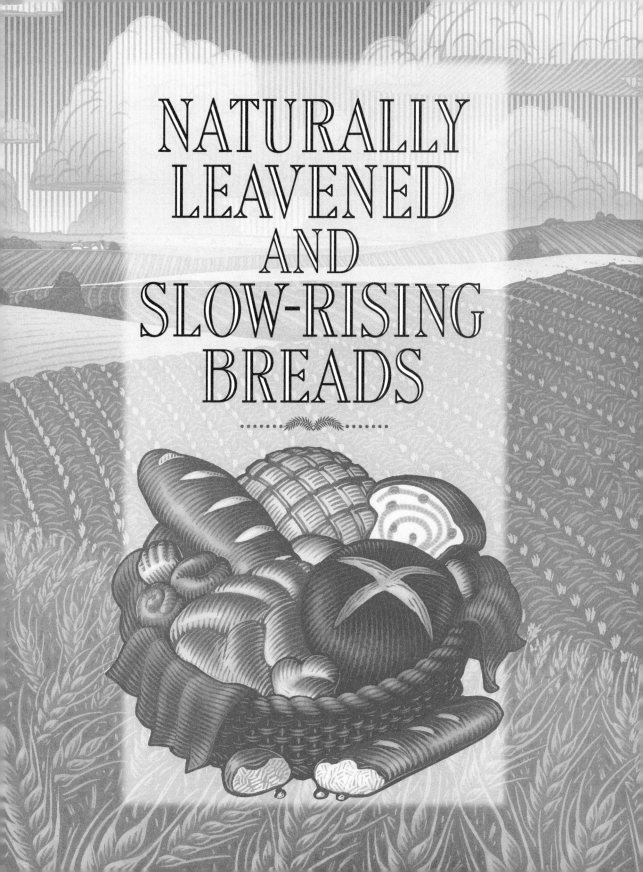

NATURALLY LEAVENED AND SLOW-RISING BREADS

OLD-FASHIONED BUTTERMILK BREAD

In *Buckeye Cookery and Practical House-keeping*, published in Minneapolis in 1877, the inspiration for this loaf is known as Winter Bread because it is "more convenient to make in winter, since a hot fire is needed to heat the milk." Sourdough bread was not admired by the anonymous ladies who compiled the recipes. Instead, they insisted that "good, sweet bread" was the goal of the urban Midwestern housewife, who had access to fresh brewer's and baker's yeast. After my great-grandmother Gertrude Rottherm Willenborg emigrated in 1888 from the Schulting family farm in north-western Germany to Cincinnati, she no doubt learned to make this type of bread—so different from the dark, dense, chewy, and slightly sour loaves she would have known growing up. She would have used a more liquid yeast, either brewer's or baker's, available in town. With this recipe, you'll get a high, light, crusty white loaf with a somewhat honeycombed crumb. You'll need to allow eight hours for the initial rising time.

MAKES 1 LOAF

FOR THE SPONGE:
1/4 teaspoon active dry yeast
3/4 cup warm (110 degrees) water
1 cup buttermilk
1/2 teaspoon salt
2 cups unbleached all-purpose flour

2 1/2 to 3 cups bread flour

1. MAKE THE SPONGE: Sprinkle the yeast over the warm water in a medium bowl and set aside to proof until foamy, about 5 minutes. Meanwhile, in a small saucepan, heat the buttermilk just until warm (110 degrees); remove from the heat.

2. WITH A WOODEN SPOON, stir the buttermilk, salt, and all-purpose flour into the yeast mixture. Cover with plastic wrap and let rise in a warm place until the sponge has doubled and is light and full of bubbles, at least 8 hours, or overnight.

3. GREASE A 9-BY-5-BY-3-INCH LOAF PAN and set aside. If desired, transfer the sponge to the bowl of an electric mixer. Stir the bread flour into the starter, 1 cup at a time, until you have a stiff dough. Using the dough hook attachment, knead the dough for 5 to 8 minutes, or until smooth and elastic, adding more flour if necessary. Or turn the dough out onto a floured surface and knead by hand. Place the dough in the prepared pan, cover with plastic wrap, and let rise in a warm place until doubled in bulk, 1 1/2 to 2 hours.

4. PREHEAT THE OVEN to 375 degrees. Bake the bread for 35 to 40 minutes, or until it is golden brown on top and sounds hollow when tapped on the bottom; an instant-read thermometer inserted into the center should register 190 to 200 degrees. Cool in the pan or on a wire rack.

PRAIRIE OVENS

············ ❧ ············

Yeast, water, flour, salt. The qualities of each of these ingredients give a particular flavor and texture to bread. Sourdough starter made from wild grapes or native plums, organic all-purpose flour, and spring water has an altogether different flavor and texture from a sponge made of active dry yeast, bleached all-purpose flour, and tap water. But another important element is the oven itself. The various types of ovens used through the Midwest contributed to the unique character of early breads.

The eastern part of the Midwest, settled in the late eighteenth and early nineteenth centuries by easterners migrating westward, had farmhouse and kitchen styles based upon the settlers' own mid-Atlantic, New England, or Southern building traditions. In the kitchen of the 1823 William Conner brick home at Conner Prairie in Noblesville, Indiana, the kitchen boasts an enormous brick cooking hearth and a brick-lined bake oven with an iron door, built into the massive kitchen wall. On baking days, a fire was started on the floor of the oven with kindling and coals from the fireplace. The fire was allowed to burn for a specified length of time. Then, when the bricks had absorbed the heat, the fire was swept out of the oven. An experienced baker could tell how hot the oven was by the flour test (how long it takes flour sprinkled on the oven floor to turn brown) or the hand test (how long you can keep your hand in the oven before you have to remove it). Breads, pastries, cakes, and pies were placed in the oven according to the temperature needed to bake them. Breads that required a hotter temperature went in first, baked treats requiring a low heat, like meringues, went in last.

In homes that did not have a bake oven, breads were baked on the hearth in a Dutch oven, a footed cast-iron pot with a concave lid. Coals were banked under, around, and on top of the Dutch oven to surround the bread with heat.

By the mid-nineteenth century, the new low two-step cast-iron stove offered greater safety and convenience, although some of the wood-fired flavor of the bake oven was lost. Wood-fired cast-iron stoves with oven compartments such as those in the 1855 Martin Franklin Handley House in Clayton, Missouri, and the Ella Sharp Museum, housed in an 1857 Greek Revival home in Jackson, Michigan, imparted a special flavor to baked goods. Looking backward from a new-millennium perspective at the old technology of the cast-iron cook stove, Nebraska folklorist Roger Welsch asks, "If it is such a backward device, why are the stews that come from its top and the breads that come from its ovens so wonderfully superior?"

In the 1860s, as a result of the Homestead Act, European immigrants went farther west to the Great Plains, where they experienced culture shock when they discovered how they would need to bake bread. Scandinavians, Germans, and Czechs were used to an abundance of wood to fire stone or brick-lined ovens. Not only did they have to learn the peculiarities of the more elaborate cook stove, they also had to learn to cook with corncobs or dried manure as fuel.

Russian Mennonite settlers on the Great Plains in the 1870s had an easier adjustment period, as they brought their own unique ovens and baking techniques that they had adapted to similar conditions on the Russian steppes. Built outdoors or into a long, thick wall separating rooms in a Russian Mennonite house, the distinctive prairie ovens were deep, making it easier to accommodate the long prairie grasses, sunflower stalks, or cornstalks that used to fire the brick-lined ovens. Like earlier bake ovens, prairie ovens were left to absorb the heat of the fire, then the smoldering fuel was swept out and the breads placed inside to bake. A long metal tray with raised edges and a handle for pulling was large enough for several round loaves of crusty white bread, or rectangular sheets of coffee cake. Today, you can see examples of these ovens in the restored farm buildings at the Kauffman Museum in North Newton, Kansas, and the Mennonite Heritage Museum in Goessel, Kansas.

Pioneers also rigged their own ovens, as Maria Schellenberg Klassen recalled in her account of traveling to their homestead in Manitoba in 1878. They stopped in the three-year-old settlement of Blumenort, Manitoba. "The villagers were most hospitable, bringing us bread and potatoes," she wrote. "We also did some of our baking—our oven being a hole in the ground with a tin around it. It worked rather well." Earlier pioneers traveling from St. Louis westward along the Oregon Trail to Oregon also rigged this kind of oven, dreaming of home, hearth, and the settled life that was still months away.

In adapting heirloom bread recipes for the modern kitchen, we know that to be really authentic, these breads would have to be baked using the oven technology available at the time. We can try to duplicate those baking methods using modern equipment, but the breads—although still wonderfully delicious—won't be exactly the same.

PRUSSIAN LEAF-WRAPPED BREADSTICKS

Immigrants from West Prussia to Russian Mennonite settlements in Saskatchewan brought with them a version of a local baking tradition—laying the dough on leaves of cabbage, kale, horseradish, or sweet calamus to bake. The practice survives in the custom of wrapping fingers of bread dough in beet leaves or other hearty, leafy greens, which are then brushed with butter and salt, baked, and served with sour cream. I learned about this tradition when I met Ted and Helen Walters at a cooking class I gave in the Detroit area. They grew up in Saskatchewan, and they described these delicious breadsticks, which their families had made. Any homemade not-too-yeasty bread recipe, prepared through the first rise, will work in this recipe. Besides having an attractive rustic appearance, the breadsticks have a delicious flavor: somehow the combination of bread dough, beet leaf, and coarse salt tastes like black olives. I serve these on a large earthenware platter, surrounding a bowl of sour cream. If you use the Old-Fashioned Buttermilk Bread dough, the recipe will need to be started the day before.

MAKES 2 DOZEN BREADSTICKS

1 recipe Old-Fashioned Buttermilk Bread dough (page 41), prepared through Step 3, Hit-the-Trail Sourdough Bread dough (page 52), prepared through Step 2, or Shaker Daily Bread dough (page 3), prepared through Step 3
24 beet or chard leaves (6 to 8 inches long), long stems trimmed, rinsed, and patted dry
6 tablespoons (3/4 stick) unsalted butter, melted
Coarse sea or kosher salt
Sour cream, for serving

A RECIPE FOR BUTTERED TOAST

The compilers of Buckeye Cookery and Practical Housekeeping, published in Minneapolis in 1877, realized the value in simple things done well. Take, for example, these directions for making buttered toast, using a toasting fork over a hot fire:

Although toast is commonly used, few know how to prepare it nicely. Take bread not too fresh, cut thin and evenly, trim off the crust-edges for the crumb-jar; first warm each side of the bread, then present the first side again to the fire until it takes on a rich, even brown color; treat the other side in the same way; butter and serve immediately. The coals should be bright and hot.

1. LINE A BAKING SHEET with parchment paper. On a floured surface, roll the dough out into a 12-inch square. With a serrated knife or a pizza wheel, cut the dough into twelve 1-inch-wide strips. Cut each strip crosswise in half, so you end up with twenty-four 6-inch-long strips. Place the strips on the prepared baking sheet. Carefully wrap a beet leaf around the middle of each strip, tucking the ends under the dough. Brush the strips with the melted butter and sprinkle with coarse salt. Cover with plastic wrap and let rise in a warm place until doubled in bulk, about 45 minutes.

2. PREHEAT THE OVEN to 375 degrees. Bake the breadsticks for 15 to 20 minutes, or until puffed and browned. Serve warm, with sour cream.

BREWHOUSE BREAD

This dark, chewy, crusty, hearty slow-risen loaf, enriched by the malty flavor of a Midwestern brew, is the perfect foil to a grilled bratwurst and a jolt of horseradish. Or try it with an aged Wisconsin Cheddar and Brew Pub Pickled Onions (*Prairie Home Cooking*, page 51) or a hearth-warmed Leelanau raclette and cornichons. The dough rises so slowly that you can make it in the morning, cover it with plastic wrap, and leave it out on the kitchen counter (at 70 to 75 degrees) all day, then come home from work and bake it for dinner.

MAKES 1 BÂTARD

½ teaspoon active dry yeast
1½ cups good-quality Midwestern ale,
*   such as Boulevard Brewery's Ten Penny*
*   Ale or Grizzly Peak Brewing Company's*
*   Steelhead Red Ale, at room temperature*
1 teaspoon salt
2 tablespoons molasses or honey
1½ cups unbleached all-purpose flour,
*   plus more for kneading if needed*
1½ cups whole wheat flour
¾ cup stone-ground graham or whole
*   wheat flour*
Yellow cornmeal, for sprinkling

1. IN A LARGE BOWL, sprinkle the yeast over the ale; set aside to proof until foamy, about 5 minutes. With a wooden spoon, stir in the salt and molasses. Stir in the flours, 1 cup at a time, until you have a stiff and slightly sticky dough.

2. TURN THE DOUGH OUT onto a floured surface and knead for 5 to 8 minutes, adding more all-purpose flour if necessary, until smooth and elastic. Place the dough in a large oiled bowl and turn to coat. Cover with plastic wrap and let rise at cool room temperature (70 to 75 degrees) for at least 8 hours, or overnight.

3. SPRINKLE A COOKIE SHEET (without sides) with cornmeal and set aside. Punch down the dough, turn it out onto a floured surface, and knead it for 2 minutes. Form the dough into a 14-inch-long bâtard, pinching and tucking the ends under, and place on the prepared cookie sheet. With a serrated knife or a razor blade, make 4 diagonal slashes across the top of the loaf. Mist the bâtard with a little water, using a plastic spray bottle.

4. PLACE A BAKING STONE or tiles on the middle rack of the oven and preheat the oven to 425

MAKING RUSTIC BREAD BOWLS

············ ❧❧ ············

Homemade bread bowls, made from doughs with body and texture, are a delicious and attractive way of serving creamy soups, chili, or thick stews. They have a free-form appearance that really adds to the presentation. (Brothy soups or stews do not work as well served in bread bowls, because the bread can get soggy very quickly.) I prefer smaller bread bowls that hold about a cup of soup or stew.

Making bread bowls is easy. To adapt a bread recipe for making bowls instead of loaves, after the dough has risen once, divide it into portions according to the amount of flour you used: $1/2$ cup flour = 1 bread bowl.

For example, if you're making Italian Bread Imperiale (page 16), let the dough rise the first time. If you used about 6 cups of flour, that means 12 bread bowls. Using a serrated knife, cut the dough in half and then cut each half into 6 equal portions. Spray the outside of twelve 6-ounce custard cups with cooking spray and set upside down on a baking sheet. On a floured surface, roll or pat each piece of dough into a free-form 7-inch circle. Mold each dough circle over an upside-down custard cup. Cover with plastic wrap and let rise in a warm place for 20 minutes, or until slightly puffy.

Meanwhile, preheat the oven to 350 degrees. Beat 1 large egg yolk with 1 tablespoon water. Brush the dough gently with this glaze. Bake the bread bowls for 10 to 15 minutes, or until golden brown. With oven mitts or pot holders, carefully lift the bread bowls from the custard cups and place right side up on a wire rack to cool.

Many of the bread doughs in this book can be baked as bowls:

Hit-the-Trail Sourdough Bread
Russian Mennonite Sour Rye Bread
Dakota Territory Sourdough Potato Bread
Old-Fashioned Buttermilk Bread
Brewhouse Bread
Life-in-the-Slow-Lane Baguettes
North Union Village Daily Bread
Wisconsin Onion Dill Bread
Swedish Rye Bread/Swedish Dipping
    Bread
Italian Bread Imperiale
Savory Sun-Dried Tomato Bread
Roasted Sweet Pepper Bread
Cheddar Chive Bread
Wheat Country Banneton

Wildflower Honey and White Whole
    Wheat Bread
Whole Wheat Cheddar Bread
Amber Waves of Grain Bread
Cracked Wheat Bread
Honey Wheat Berry Bread
Prairie Painter's Oatmeal Honey Bread
Northern Prairie Barley and Sunflower
    Bread
Blue Ribbon Whole Wheat and Soybean
    Bread
Minnesota Wild Rice Bread
Danish Pumpernickel Rye
New Maxwell Street Bollillos
Mochos

degrees. Just before baking, place a baking pan of boiling water on the lower oven shelf.

5. USING A BAKER'S PEEL, or with a quick jerk of your arms, slide the bâtard off the cookie sheet onto the baking stone. Bake for 20 minutes. Reduce the heat to 400 degrees and bake for 10 to 15 minutes longer, or until the bâtard turns a dark, reddish brown and sounds hollow when tapped on the bottom; an instant-read thermometer inserted into the center should register 190 degrees. Transfer to a rack to cool.

LIFE-IN-THE-SLOW-LANE BAGUETTES

When things, all too rarely, slow down a bit, I like to make these chewy, crusty, almost foolproof slow-risen baguettes. Like Brewhouse Bread (page 45), the dough rises so slowly that you can make it in the morning, cover it with plastic wrap, and leave it out (at 70 to 75 degrees) all day, then bake it for dinner. These baguettes also freeze and reheat well.

MAKES 2 BAGUETTES

1/2 teaspoon active dry yeast
1 1/2 cups lukewarm (90 degrees) water
1 1/2 teaspoons salt
1 tablespoon honey
1 1/2 cups unbleached all-purpose flour, plus for kneading more if needed
1 1/2 cups whole wheat flour
3/4 cup stone-ground graham or whole wheat flour
Yellow cornmeal, for sprinkling

1. IN A LARGE BOWL, sprinkle the yeast over the lukewarm water; set aside to proof until foamy, about 5 minutes. With a wooden spoon, stir in the salt and honey. Stir in the flours, 1 cup at a time, until you have a stiff and slightly sticky dough.

2. TURN THE DOUGH OUT onto a floured surface and knead for 5 to 8 minutes, adding more all-purpose flour if necessary, until smooth and elastic. Place the dough in a large oiled bowl and turn to coat. Cover with plastic wrap and let rise at cool room temperature (70 to 75 degrees) for at least 8 hours, or overnight.

3. SPRINKLE A COOKIE SHEET (without sides) with cornmeal and set aside. Punch down the dough, turn it out onto a floured surface, and knead it for 2 minutes. Divide the dough in half. Form each half into a 14-inch-long baguette, pinching and tucking the ends under, and place 2 inches apart on the prepared cookie sheet. With a serrated knife or a razor blade, make 4 diagonal slashes across the top of each loaf. Mist

IN PRAISE OF LONG-RISEN BREAD

Home-baked bread of any kind is better than anything you can buy at the grocery store. This, of course, is not saying much, since most commercial bread has the taste and texture of a cellulose sponge. Long-risen bread, however, is better than anything you can get even from a fancy bakery.
—LAURIE COLWIN, *HOME COOKING: A WRITER IN THE KITCHEN*

the baguettes with a little water, using a plastic spray bottle.

4. PLACE A BAKING STONE or tiles on the middle rack of the oven and preheat the oven to 425 degrees. Just before baking, place a baking pan of boiling water on the lower oven shelf.

5. USING A BAKER'S PEEL, or with a quick jerk of your arms, slide the baguettes off the cookie sheet onto the baking stone. Bake for 10 minutes. Reduce the heat to 400 degrees and bake for 10 minutes longer, or until the baguettes are golden brown and sound hollow when tapped on the bottom; an instant-read thermometer inserted into the center should register 190 degrees. Transfer to a wire rack to cool.

············ ⁕ ············

MRS. SHIMERDA'S BREAD

I remember how horrified we were at the sour, ashy-gray bread she gave her family to eat. She mixed her dough, we discovered, in an old tin peck-measure that Krajiek had used about the barn. When she took the paste out to bake it, she left smears of dough sticking to the sides of the measure, put the measure on the shelf behind the stove, and let this residue ferment. The next time she made bread, she scraped this sour stuff down into the fresh dough to serve as yeast.

—JIM, IN WILLA CATHER'S *MY ANTONIA*

POOLISH

Making a naturally leavened bread from a starter with no yeast is admittedly a time-consuming process that can take up to fifteen days. If you want to bake breads with much of the taste and texture of a naturally leavened, slow-risen bread but want a starter that doesn't take so much time, then rediscover what European bakers have known for centuries—poolish. There is just enough yeast in the recipe to kick-start the leavening process.

MAKES 2 CUPS

¹/4 teaspoon active dry yeast
1¹/2 cups warm (110 degrees) water
2 cups unbleached all-purpose flour,
*   preferably organic*

1. IN A MEDIUM BOWL, sprinkle the yeast over the warm water and set aside to proof until foamy, about 5 minutes. Using a hand-held mixer or a wooden spoon, beat in the flour, then continue to beat for 3 minutes. Cover with plastic wrap and let the starter rise in a warm place until it is thick and sticky, about 8 hours.

2. THE STARTER IS NOW READY to use in a recipe, or it can be stored, covered with plastic wrap, in the refrigerator for up to 3 days. Stir it down with a spoon before using, then measure it out—it will be thick and crumbly—for use in a recipe. Allow refrigerated starter to come to room temperature before using.

············ ⁕ ············

SPRING WHEAT SEMOLINA BREAD

Durum wheat, or spring wheat, is planted in the spring and harvested in the summer, mainly in the Dakotas and the Prairie Provinces of Canada. Durum wheat flour has a high gluten, or protein, content. Semolina is coarsely ground durum wheat flour, and is used in the making of pastas as well as in Italian breads and pizza doughs. When semolina is finely ground to a flour, it makes a sturdy, strong dough. This recipe produces an airy, chewy coiled loaf with a nutty, wheaty flavor and buttery yellow color. To get the characteristic crust, use a baking stone or tiles and a spray bottle to mist the dough.

MAKES 2 ROUND LOAVES

1 teaspoon active dry yeast
1 1/4 cups plus 3 tablespoons warm
    (110 degrees) water
1 1/4 cups Poolish (page 48)
2 cups durum wheat or semolina flour,
    plus about 1/3 cup for kneading
1 1/2 cups bread flour
1/3 cup yellow cornmeal, plus more for
    sprinkling
4 teaspoons coarse sea or kosher salt
1/4 cup poppy seeds

1. IN A LARGE BOWL, sprinkle the yeast over the warm water and set aside to proof until foamy, about 5 minutes. Stir in the poolish, breaking it up with your hands or the spoon. Add both flours, the cornmeal, and salt and mix, scraping and folding the dough over itself, until it gathers into a mass.

2. TURN THE DOUGH OUT onto a lightly floured surface and knead until smooth and elastic, gradually adding more durum flour as needed. (The less flour added, the lighter the bread.) Shape the dough into a ball, place in a lightly oiled large bowl, and turn to coat. Cover with plastic wrap and refrigerate for at least 8 hours, or overnight.

3. REMOVE THE DOUGH from the refrigerator and allow to come to room temperature, about 2 hours.

4. GENEROUSLY SPRINKLE a cookie sheet (without sides) with cornmeal. Punch down the dough and turn it out onto a floured surface. Divide it in half. One at a time, gently flatten each half into a 12-by-10-inch rectangle. Starting at a short side, tightly roll the dough up jelly-roll fashion into a 12-inch-long cylinder, then roll it out under your palms into a 20-inch-long rope. Coil the rope into a spiral to make a round loaf, pulling up the end of the coil in the center of the loaf for an ornamental touch (like the topknot on a brioche). Place the coils 2 inches apart on the prepared cookie sheet.

5. LIGHTLY MIST the loaves with water, using a plastic spray bottle. Cover with plastic wrap and allow to rise in a warm place until doubled in bulk, about 1 to 2 hours. Sprinkle half of the poppy seeds over each coil.

6. PLACE A BAKING STONE or tiles on the middle rack of the oven and preheat the oven to 425 degrees. Just before baking, place a baking pan of boiling water on the bottom shelf of the oven.

7. CAREFULLY PULL OUT the middle oven rack and, using a wooden peel, or with a quick jerk of your arms, slide the loaves off the cookie sheet onto the stone. Bake for 25 minutes, or until the loaves are golden and sound hollow when tapped on the bottom; an instant-read thermometer inserted into the center should register 190 to 200 degrees. Transfer the loaves to a wire rack to cool.

FRENCH CANADIAN WHEAT AND WALNUT BREAD

Versions of this French country-style bread traveled with nineteenth-century immigrants from central France to Quebec, and then on to the southernmost tip of Lake Michigan, to make the last leg of the voyage down the Kankakee River to the village of Bourbonnais in northern Illinois. From there, the recipe also went westward to French Canadian colonies such as St. Joseph in Cloud County, Kansas. By the 1860s, much of the arable farmland in eastern and central Canada had been claimed, so migrants came in a steady stream. This traditional bread—which needs three risings, including a long, slow one in the refrigerator—gets just a bit of a modern twist, with a little yeast to kick-start the rise, but basically relies on the slow-rise process of the nineteenth century. Tasting of walnuts and honey, this delicious loaf has a honeycombed crumb and a chewy bite.

MAKES 2 ROUND LOAVES

$^1/_2$ teaspoon active dry yeast
1 cup plus 2 tablespoons warm
   (110 degrees) water
$^3/_4$ cup Poolish (page 48)
5 tablespoons honey or maple syrup
$1^1/_2$ tablespoons walnut, olive, or
   canola oil
$2^3/_4$ cups unbleached all-purpose flour,
   preferably organic, plus more for
   kneading
1 tablespoon coarse sea or kosher salt
$1^1/_2$ cups walnuts, toasted and coarsely
   chopped
Yellow cornmeal, for sprinkling

1. IN THE BOWL OF AN ELECTRIC MIXER or another large bowl, sprinkle the yeast over the warm water and set aside to proof until foamy, about 5 minutes. Using a wooden spoon, stir in the poolish, breaking it up with your hands or the spoon. Beat in the honey and oil. Stir in the flour and salt and beat, scraping and folding the dough over itself, until it gathers into a mass.

2. USING THE DOUGH HOOK, knead the dough for 5 minutes, or until soft and only slightly sticky, adding more flour as needed. Or turn the dough out onto a lightly floured surface, and knead by hand. Knead the nuts into the dough until evenly distributed. Place the dough in a lightly oiled large bowl and turn to coat. Cover with plastic wrap and refrigerate for at least 8 hours, or overnight.

3. PUNCH DOWN THE DOUGH and turn it out onto a floured surface. Divide it in half. Shape each piece into a ball and place on a flour-dusted kitchen towel. Cover with plastic wrap and let rise in a warm place until doubled in bulk, 2 to 3 hours.

4. GENEROUSLY SPRINKLE a cookie sheet (without sides) with cornmeal. On a floured surface, gently flatten one of the balls of dough, then shape it into a round loaf and place on the prepared cookie sheet. Repeat with the remaining dough, leaving about 2 inches between the loaves on the cookie sheet. Cover with plastic wrap and let rise in a warm place until doubled in bulk, 2 to 3 hours.

5. AT LEAST 30 MINUTES before you want to bake, place a baking stone or tiles on the middle rack of the oven and preheat the oven to 425 degrees. Just before baking, place a baking pan of boiling water on the bottom shelf of the oven.

6. CAREFULLY PULL OUT the middle oven rack and, using a wooden peel, or with a quick jerk of your arms, slide the loaves off the cookie sheet onto the stone. Bake for 30 to 35 minutes, or until the loaves are golden brown and sound hollow when tapped on the bottom; an instant-read thermometer inserted into the center should register 190 to 200 degrees. Transfer to a wire rack to cool.

GREAT PLAINS SOURDOUGH STARTER

Sourdough bread is generally associated with San Francisco, but in fact sourdough traveled westward with pioneers during the 1840s Gold Rush and the opening of California and the Prairie Provinces of Canada for settlement. Nineteenth-century Midwestern cookbooks are full of recipes for natural yeast made from flour, water, potatoes, and, perhaps, hops. But trying to nurture homemade yeast while traveling was an impossible task—homemade yeast starters depend on the stability of home and hearth. Sourdough was more adventurous and could hit the trail, as long as the weather remained mild or the cook didn't mind sleeping with the

HAS THE STARTER STRENGTHENED ENOUGH?

Naturally leavened bread recipes call for allowing the starter to be strengthened with daily feedings of flour and water until ready for use in baking bread. How can you know for sure when it is ready? A starter ready to use for baking bread looks active. Unlike commercial yeast, which proofs into tiny bubbles that seem to foam, naturally leavened starter has bubbles about $1/4$ to $1/2$ inch in diameter. You will see many bubbles quickly forming and bursting on the surface of the starter. If there are few bubbles, or their activity seems sluggish, the starter needs to be strengthened for at least another day.

sourdough barrel to keep it warm (see Hit-the-Trail Sourdough Bread, below).

Just as there are many different recipes for homemade yeasts, there are also many for sourdough starters. Some of them are very traditional—just flour, water, and wild fruit—but also time-consuming for the home baker. This more modern version has a good success rate and produces a bread with a wonderful, chewy texture and a mild, sour flavor very similar to that of artisanal bakery sourdough. The yogurt culture helps attract the wild yeasts in the air.

MAKES 1 1/2 CUPS

1 cup nonfat milk
1/4 cup plain yogurt
1 cup unbleached all-purpose flour

1. IN A SMALL SAUCEPAN, heat the milk until lukewarm (90 degrees). Remove from the heat and stir in the yogurt. Pour the mixture into a 1-quart glass or ceramic crock, jar, or bowl. Cover with cheesecloth and let sit in a warm spot (80 to 85 degrees) for 24 hours. In cold weather, you can sit the bowl or jar on a heating pad turned to the Warm setting; on a warm day you can place the starter outside in the sun or on the kitchen counter.

2. AFTER 24 HOURS, the milk will have thickened and formed curds. Gradually stir in the flour until well blended. Cover with a non-metallic lid or plastic wrap and set in a warm place again until the starter ferments and bubbles into a thick, spongy mass, 2 to 5 days; stir once or twice a day.

3. THE STARTER IS NOW READY TO USE. Stir, cover loosely with plastic wrap, and refrigerate.

The starter will keep for 4 weeks in the refrigerator in a dormant stage before it needs to be fed again.

To feed the starter, remove 1 cup of the starter for your baking, and stir 1 cup warm (110 to 120 degrees) nonfat milk and 1 cup unbleached all-purpose flour into the remaining starter. Allow to stand in a warm place for 24 hours, or until bubbly and a clear liquid has formed on the top. Stir in the liquid, cover loosely, and refrigerate. If, at any time, the starter turns pink, develops mold, or smells rancid, throw it away and start fresh.

HIT-THE-TRAIL SOURDOUGH BREAD

Chuckwagon cooks on cattle drives along the Chisholm Trail, from the southernmost tip of Texas to the rail yards at Abilene, Kansas, would fuss over the sourdough barrel like a newborn baby. At night, the cook slept with the barrel under a blanket. During the day, the barrel traveled safely, lashed to the side of the wagon, or rested in the cool shade when the men set up camp. If the sourdough got too cold or too hot, the fermentation was adversely affected, and that meant big trouble. After all, hungry cowboys who spent all day rustling wily longhorns were in no mood to hear the cook say, "Sorry, guys, the bread didn't turn out," when they lined up for grub.

MAKES 2 ROUND LOAVES

FOR THE SPONGE:
1 cup Great Plains Sourdough Starter
   (page 51)
1¹/₂ cups warm (110 degrees) water
1 teaspoon sugar
2 cups bread flour

1¹/₂ teaspoons salt
2¹/₂ to 3 cups bread flour

1. TO MAKE THE SPONGE, combine the starter, water, sugar, and flour in a large bowl and stir with a wooden spoon until well blended. Cover

THE LAST BEST WEST

Driving east from Regina, you see the old native prairie grasses and wild western red lilies or blue flax—punctuated here and there with stands of aspen—gradually give way to an orderly scene painted in primary colors. Brilliant yellow fields of blooming canola blaze under a clear blue July sky, with a barn-red grain elevator towering over the rolling landscape in every small town.

The traditional wheat-growing farms of Saskatchewan are going to canola, as health-conscious consumers buy more and more canola oil. The forty-million-acre grain belt of Saskatchewan cuts across the middle of this Canadian Prairie Province; farther north, you would travel through birch forests before ending up in the treeless Arctic.

With the Saskatchewan prairie's extremes in temperature, from 95 degrees on a July day to way below zero during the winter, people have long been drawn to the Qu'Appelle Valley for its shelter, food, and wood. Cree Indians used to winter here, in this "Valley of the Calling Lakes." Broods of Canada geese, pintails, and blue-winged teal paddle on the surface of the lakes, while walleye pike teem below. Wild tangles of saskatoon and Juneberries are ripe for the picking, and Angus cattle graze where buffalo once did. Wheat turning golden and green gardens add more color and vigor to the summer landscape.

The richness of the soil and the promise of virtually free land began to beckon when the Canadian prairies opened up for settlement in 1881. However, it wasn't until the railroads went through in the 1890s that the real boom time came. The Canadian government encouraged other Canadians and immigrants to settle "The Last Best West." And the settlers came in droves: eastern Canadians, French Canadians, Americans, Icelanders, British, Russian Mennonites, and Ukrainians. Eastern Europeans, especially those from the steppes, had the easiest time adjusting to the big sky and seemingly endless prairie landscape.

Today, you can pause at Mallard Cove for tea, clotted cream, and a scone topped with saskatoon berry jelly, then go on to the next town to visit the onion-domed Ukrainian church, finally stopping for dinner at a local restaurant in a farther town and having Prussian Leaf-Wrapped Breadsticks (page 44) with your borscht.

with plastic wrap and let ferment in a warm place until bubbly and spongy, at least 8 to 12 hours, or overnight.

2. USING A WOODEN SPOON, stir the salt into the sponge, then stir in enough flour, $1/2$ cup at a time, so the dough is only slightly sticky. Turn the dough out onto a floured surface, sprinkle with some of the remaining flour, and knead for 5 minutes, adding more flour as necessary, until the dough is elastic and springs back when poked with your finger. Place the dough in a large oiled bowl and turn to coat. Cover with plastic wrap and let rise in a warm place until doubled in bulk, about 2 hours.

3. GREASE A BAKING SHEET and set aside. Punch down the dough and turn it out onto a floured surface. Divide it in half and form each half into a round loaf. Place 2 inches apart on the prepared baking sheet, cover with plastic wrap, and let rise in a warm place until doubled in bulk, about 1 hour.

4. PREHEAT THE OVEN to 375 degrees. Just before baking, place a pan of boiling water on the bottom shelf of the oven.

5. WITH A SHARP KNIFE or a razor blade, slash an X in the top of each loaf. Place the baking sheet on the middle shelf and bake the bread for 30 to 35 minutes, or until it sounds hollow when tapped on the bottom; an instant-read thermometer inserted into the center should register 190 to 200 degrees. Transfer to a wire rack to cool.

RYE

Throughout the nineteenth century, rye was the predominant grain in northern Europe, growing well in the relatively poorer soil and cool, moist climate. When eastern and northern European immigrants came to the prairie, they brought their knowledge of growing and harvesting rye as well as their love of sour rye bread. Today, the Prairie Provinces of Canada and the Dakotas produce most of the rye grown in North America, and most of that crop is winter rye. Like winter wheat, winter rye is drilled into the soil in autumn. Green shoots appear before the frost and stay green all winter when the plant goes dormant, with the added advantage of providing pasturage for cattle. (Cattle can nibble the rye grass without harming the roots.) In the spring, the rye starts growing again along with other prairie grasses, and it begins to turn golden in June, a signal that it is ready to be harvested.

Rye flour contains very little gluten, so using rye flour alone in a bread recipe results in a very heavy bread. That's why most rye bread recipes also include wheat flour. Rye bread also has heightened moisture-retaining properties, and you feel fuller when you eat it. Caraway seed, acidic agents like sourdough starter or yogurt, dark sweeteners like molasses or brown sugar, and onion are all traditional flavoring additions to rye bread.

RUSSIAN MENNONITE SOUR RYE BREAD

~~~

"We always had boiled potatoes the day before my mother made bread," recalls Carrie Young of growing up in the Dakotas in *Nothing to Do but Stay: My Pioneer Mother.* "Pioneer women quickly learned that bread made with potato water remained moist much longer than that made with milk or water alone." For many Scandinavian, Russian Mennonite, Polish, Bohemian, and German settlers to the Midwest, sour rye was their everyday loaf.

MAKES 2 ROUND OR REGULAR LOAVES

2 tablespoons active dry yeast
1 teaspoon sugar
1¹/2 cups warm (110 degree) water
1 cup potato cooking water
1¹/2 teaspoons salt
2 tablespoons bacon drippings, lard, or
   shortening
¹/2 cup Great Plains Sourdough Starter
   (page 51) or plain yogurt
5 cups unbleached all-purpose flour or
   bread flour, plus more if needed
2¹/2 cups stone-ground rye flour

1. IN THE BOWL OF AN ELECTRIC MIXER or another large bowl, combine the yeast, sugar, and ¹/2 cup of the warm water. With the paddle attachment or a wooden spoon, beat in the potato water, the remaining 1 cup warm water, the salt, bacon drippings, lard, or shortening, and starter. Beat in the all-purpose or bread flour, 1 cup at a time, then beat in the rye flour, 1 cup at a time, until you have a soft dough.

2. SWITCH TO THE DOUGH HOOK and knead the dough gently for 5 to 6 minutes, adding more all-purpose or bread flour if necessary, until it is elastic. Or turn the dough out onto a floured surface and knead by hand. Place the dough in a large oiled bowl and turn to coat. Cover with plastic wrap and let rise at room temperature until doubled in bulk, about 1 hour.

3. GREASE A LARGE BAKING SHEET or two 9-by-5-by-3-inch loaf pans and set aside. Punch down the dough and turn it out onto a floured surface. Divide the dough in half and form into 2 round or regular loaves. Put the loaves 2 inches apart on the prepared baking sheet or put in the prepared pans, cover with plastic wrap, and let rise in a warm place until doubled in bulk, about 1 hour.

4. PREHEAT THE OVEN to 400 degrees. Bake the loaves for 15 minutes. Reduce the heat to 375 degrees and continue baking for 30 more minutes, or until the loaves are a rich brown and sound hollow when tapped on the bottom; an instant-read thermometer inserted into the center should register 190 to 200 degrees. Transfer the round loaves to a wire rack to cool, or cool the regular loaves in the pans on a rack.

DAKOTA TERRITORY SOURDOUGH POTATO BREAD

≈≈≈

Settlers first began coming to the Dakota Territory in the 1870s. The flow increased from the 1880s through the early 1900s, when Germans, Scandinavians, and Americans from the eastern states came to stake their claims and homestead. In 1911, Nora Pfundheller King Lenartz's family came from Iowa to file a claim for free land, after her father drew a number in the land lottery. In 1913, a claim near her father's became available, and she decided to become a land holder herself, like thousands of other women in North Dakota. "Well, I was twenty-one and had no prospects of doing anything. The land was there so I took it," she wrote in her memoirs. "There were wild herds of horses that roamed over the prairie. . . . I remember one time a herd of cattle came and rubbed on the shack. . . . I thought they were going to tip it over." While roughing it in her shanty with few supplies, this is the kind of bread she would have made, keeping the starter and sponge warm near the cookstove. This makes a moist loaf with a soft, airy crumb and mild sourness. It keeps for up to a week and freezes well. The dough is heavy, so even if you use an electric mixer to mix it, knead it by hand.

MAKES 3 ROUND LOAVES

WHEN THE CRUMB JAR IS FULL

For nineteenth-century Midwestern home bakers, the process of baking bread consumed at least a part of every day. There was always yeast to make, a sponge to set, dough to mix or let rise and bake. No wonder they valued every bread crumb. Any leftovers were put in the crumb jar—or a brown paper bag tightly closed and kept in the pantry—to use in a variety of inventive and thrifty recipes. "Never throw away even a crumb of bread," the compilers of the 1877 Buckeye Cookery and Practical Housekeeping *exhorted their readers, "but save it and put it with other pieces" to use for "dressing, stuffing, puddings, griddle-cakes, etc."*

In German and Czech households, bread crumbs were sautéed in butter, perhaps with poppy seeds, then tossed with hot noodles. English and Welsh households made "puddings," or desserts, that used bread crumbs—brown bread ice cream, for which whole-meal bread crumbs were sugared and toasted in the oven (like a kind of praline), then blended into a custard and frozen; brown Betty made with layers of homemade sweetened applesauce or sliced apples, topped with buttered bread crumbs sprinkled with cinnamon, and baked; layers of sliced fruit or berries topped with buttered and sugared bread crumbs and baked to make a kind of charlotte; or a prairie plum pudding made with graham bread crumbs, raisins, dried plums, and spices. And no matter what the ethnic origin of the cook, they all dredged savory cakes of potato, salmon, whitefish, or ground chicken and veal in bread crumbs before frying.

1 cup Great Plains Sourdough Starter
 (page 51)
2 cups warm (110 degrees) water
7³/4 to 8 cups bread flour
1 cup warm mashed potatoes (can be a
 little lumpy)
²/3 cup plus 2 tablespoons milk
2 tablespoons sugar
2 teaspoons salt
2 teaspoons dillweed
1 large egg

1. TO MAKE THE SPONGE, combine the starter, warm water, and 4 cups ot the flour in the bowl of an electric mixer or another large bowl and stir until you have a smooth batter. Cover with plastic wrap and let rise in a warm place until bubbly and spongy, at least 8 to 10 hours, or overnight.

2. WITH THE PADDLE ATTACHMENT or a wooden spoon, beat the mashed potatoes, ²/3 cup of the milk, the sugar, salt, and dill into the sponge. Beat in enough of the remaining 4 cups flour, 1 cup at a time, so you have a stiff dough.

3. TURN THE DOUGH OUT onto a floured surface and knead for 8 to 10 minutes, or until it is smooth and elastic and springs back when poked

with your finger. Place the dough in a large oiled bowl and turn to coat. Cover with plastic wrap and let rise in a warm place until doubled in bulk, about 2 hours.

4. GREASE THREE 9-INCH ROUND CAKE PANS and set aside. Punch down the dough and turn it out onto a floured surface. Divide the dough into 3 portions. Form each one into a round loaf and place in one of the prepared pans. Cover with plastic wrap and let rise in a warm place until doubled in bulk, 1¹/2 to 2 hours.

5. PREHEAT THE OVEN to 375 degrees. In a small bowl, whisk together the egg and the remaining 2 tablespoons milk. With a sharp knife or razor blade, slash an X in the top of each loaf. Brush the egg glaze over each loaf.

6. PLACE A PAN OF BOILING WATER on the bottom shelf of the oven. Place the cake pans on the middle shelf and bake the bread for 30 to 35 minutes, or until it is golden brown on top and sounds hollow when tapped on the bottom; an instant-read thermometer inserted into the center should register 190 to 200 degrees. Cool in the pans or on a wire rack.

PRAIRIE PIONEER POTATO YEAST STARTER

Before there was the convenience of dried yeast, pioneers and settlers in the Heartland made their own yeast, or starter. Nineteenth-century Midwestern cookbooks give many different recipes for making homemade yeast from grated or cooked potatoes, flour, or even hops. This admittedly time-consuming starter, which takes 8 days to ferment and strengthen, is for the home baker who wants to recreate the authentic taste and texture of antique bread. The process occurs in two stages, initially attracting the yeast spores in the air and encouraging fermentation, then building up the strength of the starter in preparation for baking. Use only glass jars or plastic and ceramic bowls to make this, as the acid in the starter could damage a metal bowl. Once you have the starter made, you don't have to be tied to the twice-a-day feeding schedule. You can freeze the starter, then revive and strengthen it a few days before you're ready to bake. Always bring it to room temperature before using it in a recipe.

MAKES ABOUT 2 CUPS

1 cup warm (110 degrees) water
1 1/4 cups unbleached all-purpose flour
1 teaspoon sugar
1 teaspoon salt
1 medium potato, peeled, cooked in boiling salted water until soft, drained, and finely grated

FERMENTING THE STARTER

DAY 1. In a 4-cup glass measuring cup, mix the water, flour, sugar, and salt until well blended. Add enough of the grated potato to make 2 cups. Transfer the mixture to a quart jar or medium bowl and shake or stir to blend well. Cover with cheesecloth and let sit in a warm (80 to 85 degrees) spot for 24 hours. In cold weather, you can sit the jar or bowl on a heating pad turned to the Warm setting.

DAY 2. Stir the starter down with a wooden spoon. Cover with plastic wrap and let rest for another 24 hours in a warm spot.

DAY 3. The starter will look grayish and smell like aged blue cheese. Stir it down again; it will become foamy. Cover tightly with plastic wrap and set aside at cool room temperature (70 to 75 degrees). If, at any point, the starter turns pink, develops mold, or smells rancid, throw it away and start fresh.

STRENGTHENING THE STARTER

5 to 6 cups bread flour
3 3/4 to 4 1/2 cups lukewarm (90 degrees) water

DAY 3 OR 4. When a clear yellowish liquid (called the "hooch") has collected on the top of the starter, it means that the yeast culture has formed and the starter is ready to be strengthened in preparation for baking. Never pour off the liquid—always stir it back into the starter. You are now ready to begin feeding your starter twice a day. You will also remove some of the starter as part of the strengthening process.

DAY 5. Early in the day, remove 1 cup of the starter (it can be frozen for later use or given to a friend). Stir 1 cup bread flour and 3/4 cup lukewarm water into the remaining starter. Cover with plastic wrap and let rest for 8 to 12 hours, then stir in another 1 cup bread flour and 3/4 cup lukewarm water.

DAYS 6 TO 8. Remove 2 cups of the starter (give to a friend, freeze, or make sourdough pancakes). Stir 1 cup bread flour and 3/4 cup lukewarm water into the remaining starter. Cover and let rest for 8 to 12 hours, then stir in another 1 cup bread flour and 3/4 cup lukewarm water. Repeat this process for the next day or two, until the starter is thick, cream-colored, and foamy and you can see bubbles forming and bursting on top of it; the starter should also have a tangy, sour taste and smell. About 8 hours after the last feeding, your starter is ready for baking.

To keep the starter going, simply remove enough starter to make a bread recipe at least once every week. You can cover the starter and store it in the refrigerator for up to a week before feeding again. To maintain your starter if you haven't used it to bake, you still need to remove 1 cup of starter and discard it, then feed the remaining starter by stirring in 1 cup bread flour and 3/4 cup lukewarm water at least once a week. Remember also that you must strengthen the starter for optimal performance in baking, so plan ahead. Again, if the starter turns pink, develops mold, or smells rancid, throw it away and start fresh.

To revive a frozen starter, let it thaw and come to room temperature, then proceed with the strengthening process in preparation for baking.

.... 🌾🌿 ....

HOME

I began to think what a wonderful childhood I had. How I had seen the whole frontier, the woods, the Indian country of the great plains, the frontier towns, the building of the railroads in wild, unsettled country, homesteaders and farmers coming to take possession. I realized that I had seen and lived it all—all the successive phases of the frontier, first the frontiersman, then the pioneer, then the farmers, and the towns. Then I understood that in my own life I represented a whole period of American history.

—LAURA INGALLS WILDER, IN A SPEECH AT THE BOOK FAIR IN DETROIT, MICHIGAN, IN THE FALL OF 1937, THE YEAR *ON THE BANKS OF PLUM CREEK*, THE FOURTH BOOK IN THE "LITTLE HOUSE" SERIES, WAS PUBLISHED

PRAIRIE PIONEER TWO-DAY BREAD

🌾🌿

We've come full circle in our appreciation and enjoyment of naturally leavened breads. In the early nineteenth century, breads from natural yeasts, and then a sponge, were made by Heartland homemakers like May Woodburn Crane. The daughter of a circuit-riding minister, Crane came to Nemaha County, Kansas, in the 1860s. Years later when she wrote her memoirs, she recalled a neighbor baking bread: "Mary Clarke carefully set her sponge for the white bread Friday evening. It was well wrapped and set in a warm place to rise. Saturday morning it was mixed up before breakfast because the smartest housewives got their bread baked by noon. It should rise to twice its bulk, twice at least, and then the rolls and loaves were molded and allowed to rise to the right height and degree of lightness before baking. It must be just right."

People who grew up on Midwestern farms before World War II will remember the unique flavor of naturally leavened breads like this one. The progressive loaves you make from your starter will get better and better as the starter ages.

MAKES 2 ROUND OR REGULAR LOAVES

2 cups Prairie Pioneer Potato Yeast Starter
    (page 58)
2 cups warm (110 degrees) water
1 tablespoon wildflower, clover, or other
    light amber honey
5¹/₂ cups bread flour
1 tablespoon salt

1. TO MAKE THE SPONGE, combine the starter, warm water, and honey in the bowl of an electric mixer or another large bowl and stir with a wooden spoon until well blended. Stir in the flour, 1 cup at a time, until you have a stiff dough.

2. USING THE DOUGH HOOK, knead the dough for 5 minutes, or until smooth and elastic. Or turn the dough out onto a floured surface and knead by hand for about 8 minutes. Cover with plastic wrap and let rest for 20 minutes.

3. KNEAD THE SALT, 1 teaspoon at a time, into the dough. Place in a large oiled bowl and turn to coat. Cover with plastic wrap and let rise at cool room temperature (70 to 75 degrees) until doubled in bulk, 8 to 12 hours, or overnight.

(If the dough does not rise, you will need to strengthen your starter and start over. See page 58.)

4. GREASE A LARGE BAKING SHEET or two 9-by-5-by-3-inch loaf pans and set aside. Punch down the dough, turn it out onto a floured surface, and divide it in half. Shape it into 2 round or regular loaves and place 2 inches apart on the prepared baking sheet or put in the prepared pans. Cover with plastic wrap and let rise in a warm place for 1 hour (it will not double in bulk).

5. PREHEAT THE OVEN to 375 degrees. Bake the bread for 40 to 50 minutes, or until the loaves are golden brown and sound hollow when tapped on the bottom; an instant-read thermometer inserted into the center should register 190 to 200 degrees. Transfer the round loaves to a wire rack to cool, or cool the regular loaves in the pans on a rack.

SOURDOUGH GRAHAM BREAD

During the 1840s, physician Sylvester Graham became such a champion of whole-grain flour that coarsely ground whole wheat flour became known as "graham" flour. Urban homemakers started adding graham flour to their baking, while their country cousins felt better about using the coarser flour, or "middlings," they'd always used. Baking with this type of flour alone would produce a heavy, leaden loaf, but paired with more finely ground bread flour, graham adds body and a nutty flavor. And when you eat this slow-rising bread—it takes two days to make after your starter is ready—you're eating a living antique from the nineteenth century.

Slightly sour, densely textured, and crusty, this is Middle America's version of peasant bread. Abraham Lincoln ate this kind of bread at home in Springfield, Illinois, before he became president. Samuel Clemens ate it in Hannibal, Missouri, when he was more Huck Finn than Mark Twain. And Laura Ingalls Wilder ate this bread for Thanksgiving dinner in the Dakota Territories while living the life she would later write about.

MAKES 2 ROUND OR REGULAR LOAVES

2 cups Prairie Pioneer Potato Yeast Starter (page 58) or Artisanal Baker's Levain (page 63)
2 cups warm (110 degrees) water
1 tablespoon wildflower or other light amber honey
^{1}/$_2$ cup lard, shortening, or unsalted butter, melted
1 tablespoon salt
1^1/$_2$ cups stone-ground graham flour
4 cups bread or unbleached all-purpose flour

1. IN THE BOWL OF AN ELECTRIC MIXER or another large bowl, mix the starter with the warm water and honey. With the paddle attachment or a wooden spoon, beat in the lard, shortening, or butter, salt, and graham flour. Beat in the bread or all-purpose flour, 1 cup at a time, until you have a stiff dough.

2. SWITCH TO THE DOUGH HOOK and knead the dough for 5 minutes, or until it is smooth and elastic. Or turn the dough out onto a floured surface and knead by hand for about 8 minutes. Place the dough in a large oiled bowl and turn to

THE JOURNEY HOME

Only one word, my darling, to say we have ridden the whole day in the train, & now I am in bed for an hour to rest me before going on the platform. You & the children have been in my mind all the day, & I have been very homesick & still am. I ate a lot of chestnuts that I found in my overcoat pockets, & that brought the children very near to me, for all three of them contributed to that stock. I love you, dear, & the time seems very long, that remains yet betwixt us & meeting.
—LETTER HOME FROM MARK TWAIN, DECEMBER 13, 1884

coat. Cover with plastic wrap and let rise at cool room temperature (70 to 75 degrees) overnight, until at least doubled in bulk. (If the dough does not rise, you will need to strengthen your starter and start over. See page 58 or 64.)

3. IN THE MORNING, stir down the dough, then cover again and let rise in a warm place for about 2 hours, or until almost doubled in bulk.

4. PREHEAT THE OVEN to 375 degrees. Grease a large baking sheet or two 9-by-5-by-3-inch loaf pans and set aside. Turn the dough out onto a floured surface and cut it in half with a serrated knife. Pinch the cut edges of each portion of dough together, turn the dough seam side down, and form into a round or regular loaf. Place the loaves 2 inches apart on the prepared baking sheet or put in the prepared pans.

5. BAKE FOR 35 TO 40 MINUTES, or until the bread is golden brown and sounds hollow when tapped on the bottom; an instant-read thermometer inserted into the center should register 190 to 200 degrees. Transfer the round loaves to a wire rack to cool, or cool the regular loaves in the pans on a rack.

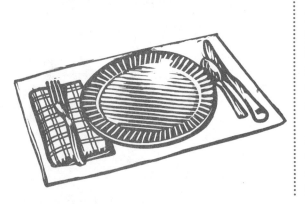

WARM GOAT CHEESE WITH FRESH BASIL, BALSAMIC VINEGAR, AND WILDFLOWER HONEY

Aromatic, crusty, hearth-baked bread deserves a worthy accompaniment. When Sarah Stegner, chef at the Ritz-Carlton Chicago, wants to entertain casually but with great taste, she serves this goat cheese in a crock, with a basket of baguettes to go with it. Sarah says you can keep your goat cheese warm by placing it on a brick or baking tile heated in the oven (or on the grill). If possible, use a regional Midwestern goat cheese such as Capriole from Indiana or Dancing Winds from Minnesota.

MAKES ABOUT 2 CUPS

1 pound fresh goat cheese
1/4 cup pine nuts
1/4 cup chopped fresh basil
1 teaspoon balsamic vinegar, or to taste
1 teaspoon wildflower or other pale amber honey, or to taste

1. PREHEAT THE OVEN to 350 degrees. Grease a 3-cup crock, soufflé dish, or ovenproof serving bowl and set aside. Puree the goat cheese in a food processor or blender. Spoon the cheese into the prepared crock and sprinkle the pine nuts on top.

2. BAKE THE GOAT CHEESE for 20 minutes, or until the pine nuts are toasted and the cheese is warmed through. (If desired, place a brick or a baking tile in the oven to heat.)

3. SPRINKLE THE GOAT CHEESE with the basil. Drizzle with the balsamic vinegar and honey, and serve with sliced baguettes, breadsticks, or flatbread.

ARTISANAL BAKER'S LEVAIN

A levain is another type of starter that is simplicity itself. The combination of organic flour, spring water, and organic grapes, plums, or even crabapples attracts the wild yeast spores in the air. The real secret ingredient is time. Once the mixture ferments and strengthens to a foamy, cream-colored, batter-like mixture, you can start baking delicious artisanal bread. The only catch is that you have to pay attention to the starter and feed it three times a day—religiously—during the strengthening process.

Making this starter and keeping it gave me a whole new appreciation for artisanal bakeries. It's like having a pet you have to feed and walk at regular intervals! But the bread I made with this levain was truly exceptional, with the dark blistered exterior, crustiness, slightly sour taste, chewy texture, and feathery crumb of true artisanal bread. I felt very accomplished after I made this. Even so, I know I won't keep feeding a starter three times a day indefinitely. So it's great to know that the starter can be frozen. About five days before you want to do artisanal baking again, just thaw the starter out and begin the strengthening process. I plan ahead to strengthen the starter for three days, make up the dough on the fourth day, and bake on the fifth. I like to have a marathon baking day, use up all the starter, and freeze the bread for later use. (For more details on this process, see Nancy Silverton's *Breads from the La Brea Bakery*, from which I adapted the blueprint for this recipe.)

MAKES ABOUT 10 CUPS
(WHEN THE STARTER HAS BEEN
STRENGTHENED ENOUGH TO BAKE WITH)

1 cup bottled spring water
1 cup organic unbleached all-purpose or bread flour
4 ounces purple or black grapes, preferably organic

FERMENTING THE STARTER

DAY 1. Whisk the spring water and flour together in an earthenware or ceramic mixing bowl. If your grapes are not organic, rinse them carefully. Place the grapes in a double thickness of cheesecloth and tie the corners together to make a pouch. Holding the pouch over the flour and water mixture, crush the grapes with your hands until about 1 teaspoon of juice falls into the bowl. Whisk the juice into the flour mixture, then place the pouch of grapes in the center of the mixture. Cover with plastic wrap and let ferment for 24 hours at cool room temperature (70 to 75 degrees).

DAY 2. The starter should gradually take on a fruity, yeasty smell. By about Day 3, it should have a bubbly or frothy appearance.

DAY 3. The starter will start to develop a pinkish liquid on top (from the grapes) called "the hooch." Stir this liquid back into the starter.

If, at any point, the starter develops mold or smells rancid, throw it away and start fresh.

1 cup unbleached all-purpose or bread flour
1 cup lukewarm (90 degrees) bottled spring water

DAY 4. The liquid that continues to form on the top of the starter may deepen in color to a dark pink. Stir the liquid back into the starter and swish the bag of grapes around in it. Stir in the flour and lukewarm water. Cover tightly with plastic wrap.

DAYS 5 THROUGH 9. Continue to check on your starter and stir the "hooch" back into it.

STRENGTHENING THE STARTER

DAY 10. Three-times-a-day feeding begins. Plan ahead so that your feeding schedule can remain the same every day. For example, I fed mine at dinnertime, then again right before bedtime, with the third feeding when I got up in the morning. That way, I could be gone all day if I had to without missing a feeding. As part of the strengthening process, you will also remove some of the starter, which can be frozen for later use or given to a friend.

• Remove the bag of grapes and discard. Pour off all but 2 cups of the starter. Whisk 1 cup bread flour and 1 cup lukewarm (80 degrees) bottled spring water into the remaining starter. Cover tightly with plastic wrap and set aside for 4 to 6 hours.

• Whisk 2^1/2 cups bread flour and 2 cups lukewarm bottled spring water into the starter. Cover tightly with plastic wrap and set aside for 4 to 6 hours.

• Whisk 5 cups bread flour and 4 cups lukewarm bottled spring water into the starter. Cover tightly with plastic wrap and let ferment for for 8 to 12 hours before repeating the feeding process.

DAYS 11 THROUGH 15. Repeat the feeding process until the starter is thick, cream-colored, and foamy and you can see bubbles forming and bursting on top of it. It should also have a tangy, sour taste and smell. About 8 hours after the last feeding, your starter is ready for baking.

To keep the starter going, maintain the three-times-a-day feeding schedule.

To revive a frozen starter, let it thaw to room temperature, then proceed with the three-times-a-day feeding schedule for 4 to 5 days before baking.

RUSTIC FRENCH BREAD

When the French adventurer Etienne de Veniard, Sieur de Bourgmont, built Fort Orleans during the winter of 1723 in what is now Brunswick, Missouri, his own comfort was a consideration. In addition to the fort itself, he had his workers construct a home for him. De Veniard was 43 and a man who had roughed it long enough. His plans for the fort speak eloquently of his wish to lead a more comfortable life: a pleasant dinner of a plump chicken from the poultry house baked with cream, kept cool in the ice house, and served with vegetables from the kitchen garden and a freshly baked loaf like this one; afterwards, a stroll in the pleasure garden to aid digestion, and a pipe smoked in front of the fire as the evening drew to a close. *Bon vieux temps!*

You will be rewarded for all the time you took to make a starter with this fantastic artisanal bread—crusty, slightly sour, chewy, and cream-colored. Made with the Prairie Potato Yeast Starter, the bread will be more sour than if made with the Artisanal Bread Baker's Levain. Use bread flour for a chewier texture, all-purpose for a softer crumb.

To make a larger French Country Boule (see the Variation below), use a stoneware cloche or mixing bowl, invert it over the dough during the final rise, and cover the loaf with it as it bakes.

MAKES 2 ROUND LOAVES OR BAGUETTES

2 cups Artisanal Baker's Levain (page 63)
or Prairie Potato Yeast Starter (page
58)
2 cups lukewarm (90 degrees) bottled
spring water
5¹/2 cups bread or all-purpose flour,
preferably organic, plus more for
kneading
¹/2 cup stone-ground graham flour or
whole wheat flour
1 tablespoon fine sea salt
Yellow cornmeal, for sprinkling

1. TO MAKE THE SPONGE, combine the levain and lukewarm water in the bowl of an electric mixer or another large bowl and stir with a wooden spoon until smooth. Stir in the flours, 1 cup at a time, until you have a stiff dough.

2. USING THE DOUGH HOOK, knead the dough for 5 minutes, or until smooth and elastic. Or

turn the dough out onto a floured surface and knead by hand for 8 minutes. Cover the dough with plastic wrap and let it rest for 20 minutes.

3. KNEAD THE SALT into the dough, 1 teaspoon at a time. Place the dough in a large oiled bowl and turn to coat. Cover with plastic wrap and let rise at cool room temperature (70 to 75 degrees) for 4 hours. Then place in the refrigerator for 8 to 12 hours, or overnight. (The dough will not increase much in bulk, but it will finish its rise during baking.)

4. GENEROUSLY SPRINKLE a cookie sheet (without sides) with cornmeal. Punch down the dough and turn it out onto a floured surface. Cut the dough in half with a serrated knife. Pinch the cut edges of each portion of dough together, place seam side down on the floured surface, and shape into a round loaf or a 16-inch-long baguette. Place the loaves about 2 inches apart on the prepared baking sheet, cover with plastic wrap, and let rise a final time in a warm spot for 45 minutes to 1 hour.

5. PLACE A BAKING STONE or tiles on the middle rack of the oven. Preheat the oven to 500 degrees. Just before baking, place a pan of boiling water on the bottom shelf of the oven.

6. WITH A SERRATED KNIFE or a razor blade, slash an X about 1 inch deep in the top of each round loaf or make four diagonal 1-inch-deep slashes in each baguette. Mist the loaves lightly with water, using a plastic spray bottle. Carefully pull out the middle rack of the oven and, using a wooden peel, or with a quick jerk of your arms, slide the loaves off the cookie sheet onto the stone. Shut the oven door and immediately turn the temperature down to 450 degrees. Bake baguettes for 20 to 25 minutes, round loaves for 30 to 35 minutes, or until the loaves are golden brown and sound hollow when tapped on the bottom; an instant-read thermometer inserted into the center should register 190 to 200 degrees. Transfer to a wire rack to cool.

FRENCH COUNTRY BOULE: In Step 4, form the dough into one large ball and place on a cornmeal-dusted cookie sheet. Cover the dough with a stoneware cloche or an inverted large stoneware mixing bowl. Preheat the oven to 500 degrees, with the baking stone or tiles placed on the middle rack. Just before baking, place a pan of boiling water on the bottom shelf of the oven. Place the cookie sheet on the baking stone or tiles, shut the oven door, and immediately turn the temperature down to 450 degrees. Bake for 55 to 60 minutes, or until the loaf is golden brown and sounds hollow when tapped on the bottom; an instant-read thermometer inserted in the center should register 190 to 200 degrees. Transfer to a wire rack to cool.

PLACE

*Is it the eagles returning to
Lecompton, old Eagle Town,
That stretch of lookout cottonwoods
on the Kaw River,*

*Or is it those rivers we measure towns by,
where we wait for flood and drought tides?*

*Or finding my grandfather
during a storm,
clouds and lightning and his face
by the window?*

*Is it the house I grew up in,
the way the sun slanted through
the front window,
warm bars of winter dust and light?*

*Is it a locus inside a muddy muscle,
the heart squeezing rivulets of blood
again, again, again.*

—DENISE LOW, *SPRING GEESE AND OTHER POEMS*
(LOW LIVES AND WRITES IN LAWRENCE, KANSAS)

HERBED POLENTA BREAD

After I thaw my Artisanal Baker's Levain, I usually plan on a bread-making marathon to use up all that starter five days later. I first strengthen the levain for three days, then make the dough on the fourth day, and bake about ten loaves of glorious artisanal bread on the fifth. As both gardeners and bakers know, bounty breeds creativity. That's how this pale gold, nubby-textured, wonderfully chewy, herb-flavored bread came about.

MAKES 2 BÂTARDS

*2 cups Artisanal Baker's Levain (page 63)
or Prairie Potato Yeast Starter (page
58)
2 cups lukewarm (90 degrees) bottled
spring water
1 teaspoon dried thyme
1 teaspoon dried oregano
5 cups bread flour, preferably organic,
plus more for kneading
1 cup finely ground polenta or yellow
cornmeal
1 tablespoon fine sea salt
1 cup cooked corn kernels
Yellow cornmeal, for sprinkling*

1. TO MAKE THE SPONGE, combine the levain and lukewarm water in the bowl of an electric mixer or another large bowl and stir with a wooden spoon until smooth. Stir in the herbs, then the flour, 1 cup at a time, and the polenta until you have a stiff dough.

2. USING THE DOUGH HOOK, knead the dough for 5 minutes, or until smooth and elastic, adding more flour as necessary. Or turn the dough out onto a floured surface and knead by hand for about 8 minutes. Cover the dough with plastic wrap and let it rest for 20 minutes.

3. KNEAD THE SALT into the dough, 1 teaspoon at a time. Place the dough in a large oiled bowl and turn to coat. Cover with plastic wrap and let rise at cool room temperature (70 to 75 degrees) for 4 hours. Then place in the refrigerator for 8 to 12 hours, or overnight. (The dough will not increase much in bulk, but it will finish its rise during baking.)

4. GENEROUSLY SPRINKLE a cookie sheet (without sides) with cornmeal. Punch down the dough and turn it out onto a floured surface. Cut the dough in half with a serrated knife. Pinch the cut edges of each portion of dough together, place seam side down on the floured surface, and shape into a 14-inch-long bâtard. Place the loaves 2 inches apart on the prepared baking sheet, cover with plastic wrap, and let rise a final time in a warm spot for 45 minutes to 1 hour.

5. PLACE A BAKING STONE or tiles on the middle rack of the oven. Preheat the oven to 500 degrees. Just before baking, place a pan of boiling water on the bottom shelf of the oven.

6. WITH A SERRATED KNIFE or a razor blade, make four diagonal 1-inch-deep slashes in each batard. Mist the loaves lightly with water, using a plastic spray bottle. Carefully pull out the middle rack of the oven and, using a wooden peel, or with a quick jerk of your arms, slide the loaves off the cookie sheet onto the stone. Shut the oven door and immediately turn the temperature down to 450 degrees. Bake for 35 to 40 minutes, or until until the loaves are golden brown and sound hollow when tapped on the bottom; an instant-read thermometer inserted into the center should register 190 to 200 degrees. Transfer to a wire rack to cool.

A Morning at WheatFields

············· ⟡ ·············

There's never a dull moment in an artisanal bakery. There's always something to do, and a unique assortment of people to do it.

At WheatFields Bakery and Café in Lawrence, Kansas, a worker regularly feeds the mammoth brick-lined steam-injected wood-burning oven from the stack of logs supplied by Fred Stewart, the elderly mayor of nearby Eudora, who cuts the wood and hauls it to Lawrence himself. The 23-metric-ton Llopis oven was installed in September 1995 by master oven mason Manuel de la Rosa of Barcelona, Spain, who had installed another oven in Brussels only the week before. The Llopis, 15 feet in diameter and 8 feet high, is capable of baking 200 loaves of bread at a time.

When I arrive early in the morning, one of the University of Kansas students who works at the bakery is shoving logs into the bottom trapdoor of the oven. "The oven doesn't ever completely cool," says Rita York, who dreams of opening her own bakery-café some day. "So a wood-burning oven is a very efficient use of heat. Wood is also a renewable resource and goes back to the earliest traditions of bread baking." The oven maintains a temperature of around 460 degrees. "If it drops to 400 degrees, it's too cool to bake our bread," she says.

As she uses a 12-foot-long peel to place loaves of ciabatta on the revolving circular oven rack, a part-time bookkeeper and a KU graduate student behind her are forming bread into loaves and placing them in banettons to rise. Others keep track of the three-times-daily feedings that WheatFields' starters or levains receive: the white and rye starters are fed at 4:00 A.M., 10:00 A.M., and again at 4:00 P.M. These starters are the heart and soul of the bakery's loaves.

WheatFields Olive Bread

⟡

Our family's all-time favorite bread, adapted from WheatFields Bakery and Café in Lawrence, Kansas. We like it with almost everything—grilled beef tenderloin, a big green salad with a garlicky dressing, a hearty soup, or a wonderful selection of cheeses. The rolls (see the Variation below) are a delicious accompaniment to summer salads and grilled foods.

MAKES 2 ROUND LOAVES

2 cups Artisanal Baker's Levain (page 63) or Prairie Potato Yeast Starter (page 58)
2 cups lukewarm (90 degrees) bottled spring water
1 teaspoon dried thyme
5 cups bread flour, preferably organic, plus more for kneading
1 cup stone-ground graham flour or whole wheat flour
1 tablespoon fine sea salt

"Artisanal bread is about the taste of a particular place," says York. "If I brought back a sourdough culture from San Francisco and kept feeding it here in Kansas, it would lose its San Francisco flavor and take on its own unique taste of the place," she says. "I just took a baking class at the San Francisco Baking Institute. Their levain out there smelled terrible. Ours smells sweet. It's all about the variety of wild yeast spores in the air, the type of organic flour you use, and where your spring water is from."

As she talks to me, York uses the long peel to remove the small rolls known as *ciabattini* that have just been baked and tosses them into a wicker basket. "I can tell by the color when they're done," she says, just as she can tell by feel when the dough is right, or by smell when the starter is right.

The starters are a simple mixture of flour, water, and those elusive wild yeast spores. At WheatFields, the flour is from organic prairie grains milled at Rocky Mountain Flour Milling in Platteville, Colorado. These flours, with beautiful names like Aspen, Meadow, and Columbine, are used in various combinations for each different type of bread. The water comes from prairie springs. The wild wheat country yeast spores are in the air everyone breathes here.

When the bakers arrive at 3:15 each morning, they weigh the levain, then add more flour and spring water in precise baker's percentages to make up different types of bread dough. They choose from containers of Kalamata olives, sunflower seeds, poppy seeds, garlic, thyme, and sun-dried tomatoes to give various flourishes to the basic bread recipes. Every loaf also contains freshly ground wheat berries or whole wheat kernels for texture. The dough then slowly rises all day, ready to be formed into loaves and baked the next morning.

1 cup brine-cured Kalamata olives, drained, pitted, and sliced
1 cup dry-cured Kalamata olives, pitted and sliced
Yellow cornmeal, for sprinkling

1. TO MAKE THE SPONGE, combine the levain and lukewarm water in the bowl of an electric mixer or another large bowl and stir with a wooden spoon until smooth. Stir in the thyme, then both the flours, 1 cup at a time, until you have a stiff dough.

2. USING THE DOUGH HOOK, knead the dough for 5 minutes, or until smooth and elastic, adding more bread flour as necessary. Or turn the dough out onto a floured surface and knead by hand for about 8 minutes. Cover the dough with plastic wrap and let it rest for 20 minutes.

3. KNEAD THE SALT into the dough, 1 teaspoon at a time. Place the dough in a large oiled bowl and turn to coat. Cover with plastic wrap and let rise at cool room temperature (70 to 75 degrees) for 4 hours. Then place in the refrigerator for 8 to 12 hours, or overnight. (The dough

will not increase much in bulk, but it will finish its rise during baking.)

4. GENEROUSLY SPRINKLE a cookie sheet (without sides) with cornmeal. Punch down the dough and turn it out onto a floured surface. Press one-quarter of the olives into the bottom half of the dough, then fold the top half over. Pinch the three sides closed, then knead the olives into the dough with the heel of your hand. Turn a quarter turn and repeat the process, until all the olives have been incorporated.

5. CUT THE DOUGH IN HALF with a serrated knife. Pinch the cut edges of each portion of dough together, place seam side down on the floured surface, and shape into a round loaf. Place the loaves 2 inches apart on the prepared baking sheet, cover with plastic wrap, and let rise a final time in a warm spot for 45 minutes to 1 hour.

6. PLACE A BAKING STONE or tiles on the middle rack of the oven. Preheat the oven to 500 degrees. Just before baking, place a pan of boiling water on the bottom shelf of the oven.

7. WITH A SERRATED KNIFE or a razor blade, slash an X about 1 inch deep in the top of each round loaf. Mist the loaves lightly with water, using a plastic spray bottle. Carefully pull out the middle rack of the oven and, using a wooden peel or with a quick jerk of your arms, slide the loaves off the cookie sheet onto the stone. Shut the oven door and immediately turn the temperature down to 450 degrees. Bake for 30 to 35 minutes, or until the loaves are deep brown and sound hollow when tapped; an instant-read thermometer inserted into the center should register 190 to 200 degrees. Transfer to a wire rack to cool.

WHEATFIELDS OLIVE ROLLS: In Step 5, cut the dough in half as directed, and shape each portion into a 16-inch-long rope. Cut each rope into eight 2-inch pieces, then cut each piece in half. Form each piece into a roll and place on the prepared baking sheet. Cover with plastic wrap and let rise for 45 minutes to 1 hour, until increased in size but not doubled. Bake as directed for 15 to 20 minutes, or until the rolls have risen and browned.

ITALIAN SLIPPER BREAD

Called *ciabatta* in Italian, this narrow oval-shaped bread is based on a recipe from Mary Kay Halston, a partner at The Corner Bakery in Chicago. Their special starter, made from organic Concord grapes, flour, and water, is fed three times a day, 365 days a year, with more flour and water. That's devotion! Their bread is baked in stone-lined, steam-injected European ovens to get that great crustiness and flavor. You can simulate it by using a baking stone or tiles and putting a pan of boiling water on the bottom shelf of the oven.

Ciabatta dough is mixed rather than kneaded, and it remains soft and batter-like. The combination of the naturally leavened starter with a yeast dough adds a wonderful depth of flavor. This recipe, which requires an electric mixer, also uses the autolyse method of letting the dough rest after mixing. The resulting loaf has a crisp crust, a somewhat chewy crumb, and a honeycombed texture.

MAKES 1 LOAF

1¹/2 cups water, at cool room temperature
(70 to 75 degrees)
1 (¹/4-ounce) package (2¹/4 teaspoons)
active dry yeast
1 cup Artisanal Baker's Levain (page 63),
Prairie Potato Yeast Starter (page 58),
or Great Plains Sourdough Starter
(page 51)
3¹/2 cups bread flour, preferably organic
1 tablespoon fine sea salt
1 tablespoon milk
1 tablespoon olive oil
Yellow cornmeal, for sprinkling

1. IN THE BOWL OF AN ELECTRIC MIXER, combine the water and yeast; set aside to proof until foamy, about 5 minutes. With the paddle attachment, on low speed, beat the levain into the yeast mixture. Beat in the bread flour, ¹/2 cup at a time, just until almost incorporated. Beat in the salt and continue mixing for about 15 minutes. Cover the mixer and bowl with a clean tea towel and let the dough rest at cool room temperature (70 to 75 degrees) for 15 minutes.

2. ON LOW TO MEDIUM SPEED, beat the milk and olive oil into the dough, then continue to beat for 10 minutes. The dough will look smooth and feel slack at this stage. Transfer the dough to a large oiled bowl, cover with plastic wrap, and let rest in a warm place until doubled in bulk, about 2 hours.

3. GENEROUSLY SPRINKLE a wooden peel or a cookie sheet (without sides) with cornmeal and set aside. Turn the dough out onto a lightly floured surface. (It will still be soft.) Flour your hands well and form the dough into an oval loaf

MODIGA

Humble bread crumbs are an important element in Sicilian-American cooking in the Heartland. In the more populated areas of Sicily, bread crumbs are known as mollica, *but in the Sicilian dialect that immigrants from Palermo and Sambuca brought with them, they were known as* modiga. *Bread crumbs are moistened with lemon juice and olive oil for* spiedini, *toasted and sprinkled over vegetables such as cauliflower or eggplant, used to coat fritters and arancini (stuffed rice croquettes), or tossed with pasta for added texture and a slightly nutty flavor. The secret is to use freshly made crumbs, for the best flavor.*

Use two- or three-day-old Italian country bread and either grate it or tear it into pieces and process into crumbs in the food processor. To toast the crumbs, heat about a tablespoon of olive oil in a large skillet and swirl it around the bottom of the pan. Add the bread crumbs and stir for several minutes with a wooden spoon until they turn a toasty brown. Toasted crumbs keep only for a day.

about 10 inches long., With your hands or two dough scrapers, carefully transfer the loaf to the prepared peel or baking sheet. Cover with plastic wrap and let rise at cool room temperature (70 to 75 degrees) until doubled in bulk, about 45 minutes.

4. FORTY MINUTES BEFORE you want to bake, place a baking stone or tiles on the middle rack of the oven and preheat the oven to 450 degrees. Just before baking, place a pan of boiling water on the bottom shelf of the oven.

5. CAREFULLY PULL OUT the middle oven rack and, using the wooden peel, or with a quick jerk of your arms, slide the loaf onto the stone. Bake the bread for 30 minutes, or until risen and deep brown; an instant-read thermometer inserted into the center should register 190 to 200 degrees. Transfer to a wire rack to cool.

VARIATION: To make Italian Slipper Bread Rolls, or *ciabattini*, in Step 4, form the dough into a 10-inch square. Using a pizza wheel, cut the dough into 2-inch squares, transferring each square, as it is cut, to the prepared peel or baking sheet (as the dough loses its shape quickly). Cover with plastic wrap and let rise at room temperature until doubled in bulk, about 45 minutes. Bake as directed for 12 to 13 minutes, or until the rolls have risen and browned.

ITALIAN SAUSAGE, PINE NUT, AND WILD MUSHROOM STUFFING

A gently flavored stuffing for the holiday bird, this is also wonderful spooned into a buttered casserole and baked for a side dish. At Thanksgiving, we were all most thankful for this accompaniment to our turkey. I used a mixture of WheatFields Olive Bread (page 68) and Spring Wheat Semolina Bread (page 49) that I had made earlier and frozen.

SERVES 8 TO 10

8 cups diced rustic bread, such as Rustic French Bread (page 64), WheatFields Olive Bread (page 68), Italian Slipper Bread (page 70), or Spring Wheat Semolina Bread (page 49)
1/2 cup (4 ounces) pine nuts
1 pound bulk Italian sausage (sweet or hot)
1/2 pound (2 sticks) unsalted butter
1 large onion, diced
4 celery stalks, diced
8 ounces mixed wild mushrooms (morels, chanterelles, oysters, shiitakes, and/or black trumpets), trimmed, rinsed, and patted dry
1/4 cup minced fresh tarragon
1/4 cup minced fresh sage
4 cups chicken stock or canned low-sodium broth
Fine sea salt to taste
1 teaspoon white pepper

1. PREHEAT THE OVEN to 350 degrees. Butter a 3-quart casserole and set aside. Spread the bread and pine nuts on a baking sheet and toast in the oven for 10 to 15 minutes, or until the pine nuts are just lightly browned. Set aside to cool. (Leave the oven on.)

2. IN A LARGE SKILLET, brown the sausage over medium-high heat, breaking up any clumps of meat. Drain off the fat and transfer the sausage to a large bowl; set aside. Wipe out the skillet with a paper towel.

3. MELT THE BUTTER in the skillet and sauté the onion and celery until softened, about 10 minutes. Add the mushrooms and sauté for 8 to 10 minutes, or until softened. Add the onion/mushroom mixture to the sausage. Stir in the toasted bread, pine nuts, and herbs and blend well.

4. SPOON THE STUFFING MIXTURE into the prepared casserole. Combine the chicken stock, salt, and white pepper in a medium bowl and pour the seasoned broth over the stuffing. Cover with aluminum foil and bake for 45 minutes. Remove the foil and bake for 15 more minutes, or until the stuffing holds together in a mass and is heated through. Serve warm.

RYE LEVAIN

The Artisanal Baker's Levain can easily be converted to a Rye Levain, over a period of about two to three days. Once you have a healthy starter (Day 15 of the Artisanal Baker's Levain recipe), simply strengthen it with rye flour instead of wheat. Organic rye flour is preferable.

2 cups Artisanal Baker's Levain (page 63)

DAY 1:

• Pour off all but 2 cups of the starter. Whisk $3/4$ cup rye flour, preferably organic, and $3/4$ cup lukewarm (90 degrees) bottled spring water into the remaining starter. Cover tightly with plastic wrap and set aside at room temperature for 4 to 6 hours.

• Whisk in 1 cup rye flour and 1 cup lukewarm spring water. Cover tightly with plastic wrap and set aside for 4 to 6 hours.

• Whisk in $1^1/4$ cups bread flour and $1^1/4$ cups lukewarm spring water. Cover tightly with plastic wrap and let ferment at room temperature for 8 to 12 hours.

DAYS 2 AND 3. Repeat the feeding process until the starter is thick, medium brown, and foamy and you can see bubbles forming and bursting on top of it. It should have a tangy, sour taste and smell. Your starter is ready for baking about 8 hours after the last feeding.

To keep the starter going, maintain the three-times-a-day feeding schedule.

To revive a frozen starter, let it thaw and come to room temperature, then proceed with the three-times-a-day feeding schedule for at least 3 days before baking.

SOUR RYE BREAD

❧

The love of sour rye bread is a remnant of European peasant culture, still alive in the Heartland. For Russian Mennonites, Norwegians, Swedes, Bohemians, and Germans, a sour rye made from natural starter was everyday bread; loaves made with finer yeast and wheat flour were reserved for special days. Dark, crusty, and hearty, this bread is delicious with smoked meats or strong cheeses. The Golden Onion Rye variation (see below) is also wonderful.

MAKES 2 BÂTARDS

2 cups Rye Levain (page 73)
2 cups lukewarm (90 degrees) bottled
    spring water
4 1/2 cups bread flour, preferably organic,
    plus more for kneading
1 cup rye flour
1/2 cup stone-ground or coarse rye flour
1 tablespoon fine sea salt
Yellow cornmeal, for dusting

1. TO MAKE THE SPONGE, combine the levain and lukewarm water in the bowl of an electric mixer or another large bowl and stir with a wooden spoon until smooth. Stir in both flours, 1 cup at a time, until you have a stiff dough.

2. USING THE DOUGH HOOK, knead the dough for 5 minutes, or until smooth and elastic, adding more bread flour as necessary. Or turn the dough out onto a floured surface and knead by hand for 8 minutes. Cover the dough with plastic wrap and let it rest for 20 minutes.

3. KNEAD THE SALT, 1 teaspoon at a time, into the dough. Place the dough in a large oiled bowl and turn to coat. Cover with plastic wrap and let rise at cool room temperature (70 to 75 degrees) for 4 hours. Then place in the refrigerator for 8 to 12 hours, or overnight. (The dough will not increase much in bulk, but it will finish its rise during baking.)

4. GENEROUSLY SPRINKLE a cookie sheet (without sides) with cornmeal. Punch down the dough and turn it out onto a floured surface. Cut the dough in half with a serrated knife. Pinch the cut edges of each portion of dough together, turn seam side down on the work surface, and shape into a 14-inch-long bâtard, pinching and tucking the ends under. Place the loaves 2 inches apart on the prepared baking sheet, cover with plastic wrap, and let rise a final time in a warm spot for 45 minutes to 1 hour.

5. PLACE A BAKING STONE or tiles on the middle rack of the oven. Preheat the oven to 500 degrees. Just before baking, place a pan of boiling water on the bottom shelf of the oven.

6. WITH A SERRATED KNIFE or a razor blade, make four diagonal 1-inch-deep slashes in each bâtard. Mist the loaves lightly with water, using a plastic spray bottle. Carefully pull out the middle rack of the oven and, using a wooden peel, or with a quick jerk of your arms, slide the loaves off the cookie sheet onto the stone. Shut the oven door and immediately turn the temperature down to 450 degrees. Bake for 40 to 45 minutes, or until the bâtards are dark brown and sound hollow when tapped on the bottom; an instant-read thermometer inserted into the center should register 190 to 200 degrees. Transfer to a wire rack to cool.

VARIATION: For Golden Onion Rye Bread, sauté 1 large onion, very finely chopped, in 3 tablespoons canola or olive oil until golden, about 7 to 10 minutes. Season with 1/4 teaspoon white pepper and 1/4 teaspoon garlic salt and set aside to cool. In Step 4, turn the dough out onto the floured surface and press one-fourth of the onion mixture into the bottom half of the dough, then fold the top half over. Pinch the three sides closed, then knead the dough with the heel of your hand. Turn a quarter turn and repeat the process, until all the onion mixture has been used. Cut the dough in half with a serrated knife and proceed as directed.

TOASTED HAZELNUT BREAD

When George Kendall trekked through the southern prairie in 1844, a generation after Lewis and Clark, he noted: "The land lies in swells; the prairies are small. . . the crab-apple, paw-paw, and persimmon are abundant, as also the hazel, pecan, and grape." It took another one hundred and fifty years before someone got the bright idea of including toasted hazelnuts in a prairie bread. The first time I tasted this bread was at a little ahead-of-its-time artisanal bakery in Topeka, Kansas, during the late 1980s. Although the bakery went out of business, I now make this bread at home, and I enjoy any leftovers in a savory bread pudding with asparagus, fresh herbs, and Fontina cheese.

MAKES 2 ROUND LOAVES OR BAGUETTES

*2 cups Artisanal Baker's Levain (page 63),
  Rye Levain (page 73), or Prairie Potato
  Yeast Starter (page 58)
2 cups lukewarm (80 to 90 degrees)
  bottled spring water
4 cups bread flour, preferably organic,
  plus more for kneading
1 cup stone-ground rye flour
1 tablespoon fine sea salt
Yellow cornmeal, for sprinkling
2 cups shelled hazelnuts, toasted and
  skinned, if desired*

1. TO MAKE THE SPONGE, combine the levain and lukewarm water in the bowl of an electric mixer or another large bowl and stir with a wooden spoon until smooth. Stir in both flours, 1 cup at a time, until you have a stiff dough.

2. USING THE DOUGH HOOK, knead the dough for 5 minutes, or until smooth and elastic, adding more flour as necessary. Or turn the dough out onto a floured surface and knead by hand for 8 minutes. Cover the dough with plastic wrap and let it rest for 20 minutes.

3. KNEAD THE SALT into the dough, 1 teaspoon at a time. Place the dough in a large oiled bowl and turn to coat. Cover with plastic wrap and let rise at cool room temperature (70 to 75 degrees) for 4 hours. Then place in the refrigerator for 8 to 12 hours, or overnight. (The dough will not increase much in bulk, but it will finish its rise during baking.)

4. GENEROUSLY SPRINKLE a cookie sheet (without sides) with cornmeal. Punch down the dough and turn it out onto a floured surface.

Press one-fourth of the hazelnuts into the bottom half of the dough, then fold the top half over. Pinch the three sides closed, then knead the dough with the heel of your hand. Turn it a quarter turn, and repeat the process until all the hazelnuts have been incorporated. Cut the dough in half with a serrated knife. Pinch the cut edges of each portion of dough together, turn seam side down on the work surface, and shape into a round loaf or a 16-inch-long baguette. Place the loaves 2 inches apart on the prepared baking sheet, cover with plastic wrap, and let rise a final time in a warm spot for 45 minutes to 1 hour.

5. PLACE A BAKING STONE or tiles on the middle rack of the oven. Preheat the oven to 500 degrees. Just before baking, place a pan of boiling water on the bottom shelf of the oven.

6. WITH A SERRATED KNIFE or a razor blade, slash an X about 1 inch deep in the top of each round

A WELL-STOCKED PRAIRIE GENERAL STORE IN THE 1860s

On the counter are baskets of eggs—three dozen for a quarter. Big jars of butter brought in by the farmers, quite soft—no ice in those days—12$\frac{1}{2}$ to 15 cents a pound and two grades. Baskets of chunks of maple sugar from the East. We made our own maple syrup, dried apples, and peaches. We used a great many dried apples during the winter. Cheese from New York, a bucket of hulled corn hominy. . . .

On the floor, barrels of flour, two grades, white and middlings, or shorts sometimes called, and meal, very coarse buckwheat flour—the kind that makes a man want someone to scratch his back. A barrel of apples from Missouri, sacks of potatoes, turnips, cabbage, pumpkins, and long-neck squashes. And back of these were barrels of New Orleans molasses, vinegar, salt pork with a big stone on top to keep the pork under the brine, salt, sugar, three grades. . . .

Kits of mackerel, two grades, the big fat ones and then the smaller ones. I don't remember the price but they were cheap and were used extensively. Around that part of the store hung up the codfish, whole, salted and tied, and hung up by tail. Also hung up around were hams, shoulders and slabs of breakfast bacon, and strings of red pepper, and then fresh meats. . . . Kegs of lard.

Back of the counter, on the shelf, were large boxes of the big square soda crackers, crocks of honey, coffee—green Rio and Mocha (we had to parch and grind it)—tea, black and Japan, in large cans, starch in bulk, bottles of catsup, cayenne, and soda and cream of tartar instead of baking powder, big glass jars of striped candy. Some spice and rice.

—GERTRUDE BURLINGAME, ABOUT GRAIGUE'S AND MORN'S GROCERY STORE IN TOPEKA, KANSAS, IN THE 1860s

loaf or make four diagonal 1-inch-deep slashes in each baguette. Mist the loaves lightly with water, using a plastic spray bottle. Carefully pull out the middle rack of the oven and, using a wooden peel, or with a quick jerk of your arms, slide the loaves off the cookie sheet onto the stone. Shut the oven door and immediately turn the temperature down to 450 degrees. Bake baguettes for 20 to 25 minutes, round loaves for 30 to 35 minutes, or until they are golden brown and sound hollow sound when tapped on the bottom; an instant-read thermometer inserted into the center should register 190 to 200 degrees. Transfer to a wire rack to cool.

SHARLOTKA WITH BRANDIED WHIPPED CREAM

A Russian version of the European charlotte, this dessert tastes like rich, festive mulled wine. The flavorings are similar to those used in a Rye Bread Torte in the 1903 *Settlement Cook Book* (published in Minneapolis). This sharlotka is adapted from a recipe by Jim Gregory, a Midwestern chef who consulted on the 1964 edition of *The Joy of Cooking*. It's a great way to use leftover homemade or bakery hearth-style rye; sliced rye bread from the grocery store will not work. Serve this as the grand finale to a celebratory meal.

SERVES 8 TO 10

1 (1-pound) loaf crusty hearth-style rye bread without caraway seeds (unsliced), such as Swedish Rye Bread (page 14), Sour Rye Bread (page 74), or Russian Mennonite Sour Rye Bread (page 55), crusts removed and torn into 1-inch pieces
Grated zest and juice of 1 orange
Grated zest and juice of 1 lemon
1 cup packed dark brown sugar
1 teaspoon ground cinnamon
1 teaspoon freshly grated nutmeg
1 cup dry red wine
1/4 cup brandy (or French Valley Spiced Pear Cordial, from Prairie Home Cooking, page 112)
6 Granny Smith apples, peeled, cored, and chopped
1 cup golden raisins, plumped in hot water and drained
1 cup red currant or raspberry jelly

FOR THE WHIPPED CREAM (OPTIONAL):
1 cup heavy cream
1 tablespoon brandy (or French Valley Spiced Pear Cordial)
1/4 cup granulated sugar

1. PLACE THE BREAD in a large bowl and add the orange zest and juice, lemon zest and juice, brown sugar, cinnamon, nutmeg, red wine, and brandy. Stir to mix well. Let stand, uncovered, until the bread has softened, about 1 hour.

2. PREHEAT THE OVEN to 350 degrees. Generously butter a 2-quart charlotte mold or soufflé dish. Spread one-quarter of the bread mixture over the bottom of the mold and press down lightly. Top with one-third each of the sliced apples and raisins. Spoon 1/3 cup of the jelly over

the fruit and nuts. Spread another quarter of the bread mixture on top of the apple layer, press down lightly, and top with another layer of the apples, raisins, and jelly. Repeat the layering process once more and spread the remaining bread mixture on top.

3. BAKE FOR 1 HOUR, or until the apples are soft and the top of the sharlotka is crusty

4. MEANWHILE, MAKE THE WHIPPED CREAM: In a medium bowl, whip the cream until soft peaks form. Beat in the brandy and granulated sugar and beat until the cream holds soft peaks again. Cover and refrigerate until ready to serve.

5. REMOVE THE SHARLOTKA from the oven and let cool for 10 minutes. Run a knife around the sides of the sharlotka to release it from the pan and carefully invert it onto a decorative plate. Serve hot or cold, with the optional whipped cream.

OZARKS
SALT-RISING BREAD

Salt-rising bread is another living antique in the Heartland, a nineteenth-century bread recipe that predates commercially packaged yeast. The use of cornmeal for the initial fermentation signals a heritage from the hilly region around the Ohio River and on into the Ozarks of Missouri, where corn, not wheat, was grown on the marginal farmland. Like breads made from a sourdough sponge, salt-rising bread depends on wild yeast spores in the air (not salt) for its leavening, although the process takes less time. It's also a tricky recipe—even the late, great James Beard complained that you couldn't always rely on salt-rising bread turning out. It has a distinct aroma when it is rising, similar to a very ripe cheese. Regardless of its pitfalls, people who like this bread *really* like it—especially toasted.

In addition to James Beard's version, I consulted three Heartland sources: a nineteenth-century recipe from North Union Shaker Village (what is now Cleveland, Ohio); J. Thompson Gill's 1881 *The Complete Bread, Cake, and Cracker Baker* (which adds that salt-rising bread was also called "milk-emptying bread" because it used milk instead of water); and *The Best Yet Cookbook*, published in Marietta, Ohio, in 1907. The secret is to keep the batter fermenting overnight at a constant temperature of 100 to 110 degrees (perhaps it was once kept warm in a bed of heated salt, hence the name); at 120 degrees or higher, the milk will curdle and the yeast spores will die. Moist and spongy, salt-rising bread does not rise as high as other breads. Because this bread is tricky to make and even trickier to find, I like to bake extra loaves and freeze them for later use.

3 cups milk
1/2 cup coarse-ground yellow cornmeal
1 3/4 teaspoons salt
2 tablespoon sugar
5 tablespoons unsalted butter
7 cups bread flour, sifted

1. IN A SMALL SAUCEPAN, scald 1 cup of the milk (heat it until small bubbles form around the edges). Place the cornmeal in a large bowl and pour the scalded milk over it. Let stand in a warm place (80 degrees) or on a heating pad set on Medium until a grainy, bubbly crust has formed on the surface, at least 6 to 7 hours, or overnight.

2. TURN THE OVEN to its lowest setting and preheat it for 15 minutes. Scald the remaining 2 cups milk in a medium saucepan. Remove from the heat and add the salt, sugar, and butter, stirring until the butter melts. Set the mixture aside to cool to 90 to 100 degrees.

3. WHISK THE WARM MILK MIXTURE into the milk and cornmeal mixture. Cover with aluminum foil, place in the oven, and turn off the oven. Let the mixture stand in the oven for at least 4 hours without opening the oven door.

4. USING AN INSTANT-READ THERMOMETER, check that the temperature of the cornmeal mixture is around 100 degrees. Briefly turn the oven on to its lowest setting if necessary. Leave the sponge in the oven for about 2 hours longer. You

will know when fermentation has occurred and the sponge is ready when the surface of the mixture has a grainy, bubbly crust and you can see bubbles rising to the surface and bursting.

5. TRANSFER THE SPONGE to the bowl of an electric mixer. With the paddle attachment, beat in the flour, 1 cup at a time. Switch to the dough hook and knead for 5 to 8 minutes, or until smooth and elastic. Place the dough in a large oiled bowl and turn to coat. Cover with plastic wrap and let rise in a warm place until doubled in bulk, about 2 hours. (If the dough does not rise, you will need to start over.)

6. GREASE THREE 9-BY-5-BY-3-INCH LOAF PANS and set aside. Punch down the dough and turn it out onto a floured surface. Divide the dough into 3 portions. Form each portion into a loaf and place in one of the prepared loaf pans. Cover with plastic wrap and let rise in a warm place until doubled in bulk, about 1 hour.

7. PREHEAT THE OVEN to 375 degrees. Bake the loaves for 15 minutes, then lower the temperature to 350 degrees and bake for 30 minutes more, or until the loaves are golden brown and sound hollow when tapped on the bottom; an instant-read thermometer inserted into the center should register 200 degrees. Cool in the pans on wire racks.

Savory Bread Pudding with Asparagus, Cheese, and Herbs

This breakfast, brunch, or light supper dish always gets rave reviews for its wonderful combination of textures and flavors. It's also a help for the cook, who can use leftover bread to make the dish, and assemble it up to 10 hours before baking.

Serves 8

6 (1-inch-thick) slices Toasted Hazelnut
    Bread (page 75), WheatFields Olive
    Bread (page 68), or other good arti-
    sanal bread, crusts removed and cut
    into 1/2-inch cubes
1 pound very thin asparagus, trimmed
2 tablespoons unsalted butter, softened
1 cup shredded Fontina cheese (4 ounces)
1 cup shredded provolone cheese (4 ounces)
6 large eggs
2 cups milk
1/2 cup chopped mixed fresh herbs (such as
    basil, parsley, chives, and/or tarragon)
Salt and white pepper to taste

1. PREHEAT THE OVEN to 250 degrees. Place the cubed bread on a baking sheet and toast in the oven for 20 minutes, or until golden. Set aside. Turn the oven temperature up to 375 degrees.

2. IN A LARGE SAUCEPAN, steam the asparagus until crisp/tender, about 1 minute. Remove from the heat, drain, and transfer to a cutting board. Cut the asparagus on the diagonal into 1-inch pieces; set aside.

3. GENEROUSLY GREASE a 13-by-9-inch baking dish with the butter. Arrange half the toasted bread cubes, half the Fontina, half the provolone, and half the asparagus in a layer in the baking dish. Make a second layer with the remaining bread cubes, cheeses, and asparagus. In a medium bowl, whisk the eggs, milk, herbs, and salt and white pepper together. Pour the egg mixture over the bread and asparagus. (The casserole can be covered and refrigerated for up to 10 hours before baking.)

4. BAKE FOR 45 TO 55 MINUTES, or until a knife inserted in the center comes out clean. Serve hot.

WHOLE-GRAIN BREADS

WILDFLOWER HONEY AND WHITE WHOLE WHEAT BREAD

Wildflower honey is one of the glories of Midwestern regional food. Made in summer when the bees visit all the prairie wildflowers in bloom, this amber honey has a true honey flavor without being too sweet. White whole wheat flour (available from mail-order sources and health food stores) is made from a variety of whole wheat with a milder flavor and lighter color, so it doesn't have to be mixed with all-purpose or bread flour to produce a delicious loaf. This recipe yields a nutty-flavored wheat bread with a tender crumb and just a touch of honeyed sweetness.

MAKES 1 LOAF

1¹/2 teaspoons active dry yeast
1 cup plus 1 tablespoon warm (110 degrees) water
¹/2 cup wildflower or other pale amber honey
¹/4 cup vegetable oil
1 teaspoon salt
3 cups white whole wheat flour, plus more if needed

FROM RED TO WHITE

Over the next decade, according to agricultural researchers and wheat breeders, Kansas will make a wholesale switch from being a red-wheat state to a white-wheat state. If this is true, the reign of the Turkey Red winter wheat variety will have ended after more than one hundred and twenty years.

The first reported Kansas wheat crop was planted in 1839 at what is now the Shawnee Indian Mission, located in the Kansas City suburb of Fairway. Between 1860 and the end of the century, farmers tried more than one hundred different varieties of wheats from the eastern states, mainly soft white and spring wheats. However, these didn't fare well in the variable climate of much of the prairie.

In 1874, the Russian Mennonites brought their Turkey Red winter wheat to Kansas from the Russian steppes. Although it was harder to grind, it fared well in the prairie climate. The "red" in its name comes from both the reddish tinge to the plant and the color of the inner bran. Because this red bran has a bitter taste, millers remove it when they grind the wheat into flour.

Now varieties of white winter wheat are looking promising. The bran from white wheat doesn't have a bitter flavor, so it doesn't have to be removed during milling. Leaving the bran in means more fiber and nutrients in the flour. In 1997, out of more than 500 million bushels of wheat grown in Kansas, more than 250,000 were of white winter wheat.

1. IN A SMALL BOWL, sprinkle the yeast over the warm water and set aside to proof until foamy, about 5 minutes. In the bowl of an electric mixer or another large bowl, combine the honey, oil, and salt and, using the paddle attachment or a wooden spoon, mix well. Add the yeast mixture, then add the flour, 1 cup at a time, mixing until you have a soft dough.

2. SWITCH TO THE DOUGH HOOK and knead the dough for 3 to 4 minutes, or until smooth and elastic, adding more flour if necessary. Or turn the dough out onto a floured surface and knead by hand. Place the dough in a large oiled bowl and turn to coat. Cover with plastic wrap and let rise at room temperature until doubled in bulk, about 1 hour.

3. GREASE A 9-BY-5-BY-3-INCH LOAF PAN and set aside. Punch down the dough and turn it out onto a floured surface. Form it into a loaf and place in the prepared pan. Cover with plastic wrap and let rise at room temperature until doubled in bulk, about 1 hour.

4. PREHEAT THE OVEN to 350 degrees. Bake the bread for about 35 minutes, until it is golden brown on top and sounds hollow when tapped on the bottom; an instant-read thermometer inserted into the center should register 190 to 200 degrees. Cool in the pan or on a wire rack.

GREAT PLAINS GRANOLA BREAD

In the 1970s, Peavey Flour Mills in Minneapolis, Minnesota, milled a granola flour that made a wonderful, nutty-tasting bread. Today, you can still make a terrific-tasting granola bread by grinding your own granola "flour" in the food processor.

MAKES 1 LOAF

1 cup granola (such as Great Plains Granola, from Prairie Home Cooking, page 5) or a flavored granola such as banana or cranberry
$1/3$ cup old-fashioned rolled oats
$1/2$ cup dried sour cherries or raisins
1 tablespoon unsalted butter
2 tablespoons honey
$1/2$ teaspoon salt
$1/2$ cup boiling water
1 cup warm (110 degrees) water
2 teaspoons active dry yeast
$2^{1}/2$ cups unbleached all-purpose flour
1 cup raisins, optional
$1/2$ cup flaked almonds, pecan pieces, or flaked coconut, optional

1. IN A FOOD PROCESSOR or blender, process the granola to coarse crumbs. Set aside.

2. COMBINE THE OATS, dried fruit, butter, honey, and salt in the bowl of an electric mixer or another large bowl. Add the boiling water and mix well with a wooden spoon; set aside to cool to lukewarm (90 degrees).

3. ADD THE WARM WATER and yeast to the oat mixture and stir to blend. Using the paddle attachment or a wooden spoon, mix in the granola crumbs and the flour, 1/2 cup at a time. Stir in the raisins and nuts or coconut, if desired. Switch to the dough hook and knead the dough gently for 7 to 10 minutes, until smooth and elastic, adding more flour if necessary. Or turn the dough out onto a floured surface and knead by hand. Place in a large oiled bowl and turn to coat. Cover with plastic wrap and let rise in a warm place until doubled in bulk, about 1 hour.

4. PREHEAT THE OVEN to 375 degrees. Grease a 9-by-5-by-3-inch loaf pan and set aside. Turn the dough out onto a floured surface and form it into a loaf. Place in the prepared pan and set aside until the dough has risen over the top of the pan, about 10 minutes.

5. BAKE THE BREAD for 35 to 40 minutes, or until it is golden brown on top and sounds hollow when tapped on the bottom; an instant-read thermometer inserted into the center should register 190 to 200 degrees. Cool in the pan or on a wire rack.

APPLE-CINNAMON GRANOLA BREAD

❧

Sweet, apple-scented, and with just a slight crunch from the granola, this Wisconsin bread makes delicious toast.

MAKES 1 LOAF

1 1/2 teaspoons active dry yeast
1/4 cup warm (110 degrees) water
3/4 cup milk
1/2 cup Honeyed Applesauce (page 87) or other sweetened chunky applesauce
1/2 tablespoon unsalted butter
3/4 teaspoon ground cinnamon
2 1/2 teaspoons salt
2 cups white whole wheat flour (available at health food stores and though mail-order)
1 1/2 cups bread flour, plus more if needed
3/4 cup granola (such as Great Plains Granola, from Prairie Home Cooking, *page 5)*

1. IN A SMALL BOWL, sprinkle the yeast over the warm water and set aside to proof until foamy, about 5 minutes. Meanwhile, in a small saucepan, scald the milk (heat it until small bubbles form around the edges); remove from the heat and let cool to lukewarm (90 degrees). In the bowl of an electric mixer or another large bowl, combine the milk, applesauce, butter, cinnamon, and salt and, using the paddle attachment or a wooden spoon, mix well. Add the yeast mixture, then beat in both flours, 1 cup at a time, and the granola, until you have a soft dough.

2. SWITCH TO THE DOUGH HOOK and knead the dough for 3 to 4 minutes, until smooth and elastic, adding more bread flour if necessary. Or turn the dough out onto a floured surface and knead by hand. Place the dough in a large oiled bowl and turn to coat. Cover with plastic wrap and let rise at room temperature until doubled in bulk, about 1 hour.

3. GREASE A 9-BY-5-BY-3-INCH LOAF PAN and set aside. Punch down the dough and turn it out onto a floured surface. Form it into a loaf and place in the prepared pan. Cover with plastic wrap and let rise until doubled in bulk, about 1 hour.

4. PREHEAT THE OVEN to 350 degrees. Bake the bread for 35 to 40 minutes, or until it is golden brown on top and sounds hollow when tapped on the bottom; an instant-read thermometer inserted into the center should register 190 to 200 degrees. Cool in the pan or on a wire rack.

FLOUR POWER

During the mid-nineteenth through the early twentieth centuries, flour mills sprang up all over the wheat-growing areas of the Heartland. At first packed in barrels or hand-sewn jute bags, freshly milled flour began to be packaged in cotton bags after 1849, when the invention of the sewing machine made this choice more cost-effective. Each mill packaged flour in its own distinctive sack, usually printed with the colorful emblem of the mill, and perhaps an idealized scene of wheat fields under a sunny sky. Thrifty Midwestern farmwives recycled those flour sacks into towels and even clothing for their children—encouraged to do so by millers' associations, who wanted consumers to keep the bags, not return them to the mills to be refilled. But it took hungry Belgians to turn flour sacks into works of art.

After the outbreak of World War I in 1914, Iowan Herbert Hoover (before he became president) formed a Commission of Relief as a private charity to help feed starving children and U.S. civilians caught in Belgium during the German occupation. Americans donated more than seven million pounds of flour—much of it shipped in 49-pound sacks of heavy cotton from Ohio, Kansas, Minnesota, and Indiana mills—to help the hungry Belgians make bread.

During the war, Belgian women and children embroidered these flour sacks in bright colors, as an act of resistance against the occupying German army, as a way to earn money, since they could sell their handiwork, and as a thank-you to the Americans. Forbidden to display flags or show the Belgian national colors—yellow, black, and red—the embroiderers found a way to sew these colors onto each flour sack. When the war was over, Herbert Hoover and his wife, Lou Henry, received more than four hundred and fifty of these embroidered works of art.

HONEYED APPLESAUCE

When Herb and Susan White of Plattsburg, Missouri, both turned fifty, they "gave it all up for chickens." Former city-slickers, the Whites made a radical change in their careers and became organic market gardeners. Today, they have fifty-seven Rhode Island Red and Barred Rock chickens, four rabbits, three cats, a dog, and thirty raised beds and nine plowed acres. Along the border of their property, beehives leased to another farmer provide delicious organic white clover honey. "It's a different life," says Herb with a bit of understatement. "If we're out somewhere, we know that when darkness falls, we have to get home to shut up the chickens in their roost." The Whites use organic apples and their own honey for this applesauce, which grandson Drew Michael eats as fast as they can make it. Dark with spices, it is wonderful served warm with homemade

Now on display at the Herbert Hoover Presidential Library in West Branch, Iowa, and the Hoover Institution in Palo Alto, California, these sacks are testimony to the creativity and quiet rebellion of the women and children who worked them. They're also a vivid reminder of how the milling industry has changed, as many of the local mills represented on the flour sacks no longer exist. On a flour sack from the Pelican River Mill Company in Elizabeth, Minnesota, an anonymous seamstress embroidered the Belgian Walloon shield with crossed American and Belgian flags, poppies, wheat, and bachelor's buttons. A sack from the Sunbury Mills in Sunbury, Ohio, shows colorful stitchery on the company seal and free-form sheaves of wheat in shades of gold.

Seamstresses also added fringe, cording, and ribbons. A rare hand-sewn jute flour bag from Sleepy Eye Flour Mills in Minneapolis was accorded special treatment—beading that accentuated the company logo, an American Indian brave. A flour sack for Zephyr High Patent Flour from the Bowersock Mills and Power Company in Lawrence, Kansas, is covered in fine Belgian lace and intricate needlework, highlighting the company's emblem of a cupid receiving a gift of bread from a butterfly.

By the end of the war in 1918, countless American flour sacks had been lifted from the mundane to the sublime. And that's when their popularity started to soar at home. During the 1920s, the Household Science Institute offered a thirty-two-page booklet entitled *Sewing with Flour Bags* with ideas for converting bags into place mats, children's clothing, toys, even curtains. In 1928, the ladies of Millard Avenue Presbyterian Church in Chicago made President Calvin Coolidge a pair of pajamas from flour sacks—a gesture of approval for his domestic policies encouraging thrift.

By the 1940s, the flour sack craze had waned. Today, a 1920s' Midwestern flour sack that would have been free with a bag of flour will cost you about $25.

biscuits or Honeymom's Rich, Buttery Scones (page 161). It can also be used as a topping for Apple Custard Kuchen (page 199), a filling for Hungarian Strudel (page 205), or a flavorful ingredient in breads such as Apple-Cinnamon Granola Bread (page 85).

MAKES 3 1/2 TO 4 CUPS

8 cups cored, peeled, and quartered tart apples, such as Lodi, Transparent, or Granny Smith (about 3 pounds apples)
1 cup clover or other mild honey
1 teaspoon fresh lemon juice
2 teaspoons ground cinnamon
1/4 teaspoon freshly grated nutmeg
1/4 teaspoon salt, or to taste

1. IN A LARGE SAUCEPAN, combine the apples and 1/2 cup of the honey, cover, and bring to a simmer. Cook until the apples are tender, about 20 minutes.

2. FOR CHUNKY APPLESAUCE, just mash the apples in the saucepan. For a smoother sauce, press the apples through a conical sieve or a food mill placed over a bowl. Stir in the the remaining ingredients. Serve warm or chilled. (The apple-sauce can be made ahead and frozen for up to 6 months.)

WHOLE WHEAT CHEDDAR BREAD

Tangy cubes of aged Cheddar make this bread rather interesting to knead and lumpy-looking on its final rise, but the taste is heaven, especially when it is still warm from the oven. For a healthy meal bursting with flavor, set a big pot of homemade vegetable soup on the stove to simmer, then put these loaves in the oven to bake. The leftover bread is delicious lightly toasted.

MAKES 2 LOAVES

3 cups unbleached all-purpose flour, plus more if needed
2 1/2 cups whole wheat or white whole wheat flour (available at health food stores and through mail-order)
1 (1/4-ounce) package (2 1/4 teaspoons) active dry yeast
2 teaspoons fine sea salt
2 1/3 cups warm (110 degrees) water
2 tablespoons canola or corn oil
1 tablespoon honey
12 ounces aged Cheddar cheese, preferably from Wisconsin, cut into 1/2-inch cubes

1. IN THE BOWL OF AN ELECTRIC MIXER or another large bowl, mix both flours, the yeast, and salt together. In a small bowl, mix the warm water, oil, and honey. Using the paddle attachment or a wooden spoon, beat the water mixture into the flour mixture until you have a smooth dough.

2. SWITCH TO THE DOUGH HOOK and knead the dough gently for 7 to 10 minutes, adding more all-purpose flour if necessary, until the dough is smooth and elastic. Or turn the dough out onto a floured surface and knead by hand. Place in a large oiled bowl and turn to coat. Cover with plastic wrap and let rise in a very warm place until doubled in bulk, about 1½ hours.

3. PUNCH DOWN THE DOUGH and turn it out onto a floured surface. Gently knead in the cheese. Divide the dough in half and let it rest for 10 minutes.

4. GREASE TWO 9-BY-5-BY-3-INCH LOAF PANS. Form the dough into 2 loaves and place in the prepared pans. Cover with plastic wrap and let rise at room temperature until doubled in bulk, about 1 hour.

5. PREHEAT THE OVEN to 350 degrees. Bake the bread for 40 to 45 minutes, or until the loaves are a rich brown on top and sound hollow when tapped on the bottom; an instant-read thermometer inserted into the center should register 190 to 200 degrees. Transfer to a wire rack to cool.

AMBER WAVES OF GRAIN: THE WHEAT FAMILY

Wheat is an ancient cereal crop. Emmer and einkorn varieties first grew wild in the Near East more than fifty thousand years ago, and archaeologists believe that wheat was the first cultivated crop, around 7000 B.C.

Wheat first came to America with the early colonists in the seventeenth century. In 1875, Russian Mennonite immigrants brought the Turkey Red hard winter wheat that is now grown in the prairie states. Today, more than thirty thousand varieties of wheat are grown all over the world, but most modern wheat varieties fall into the categories listed in the chart below.

WHEAT	PERCENT PROTEIN	USE	REGION
Durum wheat	14 to 16	Pasta, couscous, semolina flour	The Dakotas, Canada
Hard red spring	12 to 18	High-gluten bread flour	The Dakotas, Montana, Minnesota
Hard winter, red or white varieties	10 to 15	Bread flour, all-purpose flour	Kansas, Oklahoma, Texas, Nebraska, Montana, Canada
Soft	8 to 11	Cake flour	The South, Ohio, Indiana, Missouri, Illinois, the Pacific Northwest

CRACKED WHEAT BREAD

When a thrifty nineteenth-century Midwestern cook decided that leftover breakfast gruel could not be wasted, this bread was born. Old-fashioned rolled oats (not instant) also work instead of the cracked wheat, but they produce a softer-textured bread. Cracked wheat is available at larger grocery stores and at health food stores. The dough is best made in a heavy-duty mixer.

MAKES 2 LOAVES

1^1/2 cups cracked wheat
^{1}/2 cup honey or ^{3}/4 cup packed dark
   brown sugar
1^1/2 teaspoons salt
1^1/2 tablespoons unsalted butter
1^2/3 cups boiling water
2 tablespoons active dry yeast
1 cup warm (110 degrees) water
6 to 7 cups bread flour
2 tablespoons unsalted butter, melted

1. IN A MEDIUM BOWL, combine the cracked wheat, honey, salt, and butter. Pour the boiling water over the mixture, stir, and set aside for 15 minutes, or until the grain has softened and the mixture is still warm (100 degrees) but not hot.

2. IN THE BOWL OF AN ELECTRIC MIXER, sprinkle the yeast over the warm water; set aside to proof until foamy, about 5 minutes. Using the paddle attachment, beat in 1 cup of the bread flour. Mix in the cracked wheat mixture, then beat in 5 more cups bread flour, 1 cup at a time.

3. SWITCH TO THE DOUGH HOOK and knead the dough gently for 15 to 20 minutes, adding more flour if necessary, until the dough is smooth and elastic. Or turn the dough out onto a floured surface and knead by hand. Place the dough in a large oiled bowl and turn to coat. Cover with plastic wrap and let rise in a warm place until doubled in bulk, about 1^1/2 to 2 hours.

4. GREASE TWO 9-BY-5-BY-3-INCH LOAF PANS and set aside. Punch down the dough and turn it out onto a floured surface. Divide the dough in half. Form each half into a loaf and place in the prepared pans. Cover with plastic wrap and let rise in a warm place until doubled in bulk, about 45 minutes.

5. PREHEAT THE OVEN to 350 degrees. Bake the bread for 1 hour, or until the loaves are a rich brown on top and sound hollow when tapped on the bottom; an instant-read thermometer inserted into the center should register 190 to 200 degrees. Cool in the pans or on a wire rack.

DAILY GRIND WHOLE WHEAT BREAD

Wheat farmers have a bread-baking secret—the wonderful taste and texture of freshly ground wheat. Now that whole wheat berries or kernels are available at health food stores, and electric grain mills are so quiet and efficient, city folk can bake bread as delicious as that on the farm. At least that's what Jane Pigue of Greenwood, Missouri, found out. She researched a few bread recipes, and began her search for the perfect loaf of whole wheat bread. "I wanted the goodness of whole grains, but I wanted a light loaf with a tender crumb that rises high in the pan," she says.

Her bread is tender, moist, and so delicious that you won't believe it's good for you. Made with no preservatives, it will only keep at room temperature for about three days. However, you can freeze it. Fresh-ground flour is a must for this recipe, both for the texture and for the taste; packaged whole wheat flour will not give the same results. The dough stays batter-like, moist, and sticky, and there is no rising time; the wet dough rises as it bakes.

MAKES 3 LOAVES

5 to 5¹/2 cups wheat berries (hard red winter or spring wheat or hard white wheat berries, available in bulk at health food stores)
¹/2 cup honey
¹/3 cup olive oil
3¹/2 cups very warm (about 125 degrees) water
2 tablespoons instant yeast

2 tablespoons powdered dough enhancer (available through mail-order or at gourmet shops)
1 tablespoon salt
Olive oil cooking spray
1 tablespoon unsalted butter, melted

1. GRIND THE WHEAT BERRIES to a fine flour; you will have 7 to 8 cups. Put 3 cups of the flour in the bowl of an electric mixer. Using the paddle attachment, on low speed, mix in the honey, olive oil, and warm water. Add the yeast and mix for 1 minute, or until blended. Let the mixture rest for 8 minutes.

2. GRADUALLY BEAT IN 4 to 5 cups more of the flour, until the dough leaves the sides of the bowl. Add the dough enhancer and salt and mix until just blended, about 30 seconds. Switch to the dough hook and knead the dough for 8 to 10 minutes, until shiny and somewhat elastic; the dough will still be somewhat sticky.

3. PREHEAT THE OVEN to 350 degrees. Spray the inside of three 9-by-5-by-3-inch loaf pans with olive oil cooking spray and set aside. Turn the dough out onto an oiled surface and divide it into 3 equal portions. Lightly rub your hands with olive oil and form each portion of dough into a loaf, tucking the ends under. Place the loaves in the prepared pans.

4. BAKE FOR 25 TO 27 MINUTES, or until the loaves are a rich brown on top and sound hollow when tapped on the bottom; an instant-read thermometer inserted in the center should register 190 to 200 degrees. Remove the bread from the pans and brush the tops with the melted butter. Cool on wire racks.

VARIATION: Daily Grind Dill and Onion Bread makes the most delicious grilled cheese sandwiches you've ever tasted.

Add 1 tablespoon plus ¹/2 teaspoon vital wheat gluten (available at some grocery stores and through mail-order) along with the dough enhancer and salt. During the last 2 to 3 minutes of kneading, add 1 cup finely chopped onions and ¹/3 cup dried dillweed.

GRAIN MILLS

Freshly ground whole wheat flour is a revelation—it has a much richer flavor than its pale, all-purpose cousin or even packaged whole wheat flour. Home bakers who want the freshest flours possible might want to invest in an electric grain mill. I use a Bosch Whisper that grinds wheat and rye berries, barley, soybeans, and quinoa. An electric grain mill will convert about three cups of whole grains or beans into about seven cups of flour. Available through mail-order sources (see Source Guide, page 215) or at health food stores, electric grain mills are easy to use: the process is much like grinding your own coffee at the grocery store. Using an electric mill, you can grind enough flour to make three loaves of whole wheat bread in about eight minutes. Freeze any leftover flour, as the oil in the wheat germ can cause it to spoil quickly. Likewise, breads made from freshly ground wheat will keep for three days on the kitchen counter. Slice and freeze any leftover bread; then you can just take out a slice and pop it in the toaster whenever you want it.

DAILY GRIND
BLACK WALNUT
AND
APPLESAUCE BREAD

Black walnuts and apples are a taste marriage made in heaven. The addition of vital wheat gluten (available in some grocery stores and through mail-order) helps the bread to rise despite the extra weight of the walnuts and applesauce.

MAKES 3 LOAVES

6 to 7 cups wheat berries (hard red winter or spring wheat or hard white wheat berries, available in bulk at health food stores)
¹/2 cup honey
¹/3 cup olive oil
3 cups very warm (about 125 degrees) water
2 tablespoons instant yeast
2 tablespoons powdered dough enhancer (available through mail-order or at gourmet shops)
1 tablespoon plus ¹/2 teaspoon vital wheat gluten
1 tablespoon salt
1¹/2 cups Honeyed Applesauce (page 87) or other chunky applesauce
1 cup ground black walnuts, English walnuts, or pecans
Olive oil cooking spray
1 tablespoon unsalted butter, melted

1. GRIND THE WHEAT BERRIES to a fine flour; you will have 7 to 8 cups. Put 3 cups of the flour in the bowl of an electric mixer. Using the paddle attachment, on low speed, beat in the honey, olive oil, and warm water. Add the yeast and mix for 1 minute, or until blended. Let the mixture rest for 8 minutes.

2. GRADUALLY BEAT IN 4 to 5 cups of the remaining flour, until the dough leaves the sides of the bowl. Add the dough enhancer, vital wheat gluten, and salt and mix just until blended, about 30 seconds. Switch to the dough hook and knead the dough for 8 to 10 minutes, until shiny and somewhat elastic. During the last 2 to 3 minutes of kneading, add the applesauce and nuts; add more flour if necessary. (Even after kneading, the dough will still be somewhat sticky.)

3. PREHEAT THE OVEN to 350 degrees. Spray the inside of three 9-by-5-by-3-inch loaf pans with olive oil cooking spray and set aside. Turn the dough out onto an oiled surface and divide it into 3 equal portions. Lightly rub your hands with olive oil and form each portion of dough into a loaf, tucking the ends under. Place the loaves in the prepared pans.

4. BAKE FOR 25 TO 27 MINUTES, or until the loaves are a rich brown on top and sound hollow when tapped on the bottom; an instant-read thermometer inserted in the center should register 190 to 200 degrees. Remove the bread from the loaf pans and brush the tops with the melted butter. Cool on wire racks.

········· ❦❦ ···········

DAILY GRIND WHOLE WHEAT, RAISIN, AND CINNAMON ROLLS

❦❦

Leave it to a Midwesterner to find a comfort-food cinnamon roll that is actually good for you—Jane Pigue's rustic-looking whole wheat rolls, adapted here. The soft, moist dough produces a soft crumb, but it requires special handling. I have found that a flexible plastic cutting board works well as a surface on which to pat out the dough. After I've drizzled the honey and sprinkled the spices, I use two dough scrapers to help coax the dough into a jelly-roll shape. Then I use the plastic cutting board to help transfer the rolled dough cylinder to the baking sheet. I also use a dough scraper to cut the cylinder into individual rolls.

MAKES ABOUT 30 ROLLS

6 to 7 cups wheat berries (hard red winter or spring wheat or hard white wheat berries, available in bulk at health food stores)
1/3 cup olive oil
1 1/2 tablespoons honey
3 cups very warm (about 125 degrees) water
2 tablespoons instant yeast
2 tablespoons powdered dough enhancer (available through mail-order and at gourmet shops)
1 tablespoon plus 1/2 teaspoon vital wheat gluten (available at some grocery stores and through mail-order)

FOR THE FILLING:
1 1/2 tablespoons ground cinnamon
1/2 teaspoon freshly grated nutmeg
1/2 cup honey
1 cup raisins, optional, plumped in hot
	water and drained

FOR THE ICING:
8 ounces light cream cheese, softened
1/2 to 3/4 cup nonfat half-and-half
1 teaspoon vanilla extract
1 (1-pound) box confectioners' sugar

1. GRIND THE WHEAT BERRIES to a fine flour; you will have 7 to 8 cups. Put 3 cups of the flour in the bowl of an electric mixer. Using the paddle attachment, on low speed, mix in the olive oil, honey, and warm water. Add the yeast and mix for 1 minute, or until blended. Let the mixture rest for 8 minutes.

2. GRADUALLY BEAT IN 4 to 5 cups of the remaining flour, mixing until the dough leaves the sides of the bowl. Add the dough enhancer, vital wheat gluten, and salt and mix until just blended, about 30 seconds. Switch to the dough hook and knead the dough for 8 to 10 minutes, until shiny and somewhat elastic, adding more flour if necessary. (Even after kneading, the dough will still be somewhat sticky.)

3. TRANSFER THE DOUGH to a large oiled bowl and cover with plastic wrap. Refrigerate for 30 minutes to firm up the dough (the dough will almost double in bulk).

4. LINE TWO BAKING SHEETS with parchment paper and set aside. In a small bowl, mix the cinnamon and nutmeg together; set aside. Transfer the dough to an oiled surface, preferably a flexible plastic cutting board. Divide the dough

in half. Keep one half covered; set it aside or refrigerate. Rub your hands with olive oil and pat the dough out into a 9-by-15-inch rectangle. Drizzle the dough with 1/4 cup of the honey and sprinkle with half of the spices and the optional raisins, leaving a 1-inch margin of dough all around. Starting from a short end, and using two dough scrapers to help you, roll up the dough jelly-roll style. Using the flexible plastic cutting board, ease the roll, seam side down, onto a prepared baking sheet; refrigerate for 15 minutes. Meanwhile, repeat the process with the remaining dough and filling ingredients.

5. WHEN THE FIRST DOUGH CYLINDER has chilled, transfer it to an oiled surface and, using a dough scraper, cut it into fifteen 1-inch pieces. Reform each piece of dough into a coil and lay on the baking sheet. Cover with plastic wrap and let rise for 30 minutes. or until almost doubled in bulk. Repeat with the remaining cylinder of dough.

6. PREHEAT THE OVEN to 350 degrees. Bake the rolls for 25 minutes, or until lightly browned on the bottom.

7. MEANWHILE, MAKE THE ICING: In the bowl of a food processor or an electric mixer, blend the cream cheese, half-and-half, and vanilla until smooth. Add the confectioners' sugar a little at a time, processing until the icing is smooth and easy to spread.

8. WHEN THE FIRST PAN OF ROLLS has baked, let them cool for a few minutes on the pan, then spread with half of the icing. When the remaining rolls come out of the oven, let them cool for a few minutes, then spread them with the remaining icing. Serve warm or at room temperature.

AMBER WAVES OF GRAIN BREAD

᠅

Cracked grains of dull brown whole wheat. Oily, deep gold, lozenge-shaped flaxseed. Blunt stone-colored oats. Tiny pale yellow millet. When you look at a bowl full of these grains, it's like seeing the prairie grain harvest in miniature. Besides being beautiful, however, they make a bread that is deliciously good for you. Based on a recipe from the Canadian prairie made with seven-grain cereal milled in the Red River Valley, this nubby-textured bread is full of health and flavor. Any good stone-ground seven-grain cereal will work well in the recipe. Cooking the grains to soften them before adding them to the dough is an ancient technique that still works well today.

MAKES 2 REGULAR OR ROUND LOAVES

2¹/2 cups (uncooked) stone-ground
    seven-grain hot cereal (including
    cracked wheat, flaxseed, oats, and
    other cracked grains)
2 cups boiling water
¹/2 cup wildflower or other pale amber
    honey
2 tablespoons instant yeast
2 teaspoons salt
1 cup warm (110 degrees) water
About 4 cups bread flour

1. PUT THE CEREAL into a medium bowl, pour the boiling water over it, and set aside to soften for 15 minutes.

2. IN THE BOWL OF AN ELECTRIC MIXER or another large bowl, stir together the honey, yeast, salt, and warm water with a wooden spoon. Using the paddle attachment or the spoon, beat in 3 cups of the bread flour, then beat in the softened grains, with their liquid, until you have a moist, soft, heavy dough.

3. SWITCH TO THE DOUGH HOOK and knead the dough for 8 to 10 minutes, adding about 1 cup more flour, until the dough is elastic and no longer sticky. Or turn the dough out onto a floured surface and knead by hand. Place the dough in a large oiled bowl and turn to coat. Cover with plastic wrap and let rise at room temperature until doubled in bulk, about 1 hour.

4. GREASE TWO 9-BY-5-BY-3-INCH LOAF PANS or a large baking sheet and set aside. Punch down the dough and turn it out onto a floured surface. Knead it a few times. Divide the dough in half. Shape each portion into a regular or round loaf and put in the prepared loaf pans or on the baking sheet. Cover with plastic wrap and let rise in a warm spot until doubled in bulk, about 1 hour.

5. PREHEAT THE OVEN to 375 degrees. Bake the bread for 40 minutes, or until the loaves are a rich brown on top and sound hollow when tapped on the bottom; an instant-read thermometer inserted in the center should register 190 to 200 degrees. Transfer to a wire rack to cool.

HONEY WHEAT BERRY BREAD

Wheat berries, or whole wheat kernels, are available at health food stores. Use hard red winter wheat berries for the best results. This recipe produces a hearty loaf with an enhanced texture from the softened wheat berries.

MAKES 1 ROUND OR REGULAR LOAF

1/4 cup wheat berries
1 cup milk
1 (1/4-ounce) package (2 1/4 teaspoons) active dry yeast
1/4 cup warm (110 degrees) water
2 tablespoons canola oil
1/4 cup wildflower or other pale amber honey
1 teaspoon salt
2 cups bread flour
1 cup whole wheat flour, plus more if needed

1. PUT THE WHEAT BERRIES in a small saucepan with enough water to cover and bring to a boil. Remove from the heat and set aside for 1 hour to soften; drain.

2. IN A SMALL SAUCEPAN, scald the milk (heat it until small bubbles form around the edges); remove from the heat and let cool to lukewarm (90 degrees). In a small bowl, sprinkle the yeast over the warm water and set aside to proof until foamy, about 5 minutes.

3. IN THE BOWL OF AN ELECTRIC MIXER or another large bowl, combine the milk, canola oil, and honey and, with the paddle attachment or a wooden spoon, mix well. Add the yeast mixture and the salt, then beat in both flours, 1 cup at a time, until you have a soft dough.

4. SWITCH TO THE DOUGH HOOK and knead the dough for 3 to 4 minutes, adding more whole wheat flour if necessary, until the dough is elastic. Beat in the softened wheat berries. Or turn the dough out onto a floured surface and knead by hand, then knead in the wheat berries. Place the dough in a large oiled bowl and turn to coat. Cover with plastic wrap and let rise at room temperature until doubled in bulk, about 1 hour.

5. GREASE A BAKING SHEET or a 9-by-5-by-3-inch pan and set aside. Punch down the dough and turn it out onto a floured surface. Form it into a round or regular loaf and place on the prepared baking sheet or in the loaf pan. Cover with plastic wrap and let rise until doubled in bulk, about 1 hour.

6. PREHEAT THE OVEN to 375 degrees. Bake the bread for about 30 minutes, or until it is a rich brown on top and sounds hollow when tapped on the bottom; an instant-read thermometer inserted into the center should register 190 to 200 degrees. Transfer to a wire rack to cool.

PRAIRIE PIONEER CORN AND WHEAT BREAD

Nancy Kelsey, raised in Missouri and married in 1838 at age 15, was the first American woman pioneer to cross the Sierras into California in 1841. With a husband and a toddler daughter, Kelsey made her last batch of homemade bread while she waited in a makeshift camp, near what is now Kansas City, for others to join their westward-bound party. Almost eighty years later, a descendant of Kelsey's bread recipe appeared in the 1933 *Home Comfort Cook Book,* from which this golden, moist bread with a spongy texture and mellow flavor is adapted.

MAKES 2 LOAVES

2 cups water
3 cups yellow cornmeal
1 cup milk
1/4 cup sugar
1/4 cup warm (110 degrees) water
1 (1/4-ounce) package (2 1/4 teaspoons)
  active dry yeast
1 cup mashed baked sweet potato
1 teaspoon salt
3 1/2 to 4 cups bread flour

1. BRING THE WATER TO A BOIL in a medium saucepan. Gradually sprinkle 2 cups of the cornmeal into the boiling water, stirring constantly with a wooden spoon, and cook, stirring briskly, until the mixture becomes a thick porridge. Remove from the heat and set aside to cool to lukewarm (90 degrees).

2. IN A SMALL SAUCEPAN, scald the milk (heat it until small bubbles form around the edges); remove from the heat and let cool to lukewarm (90 degrees). In a small bowl, combine the sugar and warm water. Sprinkle the yeast over the water and set aside to proof until foamy, about 5 minutes.

3. IN THE BOWL OF AN ELECTRIC MIXER, using the paddle attachment, mix the sweet potato and scalded milk together. Beat in the cooked cornmeal and the remaining 1 cup cornmeal, then beat in the yeast mixture and salt. Beat in 3 cups of the bread flour, 1 cup at a time, until you have a soft dough, then beat in more flour if needed.

4. SWITCH TO THE DOUGH HOOK and knead the dough for 3 to 4 minutes, adding more flour if necessary, until the dough is elastic. Or turn the dough out onto a floured surface and knead by hand. Place the dough in a large oiled bowl and turn to coat. Cover with plastic wrap and let rise at room temperature until doubled in bulk, about 1 hour.

5. GREASE TWO 9-BY-5-BY-3-INCH LOAF PANS and set aside. Punch down the dough and turn it out onto a floured surface. Cut the dough in half, form it into 2 loaves, and place in the prepared pans. Cover with plastic wrap and let rise until doubled in bulk, about 1 hour.

6. PREHEAT THE OVEN to 350 degrees. Bake the bread for 30 minutes, or until it is a rich brown on top and sounds hollow when tapped on the bottom; an instant-read thermometer inserted into the center should register 190 to 200 degrees. Transfer the loaves to a wire rack to cool.

UTTER CONTENT

The horizon was like a perfect circle, a great embrace, and within it lay the cornfields, still green, and the yellow wheat stubble, miles and miles of it, and the pasture lands where the white-faced cattle led lives of utter content.
—WILLA CATHER, "THE BEST YEARS"

CORNMEAL PEPPER BREAD

In the Midwest, sweet corn varieties like Country Gentleman are grown for eating fresh, dent corn like Reid's Yellow Dent for making hominy, and flint corn like Seneca Red Stalker for grinding into cornmeal. On the southern fringes of the prairie, where the plains give way to the foothills of the Appalachians in southeastern Ohio or the Ozarks in southwestern Missouri, corn grown locally is still ground at riverside gristmills powered by falling water. In these areas, corn bread or salt-rising bread is still more common than wheat bread.

This yeast-risen corn bread, great for hors d'oeuvres or bite-sized buffet sandwiches, is baked in soup cans or tin bread molds for a uniform shape. Try a round of the savory bread topped with fresh goat cheese, strips of roasted red bell pepper, and arugula—or unsalted butter, paper-thin slices of salty Missouri country ham, and ripe, sweet melon.

MAKES 4 SMALL OR 2 LARGE
CYLINDRICAL LOAVES

1 ($^1/_4$-ounce) package (2$^1/_4$ teaspoons)
   active dry yeast
2 teaspoons sugar
$^1/_4$ cup warm (110 degrees) water
$^1/_2$ cup milk
8 tablespoons (1 stick) unsalted butter,
   melted and cooled
2 large eggs
1$^1/_2$ teaspoons salt
$^3/_4$ teaspoon freshly ground black pepper
$^3/_4$ teaspoon white pepper
1 teaspoon paprika
2$^1/_4$ to 2$^1/_2$ cups all-purpose flour
$^1/_2$ cup yellow cornmeal

1. IN A LARGE BOWL, sprinkle the sugar and yeast over the warm water; set aside to proof until foamy, about 5 minutes. With a hand-held electric mixer, beat in the milk, butter, eggs, salt, black and white pepper, and paprika until well blended. Add 1$^1/_2$ cups of the flour and the cornmeal and beat for 4 minutes. Beat in enough of the remaining flour, $^1/_2$ cup at a time, until you have a thick, grainy dough. Cover with plastic wrap and let rise in a warm place until doubled in bulk, 1 to 1$^1/_2$ hours.

2. HEAVILY GREASE four 10$^3/_4$-ounce clean empty soup cans or two 8$^3/_4$-by-3$^1/_2$-inch tin bread molds, opened at only one end. Punch down the dough and divide it among the cans or molds, filling each one a little less than half full. Stand the molds up, and cover each mold or can with plastic wrap. Let rise in a warm place until the dough has risen to within 1 inch of the top of the cans or molds, about 1 hour.

3. PREHEAT THE OVEN to 375 degrees. Place the cans 1 inch apart on a baking sheet, or fasten the tin cap on each bread mold and place them on their sides on the baking sheet. Bake for 30 to

35 minutes, or until the tops are browned and a wooden skewer inserted in the center of a loaf comes out clean. Run a thin spatula or knife around the inside of each can to loosen the breads, and turn the breads out onto a wire rack to cool.

4. SLICE THE BREAD into rounds to serve. (The breads can be frozen, well wrapped, for up to a month.)

PRAIRIE PAINTER'S OATMEAL HONEY BREAD

All throughout the day, Kansas artist Lisa Grossman watches the way the prairie sky meets the horizon. If the day is not too cold and the light is right, she'll grab her field box of oil paints from her Lawrence, Kansas, studio and hop in her old red truck to get in a few hours of *"plein air."* She paints the same meeting of earth and sky at least twice a week, but each time the painting is different. The clouds, sky, light, even the color of the prairie grasses can change hour by hour. Grossman might travel just ten minutes from Lawrence, an hour west to the Konza prairie near Manhattan, or two hours southwest to the Flint Hills. But not before she has packed a lunch. "I can paint with lots of distractions like wind and bugs and noise, but I've found that I can't paint if I'm hungry," she says with a laugh.

As an artist who responds so intimately to place, it's no surprise that Grossman prefers food that is grown locally. She buys organic flour and oatmeal from Kansas farms and honey from local producers to make her Oatmeal Honey Bread. "For painting outings, I do a sort of ploughman's lunch—thick slices of bread, a little mayo, cheese, and fresh garden tomatoes, preferably with some imported cracked green olives and pepperoncini on the side," she says.

MAKES 1 LOAF

1½ teaspoons active dry yeast
⅔ cup lukewarm (90 degrees) water
2 tablespoons honey
1 tablespoon instant nonfat dry milk
¼ teaspoon salt
1 tablespoon unsalted butter or
    margarine, softened
1½ cups bread flour
⅔ cups old-fashioned or quick rolled oats
    (not instant)

1. IN THE BOWL OF AN ELECTRIC MIXER or another large bowl, sprinkle the yeast over the warm water and set aside to proof until foamy, about 5 minutes. With a wooden spoon, stir in the honey, dry milk, salt, and butter or margarine, mixing well. Using the paddle attachment or wooden spoon, beat in the flour and oats.

2. SWITCH TO THE DOUGH HOOK and knead the dough for several minutes, or until shiny and elastic. Or turn the dough out onto a floured surface and knead by hand. Place the dough in a large oiled bowl and turn to coat. Cover with plastic wrap and let rise in a warm place until doubled in bulk, about 45 minutes.

3. GREASE A 9-BY-5-BY-3-INCH LOAF PAN. Punch down the dough and turn it out onto a floured surface. Form the dough into a loaf and place it in the prepared pan. Cover with plastic wrap and let rise in a warm place until doubled in bulk, about 45 minutes.

4. PREHEAT THE OVEN to 350 degrees. Bake the bread for 30 to 35 minutes, or until it is golden brown on top and sounds hollow when tapped on the bottom; an instant-read thermometer inserted into the center should register 190 to 200 degrees. Transfer to a wire rack to cool.

SPICED PERSIMMON BREAD PUDDING WITH CARAMEL SAUCE

Throughout the southern regions of the Heartland, native persimmons ripen in September, becoming soft, squishy, sweet, and mild. Like pawpaws, they have a lot of seeds, so they are used in cooking and baking rather than eaten raw. In this recipe, they become true comfort food. When the incredible aroma of this spicy bread pudding wafts through your house, you can't help but feel good. Canned pumpkin or cooked and pureed winter squash or sweet potato can be substituted for the persimmon pulp. The Caramel Sauce recipe makes a generous 2 1/2 cups, more than you think you need to serve with the bread pudding, but it will be gobbled up.

SERVES 4 TO 6

FOR THE BREAD PUDDING:
2 cups (3 to 4 slices) cubed (1/2-inch) Prairie Painter's Oatmeal Honey Bread (page 99), Challah (page 5), or The Miller's Cinnamon and Raisin Bread (page 20)
1/2 cup chopped pecans
4 tablespoons (1/2 stick) unsalted butter, softened
1/2 cup granulated sugar
1/2 cup packed brown sugar
3 large eggs
1 teaspoon ground cinnamon
1/2 teaspoon ground allspice
1/2 teaspoon freshly grated nutmeg

¹/2 teaspoon salt
¹/2 cup heavy cream
1 cup native or Asian persimmon pulp
   (see headnote)

FOR THE CARAMEL SAUCE:
1 cup heavy cream or evaporated milk
   (low-fat or nonfat works well)
1 teaspoon vanilla extract
1 cup granulated sugar
³/4 cup water

1. PREHEAT THE OVEN to 350 degrees. Generously butter an 8-inch square baking dish and set aside. Spread the bread cubes and pecans on a baking sheet and toast in the oven for about 10 minutes; set aside to cool. (Leave the oven on.)

2. IN A LARGE BOWL, with a hand-held electric mixer, cream the butter and both sugars. Add the eggs one at a time, beating well after each addition. Add the spices and salt, then beat in the cream and persimmon pulp until smooth.

3. SCATTER THE BREAD CUBES and pecans over the bottom of the prepared baking dish and pour the batter over them. Cover the pan with aluminum foil and bake for 30 minutes. Remove the foil and continue to bake for 15 minutes more, or until the bread pudding is risen and browned on top and a toothpick inserted in the center comes out clean. Let cool for 15 minutes before serving.

4. WHILE THE BREAD PUDDING IS BAKING, make the caramel sauce: Combine the cream and vanilla in a measuring cup and heat in the microwave until hot (or combine in a saucepan and heat over low heat); set aside. Combine the sugar and water in a heavy pan and stir over low heat to dissolve the sugar. Turn the heat up to medium-high and bring to a boil. Cook, watching carefully but not stirring, until the caramel is golden brown, about 10 minutes. Immediately remove from the heat (or the caramel will get too dark and become bitter). With a heavy-duty oven mitt on each hand, pour in the cream and whisk to blend (the hot caramel may splatter your hands a bit as you do this).

5. SERVE THE BREAD PUDDING WARM, drizzled with the warm caramel sauce.

NORTHERN PRAIRIE BARLEY SUNFLOWER BREAD

Nineteenth-century author Hamlin Garland's family farmed in rural areas across the upper Midwest. The most frenetic activity came in the summer, when during a four-week period, three different crops of grain ripened: barley first, then wheat and oats. "Day by day I studied the barley as it turned yellow, first at the root and then at the neck (while the middle joints, rank and sappy, retained their blue-green sheen)," he wrote, "until at last the lower leaves began to wither and the stems to stiffen in order to uphold the daily increasing weight of the milky berries. . . . Reaping generally came about the 20th of July, the hottest and driest part of the summer, and was the most pressing work of the year. It demanded early rising for the men, and it meant an all-day broiling over the kitchen stove for the women," he recalled. While the men harvested, threshed, and gleaned barley kernels to be aged in sacks in upper Midwestern threshing barns, the sunflowers kept growing in the gardens, turning their heads to face the sun, and finally giving up their seeds in late August or early September. Then this hearty bread could be made.

HOME

Mary Dodge Woodward grew up in Vermont and moved to Wisconsin when she married. With her sons, she later moved to a farm near Fargo, North Dakota, after her husband died. This is a passage from her diary, dated June 16, 1886, soon after she moved to North Dakota.

Later we went over to the Hayes place and gathered flowers, a great basket full. We stopped the horses on the way back to watch the sunset. Nowhere except in Dakota have I seen anything so beautiful. One can see for miles and miles in one long, unbroken stretch. The prairies are dotted with farm houses, the windows gleaming in the setting sun. I sometimes long for my trees and hills at home, yet nothing can excel this enchanting endless view. The sun flattens on the prairie until it looks like a sea of fire as it disappears from the horizon.

MAKES 1 LOAF

2¹/2 cups bread flour
1 cup barley flour (available at health food stores) or freshly ground barley
1 (¹/4-ounce) package (2¹/4 teaspoons) active dry yeast
1 teaspoon salt
¹/2 cup roasted salted sunflower seed kernels, plus more for sprinkling
1 tablespoon sunflower, canola, or vegetable oil
1¹/4 cups warm (110 degrees) water
1 tablespoon unsalted butter, melted

1. IN A LARGE BOWL, stir the flours together with a wooden spoon, then stir in the yeast, salt, and sunflower seed kernels. Make a well in the center of the dry ingredients, pour in the oil and warm water, and stir until a soft dough forms.

2. TURN THE DOUGH OUT onto a floured surface and knead for 8 to 10 minutes, or until elastic. Place the dough in a large oiled bowl and turn to coat. Cover with plastic wrap and let rise in a warm place until doubled in bulk, 2 to 2 1/2 hours.

3. PREHEAT THE OVEN to 350 degrees. Grease a 9-by-5-by-3-inch loaf pan. Turn the dough out onto a floured surface, form into a loaf, and place in the prepared pan. Brush the top of the loaf with the melted butter and sprinkle with additional sunflower seed kernels.

4. BAKE FOR 40 TO 50 MINUTES, or until the loaf is golden brown on top and sounds hollow when tapped on the bottom; an instant-read thermometer inserted in the center should register 190 to 200 degrees. Let cool in the pan or on a wire rack.

BREAD-CRUMBED BLUE CHEESE SOUFFLÉ

As a luncheon or a light dinner, this recipe is a sophisticated way to use up leftover blue cheese and bread crumbs. You can serve the individual soufflés still in their ramekins, but they unmold easily, and I like to serve them on baby greens lightly dressed with a homemade vinaigrette.

SERVES 4

3 tablespoons unsalted butter, softened
1/2 cup homemade dried bread crumbs
2 teaspoons all-purpose flour
1/4 cup milk
4 ounces blue cheese, preferably Maytag
  Blue, crumbled
1 large egg, separated
1/4 teaspoon salt
1/4 teaspoon cayenne pepper
1/4 teaspoon white pepper
2 large egg whites, at room temperature
1/4 teaspoon cream of tartar

1. PREHEAT THE OVEN to 375 degrees. Butter four 6-ounce ramekins with 2 tablespoons of the butter. Dust the insides of the ramekins with the bread crumbs and set aside.

2. IN A MEDIUM SAUCEPAN, melt the remaining 1 tablespoon butter over medium heat. Whisk in the flour and cook, whisking, for 2 minutes. Slowly whisk in the milk and continue whisking until the sauce has thickened, about 2 minutes. Add half the blue cheese and whisk until smooth. Remove the pan from the heat and whisk in the egg yolk, salt, and red and white pepper. Set aside.

3. IN A LARGE BOWL, with a hand-held electric mixer, beat the 3 egg whites with the cream of tartar until soft peaks form. Gently fold the egg whites into the cheese mixture. Spoon enough of the soufflé mixture into the ramekins to fill them one-third full. Scatter the remaining blue cheese on top of the soufflé mixture, then top with the remaining soufflé mixture. Place the ramekins in a baking pan and add enough hot water to reach halfway up the sides of the ramekins.

4. PLACE THE BAKING PAN in the oven and bake for 16 to 20 minutes, or until the soufflés have risen and browned on top and a toothpick inserted in the center comes out clean. Remove from the oven and remove the ramekins from the water bath. Let the soufflés cool for 10 minutes.

5. SERVE THE SOUFFLÉS in the ramekins or invert each one into your hand and then place right side up on top of dressed greens.

BLUE RIBBON WHOLE WHEAT AND SOYBEAN BREAD

Soybeans are a relatively new Midwestern farm crop. First grown in China more than five thousand years ago, soybeans arrived in the United States as ballast in a Yankee clipper ship carrying an 1804 China trade cargo. The first commercial American crop was planted in 1929, intended for soy sauce. Since then, the cultivation and use of soy has greatly expanded, with hundreds of horticulturally developed varieties finely tuned to the minute changes in climate from the Canadian prairies south to Indiana and Ohio. During the 1950s and '60s, soybeans became an essential part of the typical Iowa farm triad, along with corn and hogs.

Prairie bread bakers who grind their own grain have discovered that freshly ground soybean flour is delicious in bread. Try this even if you don't grind your own grain—you can find soy flour in better grocery and health food stores. This recipe is adapted from one that won Emogene Harp a blue ribbon at the Kansas State Fair. The dough will smell and taste a little like bean sprouts, but that disappears during baking, to give you a fine-textured, mild-flavored bread.

MAKES 2 LOAVES

1 tablespoon plus 1/4 teaspoon active dry yeast
1 1/2 cups warm (110 degrees) water
2 large eggs, beaten
1/2 cup soy or canola oil
1/4 cup honey
2 teaspoons salt
3 cups all-purpose flour, plus more for kneading
1 cup soybean flour, preferably freshly ground
2 cups whole wheat flour, preferably freshly ground
2 tablespoons unsalted butter or soy margarine, melted

1. IN THE BOWL OF AN ELECTRIC MIXER or another large bowl, sprinkle the yeast over the warm water and set aside to proof until foamy, about 5 minutes. With the paddle attachment or a wooden spoon, beat in the eggs, oil, honey, and salt. Beat in both flours, 1 cup at a time, until you have a stiff dough that does not stick to the bowl.

2. TRANSFER THE DOUGH to an oiled surface. Rub your hands with oil and knead the somewhat sticky dough, adding more all-purpose flour as necessary, until smooth and elastic, 8 to 10 minutes. Place the dough in a large oiled bowl and turn to coat. Cover with plastic wrap and set aside to rise in a warm place until doubled in bulk, about 1 hour.

3. GREASE TWO 9-BY-5-BY-3-INCH LOAF PANS and set aside. Punch down the dough and turn it out onto a floured surface. Cut it in half with a serrated knife. Shape each half into a loaf and place in the prepared pans. Cover with plastic wrap and let rise in a warm place until doubled in bulk, 45 to 60 minutes.

4. PREHEAT THE OVEN to 375 degrees. Bake the bread for 35 minutes, or until the loaves are golden brown and sound hollow when tapped on the bottom; an instant-read thermometer inserted into the center should register 190 to 200 degrees. Brush the tops of the warm loaves with the melted butter or margarine and let cool in the pans or on a wire rack.

MINNESOTA WILD RICE BREAD

❧

When people who live in the Minneapolis-St. Paul area plan to entertain, a visit to one of the Wuollet Bakeries is often a first stop on the shopping list. This dense and hearty round loaf, inspired by one of the bakery's breads, is delicious sliced and eaten with cheeses or sliced meats. It's also delicious hollowed out and filled with a creamy dip or a hearty soup or stew. I cook and then freeze wild rice ahead of time to have on hand for recipes like this one.

MAKES 2 ROUND LOAVES

---

1 1/2 cups warm (110 degrees) water
2 (1/4-ounce) packages (1 1/2 tablespoons) active dry yeast
1/3 cup wildflower, clover, or other pale amber honey
1 1/2 teaspoons salt
2 teaspoons white pepper
3 1/2 to 4 cups bread flour, plus more for kneading if needed
1/2 cup stone-ground rye flour
2 cups cooked wild rice
1 tablespoon unsalted butter, melted

1. IN THE BOWL OF AN ELECTRIC MIXER or another large bowl, sprinkle the yeast over the warm water and set aside to proof until foamy, about 5 minutes. Using the paddle attachment or a wooden spoon, beat in the honey, salt, and white pepper, then beat in both flours, 1 cup at a time, until you have a soft dough. Beat in the rice.

2. SWITCH TO THE DOUGH HOOK and knead the dough until it is smooth and elastic, about 8 to 10 minutes, adding more bread flour if necessary. Or turn the dough out onto a floured surface and knead by hand. Place the dough in a large oiled bowl and turn to coat. Cover with plastic wrap and set aside to rise in a warm place until doubled in bulk, 1 1/2 to 2 hours.

3. GREASE A BAKING SHEET and set aside. Punch down the dough and turn it out onto a floured surface. Cut it in half with a serrated knife. Shape each half into a 6-inch round loaf and place on the prepared baking sheet. Cover with plastic wrap and let rise in a warm place until doubled in bulk, 40 to 50 minutes.

4. PREHEAT THE OVEN to 375 degrees. Bake the bread for 30 to 35 minutes, or until the loaves are dark brown and sound hollow when tapped on the bottom; an instant-read thermometer inserted into the center should register 190 to 200 degrees. If necessary, during the last 10 minutes of baking, cover the tops of the loaves with a tent of aluminum foil to prevent overbrowning.

5. AS SOON AS THEY COME OUT of the oven, brush the tops of the loaves with the melted butter. Transfer to a wire rack to cool.

WISCONSIN ONION DILL BREAD

Inspired by a bread served at the Sun Porch Café in Madison, Wisconsin, this recipe makes a hearty, flavorful bread that is perfect paired with a regional cheese such as an aged Wisconsin Cheddar, an Illinois Brie, or an Indiana chèvre. The dough can also be used to make delicious dinner rolls (see the Variation below).

MAKES 2 LOAVES

3/4 cup buttermilk
2 large eggs
3/4 cup warm (110 degrees) water
1/4 cup wildflower or clover honey
1 tablespoon molasses or sorghum
  (available in larger grocery stores)
2 3/4 teaspoons active dry yeast
1 medium yellow onion, cut in half
1/4 cup canola or corn oil
4 cups bread flour, plus more if needed
2 cups whole wheat flour
3 tablespoons dillweed
1 1/2 teaspoons salt

1. IN A SMALL SAUCEPAN, heat the buttermilk until warm (110 degrees); remove from the heat. In a medium bowl, stir together the eggs, warm buttermilk, warm water, honey, molasses or sorghum, and yeast. Set aside to proof until foamy, about 5 minutes.

2. COMBINE THE ONION AND OIL in a food processor or blender and process to a puree.

3. COMBINE BOTH FLOURS, the dill, and salt in the bowl of an electric mixer or another large bowl. Using the paddle attachment or a wooden spoon, beat in the yeast mixture, then beat in the onion puree until you have a firm dough.

4. SWITCH TO THE DOUGH HOOK and knead the dough for 5 to 7 minutes, or until shiny and elastic, adding more bread flour if necessary. Or turn the dough out onto a floured surface and knead by hand. Place the dough in a large oiled bowl and turn to coat. Cover with plastic wrap and set aside in a warm place to rise until doubled in bulk, about 1 hour.

5. GREASE TWO 9-BY-5-BY-3-INCH LOAF PANS and set aside. Punch down the dough and transfer to a floured surface. Cut the dough in half with a serrated knife. Form each half into a loaf and place in the prepared pans. Cover with plastic wrap and let rise in a warm place to rise until doubled in bulk, about 1 hour.

6. PREHEAT THE OVEN to 350 degrees. Bake the loaves for 35 to 40 minutes, or until they are reddish brown on top and sound hollow when lightly tapped on the bottom; an instant-read thermometer inserted into the center should register 190 to 200 degrees. Cool in the pans on a wire rack.

VARIATION: For Wisconsin Onion Dill Rolls, in Step 5, grease two 9-inch round pans and set aside. Punch down the dough and cut it in half as directed, then cut each half into 12 pieces. Roll each piece into a ball and place the rolls in the prepared pans. Cover with plastic wrap and let rise until doubled in bulk, about 1 hour. Bake the rolls for 10 to 15 minutes, or until they are reddish brown and sound hollow when tapped on the bottom. Cool on wire racks.

WHEAT COUNTRY BANNETON

꧁ ꧂

When dough is left to rise in a flour-dusted cloth-lined or natural wicker basket—a banneton—the loaf takes on the imprint of the weave so the flour looks like snow dusting the ridges of a hillside. Baskets with prominent weaves and ridges 1/2 to 1 inch apart work best. Bakeries throughout the Heartland—from La Châtelaine in Columbus, Ohio, to the Corner Bakery in Chicago to Hahn's Original Hearth Oven Bakery in Iowa's Amana colonies to Clasen's in Madison, Wisconsin—use this easy method to produce round loaves that are as pleasing to look at as they are to eat. You can order bannetons from mail-order sources or find them at specialty baking and gourmet shops (see Source Guide, page 215), or simply use an unvarnished round wicker basket lined with a clean tea towel well dusted with flour. This recipe features the "autolyse" method preferred by some Heartland bakers. After the dough is mixed, it is allowed to rest for 10 to 12 minutes so it relaxes and becomes easier to handle, requiring less flour during kneading.

MAKES 1 ROUND LOAF

1 (1/4-ounce) package (2 1/4 teaspoons)
    active dry yeast
1 1/4 cups warm (110 degrees) water
1/4 cup wildflower or clover honey
1 tablespoon canola, corn, or other
    vegetable oil
1 teaspoon fine sea salt
1/2 cup dark rye meal or (uncooked) seven-
    grain hot cereal
2 3/4 to 3 1/4 cups all-purpose flour
Yellow cornmeal, for sprinkling

1. IN THE BOWL OF AN ELECTRIC MIXER or another large bowl, sprinkle the yeast over 1/4 cup of the warm water and set aside to proof until foamy, about 5 minutes. Using the paddle attachment or a wooden spoon, beat in the remaining 1 cup warm water, the honey, oil, salt,

A RECIPE FOR THE GOOD LIFE

············ ❧ ············

In the nineteenth century, baking bread—a days-long process—was one of the domestic activities that helped create a home life. Marie Eck Mosiman remembers her Russian Mennonite Grandmother Siebert's bread-baking ritual:

> Two evenings before baking day, grandmother would get the yeast from the butter well. In the days before refrigeration, every farm woman placed perishable food items like butter into a box or container tied to a rope and hung them in the well, just above the water level, to keep them as cool as possible during warm weather. . . . To the yeast, Grandmother added potato water and one or two mashed potatoes and some sugar. This mixture she let stand overnight. The next morning she took two cups of the yeast and potato mixture out for bread making and the other cup was saved in a quart jar in the butter well for the next baking.

Later that day, after the starter had risen, Grandmother Siebert mixed in more water, sugar, salt, and flour and let the dough rise in a warm place. Finally, on the third morning, the dough was ready to be baked. She made six loaves of bread twice a week.

Likewise, in most other Midwestern households, two days a week were set aside for the actual baking of bread, although its preparation required daily activity. The compilers of the 1877 *Buckeye Cookery and Practical Housekeeping* give these "general suggestions" for a smoothly run household: "On Monday, wash; Tuesday, iron; Wednesday, bake and scrub kitchen and pantry; Thursday, clean the silver-ware, examine the pots and kettles, and look after storeroom and cellar; Friday, devote to general sweeping and dusting; Saturday, bake and scrub kitchen and pantry floors, and prepare for Sunday."

During her youth in Red Cloud, Nebraska, author Willa Cather found that while women were doing these everyday chores, more went on than just work. When the Bohemian farm women worked together, they told stories, shared information, and solved problems. "I have

and rye meal until well blended. Add 2 cups of the flour and beat for 5 minutes, or until the dough is smooth and soft. Cover and let rest for 10 to 12 minutes.

2. SWITCH TO THE DOUGH HOOK attachment and knead the dough for 5 to 7 minutes, adding enough of the remaining flour so the dough is smooth and elastic. Or turn the dough out onto a floured surface and knead by hand.

Place the dough in a large oiled bowl and turn to coat. Cover with plastic wrap and let rise until doubled in bulk, about 1 hour.

3. PUNCH DOWN THE DOUGH, cover again, and let rest for 10 minutes.

4. DUST A BANNETON WELL with flour or line a 10-inch round wicker basket with a clean tea towel and dust the towel with flour. Shape the

never found any intellectual excitement any more intense than I used to feel when I spent a morning with one of those old women at her baking or butter making," Cather wrote in 1913, "as if I had actually got inside another person's skin."

But all this was soon to change. New technology spurred products such as readily available all-purpose flour and packaged yeast—welcome convenience foods that radically altered not only the types of breads that Midwesterners made, but also the domestic activity of the household. As Anne Mendelson writes in *Stand Facing the Stove*, by the 1931 publication of the first edition of *The Joy of Cooking*, women like its author Irma Rombauer were "long removed from everyday knowledge of bread baking. Both American living routines and American taste—aided by American grain-milling technology—had firmly rejected the sturdy-textured bread that had been familiar to everyone when wheat flour still contained most of the germ and making up the bread was a necessary part of the household schedule." American women were also isolated in their state-of-the-art kitchens.

Gone were the heartier, whole-grain pioneer breads, and in their place the sweetened, yeasty breads we now associate with the term "homemade." Gone, also, was the need for hands-on help in preparing food, now that a machine could take the place of a kitchen assistant.

But what goes around, comes around.

Generations after women were liberated from daily baking chores, we are interested anew in the days-long process of making slow-rising, naturally leavened breads or the complicated technique for making rich, buttery Danish pastry. Today, baking is a personal accomplishment, not a household necessity. And now that one person can easily make a seven-course dinner for eight with the help of culinary technology, we are eager to reclaim the easy-going camaraderie of cooking and baking with friends.

I love to make homemade bread, rolls, or pastries at least once a week. And once a month, I gather with my cookbook club friends at one of our homes to read, discuss, cook, bake, and sample the dishes that we have made from the books we have read. These are two not-so-secret ingredients in my personal recipe for the good life.

dough into a ball and place it in the prepared banneton or basket. Cover with a tea towel and let rise in a warm place until doubled in bulk, about 45 minutes.

5. PREHEAT THE OVEN to 375 degrees. Generously sprinkle a baking sheet with cornmeal. Carefully and quickly invert the dough onto the baking sheet, so that the paterned side is up.

Bake the bread for 35 to 40 minutes, or until the top is a rich brown and the loaf sounds hollow when tapped on the bottom; an instant-read thermometer inserted into the center of the loaf should register 190 to 200 degrees. Cool on a wire rack.

DAIRY COUNTRY CHEESE FONDUE

During the late 1960s and early '70s, the popularity of fondue coincided with the emergence of Julia Child and the awakening American interest in European food. Coming home from college at that time, half-starved, I would look forward to my mother's newest culinary creations. When she made Julia Child's French bread and served cheese fondue with it, I could banish the horrible memories of college dorm food. By the late 1990s, Midwestern cheese makers and bakers had rediscovered their roots, paving the way for the return of fondue to the restaurant scene in Chicago and Minneapolis. With cheese from Wisconsin and Minnesota, a Heartland brew, and bread from your own kitchen or an artisanal bakery, you can invite your friends over for a dip in the pot, a green salad, and a fruit dessert—all washed down with a little more brew. Try a cube of bread dipped in fondue, eaten together with a bite of salad dressed with Garlic and Lemon Vinaigrette (page 5)—heaven. An electric fondue pot works best.

SERVES 8

1 garlic clove, halved
1 cup full-bodied ale
3/4 pound raclette (preferably Leelanau) or
    brick cheese, grated
1/2 pound Gruyère cheese, grated
1/2 teaspoon white pepper
1/2 teaspoon sweet Hungarian paprika

1 loaf Wheat Country Banneton (page 107), Rustic French Bread (page 64), French Canadian Wheat and Walnut Bread (page 50), or Spring Wheat Semolina Bread (page 49), cut into 2-inch cubes

1. WIPE THE INSIDE of your fondue pot with the cut sides of the garlic and discard the garlic. Add the ale to the pot and bring to a simmer over medium heat. Gradually add the cheese, stirring constantly in a figure-eight pattern. Once the cheese is melted, heat for another 3 minutes, stirring, then add the white pepper and paprika.

2. TRANSFER THE FONDUE POT to its stand over a flame, or turn the heat on an electric pot down to low to keep the fondue warm. Give each guest a fondue fork to dip pieces of bread into the fondue.

DANISH PUMPERNICKEL RYE

Known as *rugbrod*, this dark, dense loaf is the preferred bread for *smorrebrod*, open-faced Danish sandwiches. It's just as good sliced paper-thin and spread with fresh butter. To make three cylindrical loaves, see the Variation, following.

MAKES 2 LOAVES

4¼ cups water
1½ cups pumpernickel (dark rye) meal
¼ cup sugar
3 tablespoons dark molasses
¼ cup unsweetened cocoa powder
2 (¼-ounce) packages (1½ tablespoons)
    active dry yeast
4 cups bread flour
1 cup rye flour
1 tablespoon salt
1 tablespoon unsalted butter, melted

1. BRING 3½ CUPS OF THE WATER TO A BOIL in a large saucepan. Add the rye meal, reduce the heat, and simmer for 10 minutes, stirring occasionally, until it becomes a thick porridge. Remove from the heat and let cool to lukewarm (90 degrees).

2. TRANSFER THE RYE PORRIDGE to the bowl of an electric mixer. Using the paddle attachment, beat in the remaining ¾ cup water, the sugar, molasses, cocoa powder, and yeast. Beat in both flours, 1 cup at a time, and the salt until you have a stiff dough. Switch to the dough hook and knead the dough for 6 to 8 minutes, or until shiny and elastic.

3. GREASE TWO 9-BY-5-BY-3-INCH LOAF PANS and set aside. Turn the dough out onto a floured surface and cut it in half with a serrated knife. Press each portion of dough into one of the prepared loaf pans, so that the dough reaches into the corners of the pan. With a fork, prick the dough all the way through to the bottom of the pan 8 or 9 times. (This helps the heavy dough rise evenly.) Cover with plastic wrap and let rise in a warm place until doubled in bulk, 1½ to 2 hours.

4. PREHEAT THE OVEN to 375 degrees. Brush the tops of the loaves with the melted butter. Bake for 1 hour, or until the tops are dark brown and the loaves sound hollow when tapped on the bottom; an instant-read thermometer inserted into the center should register 200 degrees. Transfer to a wire rack and let cool for several hours, or overnight, before serving.

5. TO SERVE THE BREAD, slice very thin.

VARIATION: For round loaves, bake the bread in three greased (8¾-by-3½-inch) tin bread molds (see Cornmeal Pepper Bread, page 98). In Step 2, open each mold only at one end and fill a little less than half-full with the dough. Stand each mold upright, cover with plastic wrap, and let rise in a warm place until the dough has risen to within 1 inch of the top of the molds, about 1 hour. Fasten the cap on each mold and place them on their side on a baking sheet. Bake for 35 to 45 minutes.

ROLLS
AND
BUNS

FARMHOUSE ROLLS

Growing up on a farm in Rayville, Missouri, Bonnie Knauss "always cooked," because there were always lots of people to feed. Extra farm hands at haying and wheat harvest time. The minister and his family after church one Sunday a month. Family members for birthdays and special occasions. Knauss has a vivid childhood memory of traveling to a relative's home for dinner, sitting in the back seat of the family car with a large Harzfeld's Department Store suit box on her lap full of pans of homemade rolls that were still rising. Today she makes those same Parker House–style rolls that her grandmother and mother did on the farm. "The old-fashioned egg bread dough is very versatile and forgiving of any treatment," she says. "It really doesn't care whether you knead it much or not. It will allow refrigeration at any of the stages. And it makes wonderful cinnamon rolls or even tasty egg bread loaves."

Makes 32 rolls

*1 (1/4-ounce) package (2 1/4 teaspoons)
    active dry yeast*
1/4 cup warm (110 degrees) water
1 1/4 cups boiling water
2/3 cup shortening
2 large eggs, beaten
1/2 cup sugar
1 teaspoon salt
5 cups all-purpose flour
*4 tablespoons (1/2 stick) unsalted butter,
    melted*

1. IN A SMALL BOWL, sprinkle the yeast over the warm water and set aside to proof until foamy, about 5 minutes. In the bowl of an electric mixer or another large bowl, pour the boiling water over the shortening and let stand until lukewarm (90 degrees).

2. USING THE PADDLE ATTACHMENT or a wooden spoon, beat the eggs, sugar, salt, and 1 cup flour into the shortening mixture. Beat in the yeast mixture. Continue adding the remaining flour, 1/2 cup at a time, until the dough is too stiff for the paddle. Switch to the dough hook or turn the dough out onto a floured surface and knead in the rest of the flour.

3. PLACE THE DOUGH in a large oiled bowl and turn to coat. Cover with plastic wrap and let rise in a warm place until doubled in bulk, 1 to 1 1/2 hours; or let rise in the refrigerator for at least 4 hours, or overnight.

4. PUNCH DOWN THE DOUGH and turn it out onto a floured surface. Roll it out to a 1/2-inch-thick rectangle. With a 2 1/2-inch biscuit cutter or round cookie cutter, cut out circles of dough. Brush each circle of dough with melted butter and fold over to make a semicircle. Pinch the edges closed. Place the rolls, touching one another, in two ungreased 9-inch round cake pans. Cover with tea towels and let rise again until doubled in bulk, 1 to 1 1/2 hours.

5. PREHEAT THE OVEN to 350 degrees. Bake the rolls for 17 to 20 minutes, or until slightly browned. Serve warm.

WHITE LADIES

············ ✦ ············

When the crude log cabin or sod house gave way to a white Victorian farmhouse, it meant the Heartland family was settled, and the wilderness was turning into civilization.

Such marks of civilization are evident in rural communities throughout the prairie. Some of these Victorian farmhouses have pretentious Gothic windows as portrayed in Grant Wood's *American Gothic* house in Eldon, Iowa. Others proclaim an ethnic heritage, as evidenced by the light blue trim and elegant scrolled gingerbread found on the "white ladies" favored by Swedish builders in Lindsborg, Kansas.

Poet Justin Isherwood, who lives and farms in Plover, Wisconsin, knows these white farmhouses well:

They were Victorians, standing like Victorians must; straight, unflinching, haughty-eyed; they were what the land needed. They were to agriculture, to landscape, prairie, and field what the log cabin had been to the pioneer. More sophisticated than logs, genteel yet fortress-like, girdled, braced, whale-boned Victorians, with a touch of lace. . . .

They calmed the farmstead, smoothed its hair, petted its forehead, gentled the frantic stray sheds, clucked and nuzzled the raw ends into a self-protective circle, a pack of mutually dependent animals against the emptiness of land. I was raised by a white lady and so was everybody I knew. . . .

BETTER-THAN-BLESSED POTATO ROLLS

"When I get in a cooking mood," Debbie Givhan-Pointer says, "I go to my kitchen in the basement and play my 'Better Than Blessed' gospel music, and I can stay there all day." As a preacher's wife, Debbie loves to try new recipes at dinners she hosts at her home, usually to entertain members of the Greater Mount Lebanon Missionary Baptist Church in Kansas City, Missouri. Potluck dinners after church on Sunday are also occasions for cooking up something special, like her mashed potato dinner rolls. This recipe produces light, airy, moist rolls that keep and freeze well. Debbie usually makes up a large batch and freezes some to have on hand.

MAKES ABOUT 3 DOZEN ROLLS

1 (¹/4-ounce) package (2¹/4 teaspoons)
    active dry yeast
¹/2 cup warm (110 degrees) water
1 cup milk
²/3 cup shortening
³/4 cup sugar
2 teaspoons salt
1 cup mashed potatoes
2 large eggs, beaten
6 to 6¹/2 cups all-purpose flour
8 tablespoons (1 stick) unsalted butter,
    optional, melted

1. IN A SMALL BOWL, sprinkle the yeast over the warm water and set aside to proof until foamy, about 5 minutes. In a small saucepan, scald the milk (heat it until small bubbles form around the edges); remove from the heat.

2. COMBINE THE SHORTENING, sugar, and salt in a large bowl. Add the hot milk and stir with a wooden spoon until the shortening has melted. Stir in the mashed potatoes and eggs, then stir in 1 cup of the flour until well blended. Beat in the yeast mixture, then beat in 5 more cups of flour to make a soft dough. Turn the dough out onto a floured surface, cover with a clean tea towel, and let rest for 10 minutes.

3. KNEAD THE DOUGH until smooth and elastic, adding more flour if necessary. Place the dough in a large oiled bowl and turn to coat. Cover with plastic wrap and refrigerate for 2 hours. (The dough can be refrigerated for up to 3 days.)

4. ABOUT 2 HOURS BEFORE you're ready to bake, grease three 9-inch cake pans. Pinch off about ¹/4 cup of the dough at a time and roll into balls; place 12 rolls in each prepared pan. Cover with plastic wrap and let rise in a warm place for 1 to 1¹/2 hours, or until doubled in bulk.

5. PREHEAT THE OVEN to 425 degrees. Bake the rolls for 15 minutes, or until risen and browned. If desired, brush with the melted butter while still hot. Serve warm.

HERBED SQUASH ROLLS

You'll be tempted to eat these golden rolls, warm and savory with the scent of herbs, right out of the oven. They can go uptown made into sophisticated cocktail sandwiches filled with poached chicken, tiny steamed green beans, and aïoli. Or they can go down home as part of an autumn dinner centered around roast duck, pheasant, or chicken. For the herbed topping, I sometimes just use the Parisien Bonnes Herbes mixture from Penzey's in Milwaukee (see Source Guide, page 215).

MAKES 2 DOZEN ROLLS

1 tablespoon active dry yeast
1/4 cup warm (110 degrees) water
2/3 cup milk
1 1/3 cups pureed cooked winter squash or pumpkin or thawed frozen winter squash
2/3 cup packed brown sugar
1/2 teaspoon salt
4 tablespoons (1/2 stick) unsalted butter, melted
3 1/2 to 4 cups unbleached all-purpose flour

FOR THE HERB TOPPING:
1/4 teaspoon dried chives
1/2 teaspoon dillweed
1/4 teaspoon dried basil
1/4 teaspoon dried tarragon
1/4 teaspoon dried chervil
1/2 teaspoon white pepper

Melted butter, for brushing

1. IN A SMALL BOWL, sprinkle the yeast over the warm water and set aside to proof until foamy, about 5 minutes. In a small saucepan, scald the milk (heat it until small bubbles form around the edges). Transfer to the bowl of an electric mixer or another large bowl.

2. ADD THE SQUASH to the milk and beat with the paddle attachment or a wooden spoon until smooth. Beat in the brown sugar, salt, butter, and yeast mixture. Beat in the flour, a little at a time, until you have a pliant but not stiff dough.

3. SWITCH TO THE DOUGH HOOK and knead until the dough is smooth and elastic, about 5 minutes. Or turn the dough out onto a floured surface and knead by hand. Place the dough in a large oiled bowl and turn to coat. Cover with plastic wrap and let rise in a warm place until doubled in bulk, about 1 hour.

4. GREASE TWO BAKING SHEETS. Punch down the dough and turn it out onto a floured surface. Cut the dough in half, then cut each half into 12 equal pieces. Form each piece into a roll and place about 1 inch apart on the prepared baking sheets. Cover with a tea towel and let rise in a warm place for 30 minutes, or until almost doubled in bulk.

5. PREHEAT THE OVEN to 375 degrees. Bake the rolls for 20 minutes, or until risen and browned.

6. WHILE THE ROLLS ARE BAKING, make the herb topping: Combine all the ingredients in a small bowl. Brush the hot rolls with melted butter and sprinkle with the herb mixture. Serve warm.

IOWA CORN CLOVERS

Ada Lou Roberts grew up on a farm in Iowa at the turn of the nineteenth century, helping her grandmother bake the daily bread "in big old gray-agate enameled baking pans which held four loaves each." Later she moved to New York City for a career in women's magazines. An avid bread baker whose trademark was a pinch of dried ginger to help the yeast work, she wrote *Favorite Breads from Rose Lane Farm* (published in 1960), from which this recipe is adapted. Indicative of her times, she suggested these rolls to accompany a dinner of creamed chipped beef, baked potatoes, radishes, and piccalilli. With their light yet crumbly texture, the rolls would go well today with Easter ham, homemade soups, or a grilled chicken Caesar salad. They would also be delicious with the addition of grated sharp cheese or dried herbs.

MAKES ABOUT 2 DOZEN ROLLS

119

*¹/4 cup plus 1 cup warm (110 degrees)
    water*
¹/4 cup plus 1 teaspoon sugar
¹/4 teaspoon ground ginger
*2 (¹/4-ounce) packages (1¹/2 tablespoons)
    active dry yeast*
*1 cup yellow cornmeal, plus more for
    sprinkling*
3 to 3¹/2 cups all-purpose flour
¹/2 cup instant nonfat dry milk
2 large eggs, beaten
³/4 cup sour cream
2 teaspoons salt
1 teaspoon white pepper
*8 tablespoons (1 stick) unsalted butter,
    melted*

1. IN A SMALL BOWL, combine ¹/4 cup of the warm water, 1 teaspoon of the sugar, and the ginger. Sprinkle the yeast over the water and set aside to proof until foamy, about 5 minutes.

2. IN A LARGE BOWL, using a wooden spoon, mix the cornmeal, the remaining ¹/4 cup sugar, 3 cups of the flour, and the dry milk together. Stir in the yeast mixture, eggs, sour cream, salt, and white pepper, mixing until the dough leaves the sides of the bowl.

3. TURN THE DOUGH OUT onto a floured surface and knead until smooth and elastic, about 5 minutes. Place the dough in a large oiled bowl and turn to coat. Cover with plastic wrap and let rise in a warm place until doubled in bulk, about 1 hour.

4. GREASE TWO MUFFIN TINS. Sprinkle about ¹/4 teaspoon cornmeal into each muffin cup and set aside. Punch down the dough and turn it out onto a floured surface. Cut it into 4 equal parts

with a serrated knife. Cut each quarter of dough into 6 equal portions, then divide each portion into 4 small pieces. Roll each piece into a ball. For each muffin, dip 4 of the small balls in the melted butter and place in a prepared muffin cup. Cover the muffin tins with clean tea towels and set aside to rise in a warm place until doubled in bulk, about 45 minutes to 1 hour.

5. PREHEAT THE OVEN to 425 degrees. Bake the corn clovers for 12 to 15 minutes, until risen and browned. Serve warm.

.... ～✣～ ....

GARDEN
PEPPER RELISH

～✣～

In early September, quilt designer Gerry Kimmel-Carr often takes a few moments to sit on a garden bench and watch the butterflies flutter in her Liberty, Missouri, garden. As she looks at the neat patterns of strawberries, chives, lavender, sage, oregano, parsley, thyme, nasturtiums, peppers, and tomatoes, then out to the colonnade of apple trees that line the front yard, she sees an edible landscape and the promise of delicious meals to come. She loves to serve this savory jelly with cream cheese as a topping for homemade rolls.

MAKES 5 HALF-PINTS

GREAT-GRANDMOTHER'S CLOVERLEAF ROLLS

.... ⚜ ....

Written in faded fountain pen ink in my grandmother's household book—a dark brown composition notebook—is this recipe from her mother, Gertrude Rottherm Willenborg, from the 1920s. Because my grandmother would have watched her mother make these and knew the method, the recipe itself is written in a kind of shorthand.

(twentieth-century recipe)
3 tablespoons lard
$1/4$ cup sugar
1 teaspoon salt
$3/4$ cup milk

Put the lard, sugar, and salt in a bowl. Heat the milk and pour it over the above and let it cool. Dissolve 1 cake yeast in $1/2$ cup warm water, then stir into the above. Beat one egg in a cup and add to the above. Then add $3 1/2$ cups sifted flour. Cover and put in the icebox. Two hours before baking, make into small rolls and dip into melted butter.

Bake 15 minutes.

.... ⚜ ....

Today when our far-flung family gathers for holidays, my mother, my sister, and I make this updated version to go with our typical menu: grilled beef tenderloin served with a dollop of sour cream, horseradish, and bacon sauce; grilled asparagus; potato casserole; a green salad with blue cheese crumbles; and pear and almond tart for dessert.

(twenty-first century recipe)
3 tablespoons unsalted butter
$1/4$ cup sugar
1 teaspoon salt
$3/4$ cup milk
1 ($1/4$-ounce) package ($2 1/4$ teaspoons)
active dry yeast
$1/2$ cup warm (110 degrees) water
1 large egg, beaten
$3 1/2$ cups all-purpose flour
6 tablespoons ($3/4$ stick) unsalted butter,
melted

Put the butter, sugar, and salt in a large bowl. In a small saucepan, heat the milk until warm; pour it over the butter mixture and let cool. In a small bowl, sprinkle the yeast over the warm water; set aside to proof until foamy, about 5 minutes.

Stir the yeast mixture into the butter mixture. Beat in the egg, then beat in the flour until you have a soft dough. Cover and refrigerate.

Two hours before baking, turn the dough out onto a floured surface and divide it in half. Divide each half into 6 equal portions, then divide each portion into 3 pieces. Roll each piece into a ball, dip into the melted butter, and place in a muffin tin, 3 balls to a muffin cup. Cover with plastic wrap and let rise in a warm place until doubled in bulk, about $1 1/2$ hours.

Preheat the oven to 350 degrees. Bake the rolls for 15 minutes, or until golden brown. (Makes 1 dozen rolls.)

6 large bell peppers (a combination of
  4 red and/or yellow and 2 green),
  cored, seeded, and chopped
2 large onions, chopped
3 cups cider vinegar
1 1/2 cups sugar
1 tablespoon salt
2 teaspoons celery seeds
1 teaspoon mustard seeds
2 teaspoons turmeric
1 teaspoon dried tarragon

1. PUT ALL THE INGREDIENTS for the relish into a large heavy pot and bring to a boil. Cook for 15 to 20 minutes, or until slightly thickened.

2. MEANWHILE, sterilize 5 half-pint jars; keep the jars warm.

3. LADLE THE RELISH into the hot jars, leaving about 1/2 inch of headspace. Wipe any excess from the rims and cap the jars according to the manufacturer's directions. Process the jars in a boiling-water bath for 10 minutes. Let the jars cool, and test for a seal. Store in a cool, dark place; refrigerate after opening.

FLY-OFF-THE-PLATE ROLLS

In 1925, Earl May began broadcasting on KMA Radio-960 from Shenandoah, Iowa, to boost his fledgling seed business. The station aired practical information designed to help with day-to-day activities in Midwestern kitchens. Hosting the daily radio programs—"Home Hour," "The Stitch and Chat Club," and "The KMA Party Line"—was a changing roster of personable, lively women such as Leanna Driftmier, who became known as KMA Radio Homemakers. Driftmier's "Kitchen-Klatter" show inspired Iowa homemakers long before self-help books were a major industry. Her program sponsored many different contests, including one that involved weight loss; those who shed the most pounds were invited to prove it by weighing in at the Driftmier home. Then all the contestants sat down to a huge covered-dish dinner!

Listeners also sent in recipes like this one, and attested to their virtues on the air. Rising high and light in the pan, with a tender, feathery crumb, these rolls *will* fly off the plate as soon as your guests taste them. They're similar to the "throwed rolls" offered in country cafés throughout central Missouri. Because the dough is soft and a little sticky, you almost throw rather than place each roll in the pan; any imperfections disappear during the final rise.

MAKES 16 ROLLS

1/4 cup plus 1 1/2 tablespoons sugar
1 1/2 cups lukewarm (90 degrees) water
1 (1/4-ounce) package (2 1/4 teaspoons)
  active dry yeast
3 3/4 to 4 1/2 cups all-purpose flour
3 tablespoons instant nonfat dry milk
1 teaspoon salt
1 large egg, beaten
3 tablespoons canola or corn oil
Melted butter, for brushing

1. IN A SMALL BOWL, combine 1 1/2 tablespoons of the sugar and 1/2 cup of the lukewarm water.

Sprinkle the yeast over the water and set aside to proof until foamy, about 5 minutes.

2. IN A LARGE BOWL, combine 3 cups of the flour, the dry milk powder, and salt. Pour the yeast mixture over the flour mixture. With a wooden spoon, stir in the remaining $1/4$ cup sugar and 1 cup lukewarm water, the egg, and oil until you have a batter-like dough.

3. TURN THE DOUGH OUT onto a floured surface. Flour your hands and the dough and knead for 7 to 10 minutes, using a dough scraper to fold the dough over on itself. Knead in up to $1^1/2$ cups more flour as necessary, until the dough is soft and slightly sticky. Place the dough in a large oiled bowl and turn to coat. Cover with plastic wrap and set aside in a warm place to rise until doubled in bulk, 45 to 60 minutes.

4. GREASE TWO 9-INCH ROUND CAKE PANS and set aside. Turn the dough out onto a floured surface. Cut the dough in half with a dough scraper, then cut each piece in half again. Cut each quarter of dough into 4 equal portions, and form each portion loosely into a roll. Place 7 rolls around the perimeter and 1 roll in the middle of each prepared pan. Prick each roll twice with the tines of a fork. Cover with clean tea towels and let rise in a warm place until doubled in bulk, about 45 minutes.

5. Preheat the oven to 350 degrees. Bake the rolls for 15 minutes, or until risen and browned. Brush with melted butter and serve warm.

BUTTERMILK CRESCENT ROLLS

Mellow-tasting and slightly chewy, these rolls are a delicious contrast to the more common yeasty dinner roll. Start the dough in the afternoon if you want to make these flavorful rolls for dinner, as they take about four hours from start to finish.

MAKES 1 DOZEN ROLLS

$3/4$ cup buttermilk
4 tablespoons ($1/2$ stick) unsalted butter
1 tablespoon active dry yeast
$1/4$ cup warm (110 degrees) water
3 to $3^1/2$ cups unbleached all-purpose flour
2 tablespoons sugar
1 teaspoon salt
$1/4$ teaspoon baking soda
1 large egg, beaten, for egg glaze

1. IN A SAUCEPAN, combine the buttermilk and butter and heat until the butter melts. Remove from the heat and set aside to cool. In a small bowl, sprinkle the yeast over the warm water; set aside to proof until foamy, about 5 minutes.

2. IN THE BOWL OF AN ELECTRIC MIXER or another large bowl, combine 1 cup of the flour, the sugar, salt, and baking soda. Using the paddle attachment or a wooden spoon, beat in the buttermilk and yeast mixtures. Beat in 2 cups more flour, 1 cup at a time.

3. SWITCH TO THE DOUGH HOOK and knead the dough for 5 to 8 minutes, or until elastic, adding more flour as necessary. Or turn the dough out onto a floured surface and knead by hand. Place the dough in a large oiled bowl and turn to coat. Cover with plastic wrap and let rise in a warm place until doubled in bulk, 1 1/2 to 2 hours.

4. GREASE A LARGE BAKING SHEET. Punch down the dough and turn it out onto a lightly floured surface. Roll the dough into an 11- to 12-inch circle, then cut the circle into 12 triangles. Starting with the wide end, roll up each triangle, then place seam side down on the baking sheet and form into a crescent. Cover with tea towels and let rise in a warm place until doubled in bulk, about 1 hour.

5. PREHEAT THE OVEN to 375 degrees. Brush the crescents with the egg glaze and bake for 20 minutes, or until the rolls are puffed and browned. Serve hot.

BOHEMIAN SOUR RYE KNOTS

In her short story "The Bohemian Girl," Willa Cather describes the beauty of the prairie grain harvest: "The moonlight flooded that great, silent land. The reaped fields lay yellow in it. The straw stacks and poplar windbreaks threw sharp black shadows. The roads were white rivers of dust. The sky was a deep, crystalline blue, and the stars were few and faint. Everything seemed to have succumbed, to have sunk to sleep, under the great, golden tender, midsummer moon." When the grain harvest is over, it's time to celebrate with these unusual rolls, which can accompany a sophisticated dinner. The secret to their sour rye flavor is plain yogurt, not a sourdough starter. Lard is the traditional cooking medium for the onions, but you can substitute vegetable oil. Make sure the sautéed onions have completely cooled before you add them to the dough.

MAKES ABOUT 3 DOZEN ROLLS

1/3 cup lard or canola oil
1 onion, finely chopped
3 1/2 teaspoons active dry yeast
1/2 teaspoon sugar
1/4 cup warm (110 degrees) water
2 1/4 cups plain yogurt
2 1/2 tablespoons caraway seeds
1 tablespoon salt
1 1/2 teaspoons white pepper
2 large eggs
2 1/2 cups stone-ground rye flour
2 to 2 1/2 cups unbleached all-purpose flour
Yellow cornmeal, for dusting
1 large egg yolk, beaten with 1 tablespoon water, for egg glaze
1/4 cup coarse sea or kosher salt

1. HEAT THE LARD or oil in a medium skillet and sauté the onion until it begins to turn golden, about 12 minutes. Remove from the heat and set aside to cool.

2. IN THE BOWL OF AN ELECTRIC MIXER or another large bowl, sprinkle the yeast and sugar over the warm water; set aside to proof until foamy, about 5 minutes.

3. USING THE PADDLE ATTACHMENT or a wooden spoon, beat the yogurt, caraway seeds, salt, and white pepper into the yeast mixture. Beat in the eggs. Beat in the rye flour, 1 cup at a time, then beat in enough of the all-purpose flour until you have a soft but no longer sticky dough.

4. SWITCH TO THE DOUGH HOOK and knead the dough for 5 to 7 minutes, or until elastic. Or turn the dough out onto a floured surface and knead by hand. Place the dough in a large oiled bowl and turn to coat. Cover with plastic wrap and let rise in a warm place until doubled in bulk, about 2 hours.

5. DUST 3 LARGE BAKING SHEETS with cornmeal and set aside. Turn the dough out onto a floured surface and cut it into thirds. Roll each third into a 12-inch square and cut the dough into 12 strips. Tie each strip into a loose single knot and place the knots about 1 inch apart on the prepared baking sheet. Repeat the process until all the dough is used. Cover with tea towels and let rise in a warm place for 30 minutes.

6. PREHEAT THE OVEN to 350 degrees. Brush the knots with the beaten egg yolk and sprinkle with coarse salt. Bake for 20 to 25 minutes, or until golden brown. Serve hot.

GERMAN SOFT PRETZELS

I grew up in a German/Irish family that loved to have a good time. Family gatherings were always occasions for singing, playing the piano or cards, telling stories and jokes, with the cousins playing hide and seek in back bedrooms or kick the can outside. One evening in the 1950s, my cousins invited the extended family over to make homemade pretzels. The men brought jugs of locally brewed beer, the women had the pretzel dough ready to be shaped, and everyone kept the kids from getting too close to the lye, which gives pretzels their distinctive flavor but is very caustic. (Store the remaining lye carefully.) This is the pretzel recipe. Now, go and make your own fun! Serve with a hearty mustard or Midwestern cheese.

MAKES ABOUT 3 DOZEN PRETZELS

2 (1/4-ounce) packages (1 1/2 tablespoons) active dry yeast
1 1/2 cups warm (110 degrees) water
About 5 cups unbleached all-purpose flour
1 teaspoon Red Devil lye (available at hardware or plumbing supply stores)
1 cup water
1 cup coarse sea, kosher, or pretzel salt

1. IN THE BOWL OF AN ELECTRIC MIXER or another large bowl, sprinkle the yeast over the warm water and set aside to proof until foamy, about 5 minutes. With the paddle attachment or wooden spoon, beat in enough of the flour, 1 cup at a time, until you have a stiff dough.

2. SWITCH TO THE DOUGH HOOK and knead the dough for 5 to 8 minutes, until smooth and elastic, adding more flour if necessary. Or turn out the dough onto a floured surface and knead by hand. Place the dough in a large oiled bowl and turn to coat. Cover with plastic wrap and let rise in a warm place until doubled in bulk, 1 to 1 1/2 hours.

3. LINE TWO BAKING SHEETS with aluminum foil, grease the foil, and set aside. Punch down the dough and turn it out onto a floured surface. With a serrated knife, cut the dough in half. Roll one half of the dough into a 1-inch-thick rectangle. With the serrated knife or a pizza wheel, cut the dough into 1-inch-wide strips. Form each strip into a pretzel shape and place on the prepared baking sheet. Repeat with the remaining dough. Cover with plastic wrap and let rise in a warm place until doubled in bulk, 45 minutes to 1 hour.

4. PREHEAT THE OVEN to 375 degrees. In a small enameled or other noncorrosive saucepan, mix the lye and water together. Bring to a boil, then immediately remove from the heat. Using tongs, dip each pretzel into the lye solution so that it is completely coated, then return to the baking sheet.

5. SPRINKLE THE PRETZELS with coarse salt and bake for 15 to 18 minutes, or until browned. Transfer to wire racks to cool.

VARIATION: To make Pretzel Sticks, place the strips of dough on the prepared baking sheet. Using a plastic brush (with no metal parts), brush the strips with the lye solution. Sprinkle with the salt and bake for 12 to 15 minutes, or until well browned. Transfer to racks to cool.

THRESHING DAY BUNS

During the winter wheat harvest throughout the Great Plains, lunch is eaten in the fields, or more precisely, in the air-conditioned combine. Most often, lunch means a sandwich on homemade bread or rolls like these, a piece of fruit, and a cool drink—as the 100-degree heat can make the wheat fields seem to shimmer. The sponge method produces a feathery texture (be sure to allow for its 6-to-8-hour rising time), and the extra sugar helps create a thin and somewhat crisp crust.

MAKES 2 DOZEN BUNS

FOR THE SPONGE:
1/4 teaspoon active dry yeast
1 1/2 cups warm (110 degrees) water
2 cups unbleached all-purpose flour

1/2 cup warm (110 degrees) water
1 cup plus 1/2 teaspoon sugar
1 (1/4-ounce) package (2 1/4 teaspoons) active dry yeast
1 cup milk
3 tablespoons unsalted butter, melted
1 teaspoon salt
5 to 6 cups unbleached all-purpose flour

1. MAKE THE SPONGE: In a medium bowl, sprinkle the yeast over the warm water; set aside to proof until foamy, about 5 minutes. With a wooden spoon, stir in the flour until you have a smooth batter. Cover with plastic wrap and let rise in a warm place until doubled in bulk, 6 to 8 hours.

2. IN A SMALL BOWL, combine the warm water and ¹/2 teaspoon of the sugar. Sprinkle the yeast over the water and set aside to proof until foamy, about 5 minutes. In a small saucepan, heat the milk until warm (110 degrees); remove from the heat.

3. IN THE BOWL OF AN ELECTRIC MIXER or another large bowl, combine the milk and the remaining 1 cup sugar. Using the paddle attachment or a wooden spoon, beat in the butter, salt, and the yeast mixture. Beat in the sponge, then beat in the flour, ¹/2 cup at a time, until you have a pliant but not stiff dough.

4. SWITCH TO THE DOUGH HOOK and knead the dough for about 5 minutes, until it is smooth and elastic. Or turn the dough out onto a floured surface and knead by hand. Place the dough in a large oiled bowl and turn to coat. Cover with plastic wrap and let rise in a warm place until doubled in bulk, about 1 hour.

5. GREASE TWO BAKING SHEETS. Punch down the dough and turn it out onto a floured surface. Cut the dough in half, then cut each half into 12 equal pieces. Form each piece into a ball and place 1 inch apart on the prepared baking sheets. Cover with tea towels and let rise in a warm place for 30 minutes, or until almost doubled in bulk.

6. PREHEAT THE OVEN to 375 degrees. Bake the buns for 20 minutes, or until risen and browned. Serve warm. (These can be frozen for up to 3 months.)

THE KANSAS WHEAT HARVEST

············ ❧❦ ············

It's dusk on the prairie. Where Cheyenne and buffalo once roamed and cowboys drove herds of longhorn cattle northward along the Chisholm Trail, today a patchwork of golden squares outlined in dark green spreads out like a living quilt. The wind rustles the papery stalks of ripe wheat, sending the smell of dried grass and warm earth rising into the evening air. Wheat, premier of all prairie grasses, has made its indelible mark on the landscape.

Here in a triangle of Kansas country towns about thirty miles north of Wichita—Newton, Moundridge, and Goessel—wheat makes its own unique imprint on the lives of farmers and townspeople alike.

It's also what connects the wheat-farming Wenger family and other descendants of the original wheat-farming families in the area. Wheat is the reason they came here from the Ukraine over a century ago, responding to Santa Fe Railroad ads promising "good soil for wheat, corn, and fruit." In 1874, the first Russian Mennonite families brought sacks full of the reddish-brown seeds that would dramatically change the land. As at home on the Kansas prairie as it was on the Russian steppes, Turkey Red winter wheat and its more than two hundred varieties of descendants—including the Pioneer 2163 and Karl 92 hybrids the Wengers plant and harvest—have transformed the prairie into the nation's Breadbasket.

At the close of the first day of harvest, the sun is setting in the western quadrant of the big sky. The wind has shifted, blowing out the oppressive heat of the day that rose to nearly 100 degrees, and breezing in cooler air. In the east, a massive thunderhead dazzles in sunset colors of mauve, coral, rose, and blue.

To Merle Wenger, a forty-four-year-old conservative Mennonite farmer who is combining the first of 900 acres of ripening wheat, the scenery is incidental. He has his eye on the dwindling sun, the threatening eastern sky. And on all of the wheat that needs to be cut yet. "There's a big white combine," he says, pointing to the miles-high storm in the distance, "that could take care of this field in five minutes."

Already he's had to repair a sickle on one combine, staying up late at night to hammer out the razor-sharp blades. And then a tire blew on the other. "They're my teenagers," Merle says of his expensive and temperamental equipment.

And then there's all the help to contend with. "We have too much help at harvest," Merle's 42-year-old wife Lena dryly remarks. "Everyone wants something to do." Merle and 20-year-old daughter Angela clamber up the six-foot ladders to drive the giant two-story-high air-conditioned combines that cut the wheat, then separate the kernels from the straw, storing the kernels in the bin and blowing the chaff and straw back onto the field. As the bins on each combine fill up, Angela's husband, Royce, sees the signal and drives up parallel to the combine in his wheat cart. With as little wasted time and energy as possible, a chute on the top of the combine's bin is hooked up to the wheat cart and transfers the harvested wheat onto the cart. Royce then takes the load of wheat—over 200 bushels—to the wheat truck waiting on the dirt road. From there, Lena will drive the fully laden wheat truck to the grain elevator in Newton. Everyone stays in touch by radio or cell phone, a technological innovation that had to meet the approval of the Wenger's strict church committee.

Teenaged Emily, who, like most conservative Mennonite children, is finished with formal schooling at age 14, is on cooking duty preparing dinners and suppers that everyone can eat while they work. Even younger siblings Dwayne and Julie have a part to play, putting the meals together and transporting them to the fields.

Lena and other wheat truck drivers endure long lines at the co-op, as each truckload from neighboring farms waits to be weighed, tested, and emptied. Pulling up to the co-op office window, much like a fast food drive-through, the full truck is first weighed. Then a worker climbs to the top and inserts a copper tube into the wheat kernels to get a sample. In a matter of seconds, the sample is dumped into a small machine that evaluates the moisture content. Next, the sample is quickly sifted for impurities like weeds, stones, or seeds.

And only then is the price configured; the lower the moisture content and impurity level, the higher the price—about $6 per bushel today. Last year, the price ranged from $3 to more than $5 per bushel. To put this in perspective, wheat farmers like Merle Wenger receive about 5 cents for the wheat in a 1-pound loaf of bread that sells in grocery stores for about 75 cents.

An average bushel of wheat weighs 60 pounds, but this year, some farmers are getting 63 pounds to the bushel, meaning heavier wheat berries—another good sign. A girl hands Lena the ticket, and her truck moves on to the grain elevator.

Like a huge tower with a garage opening on the ground level, the grain elevator is a noisy, dusty place during harvest. Lena's truck pulls into the opening, guided by two seasonal workers. At their signal, she raises the truck bed and dumps the grain onto the grates that form the floor. Wearing hospital masks in the hot powdery wind tunnel, the workers "scoop truck" to clear out the grain quickly. The machinery hums so loudly you have to shout to be heard as the grain travels by underground auger up into the elevator. When the truck is empty, Lena moves it on to be weighed again so the weight of the wheat can be calculated, then drives back to the field for another load.

Even when darkness finally falls and everything is quiet, it will still be a night of restless sleep until the harvest is safely in. This year's wheat crop is much better than anyone expected: more than 40 bushels per acre on Merle's worst field; more than 55 on the best. A good wheat crop is between 35 and 45 bushels. Good news—so far.

NEW MAXWELL STREET BOLILLOS

Every Sunday in Chicago's historic New Maxwell Street Market, Mexican vendors sell everything from old machine parts and men's socks to homemade tamales and *hurachies* (sandal-shaped corn flatbread topped with tomatillo sauce). Bolillos, crusty hard rolls with a chewy crumb, make hearty sandwiches, or *tortas*, for market-goers, with fillings such as chorizo sausage, cheese, and pinto beans, or taco-seasoned ground beef, strips of sautéed red and green bell pepper, and cubes of fried potato.

At La Posada Market on Kansas City's Southwest Boulevard, owner Esther Rogers fills freshly baked bolillos with homemade *carnitas*, slow-roasted morsels of spiced pork.

Bolillos are also good for breakfast with butter and homemade preserves. Or, when cut in half lengthwise, brushed on the cut side with a garlicky vinaigrette, and topped with a grilled vegetable filling, they make great sandwiches for a tailgate party or picnic.

MAKES 16 ROLLS

1 (¼-ounce) package (2¼ teaspoons)
    active dry yeast
¼ cup warm (110 degrees) water
6 to 6¾ cups all-purpose flour
2 teaspoons salt
1 tablespoon sugar
2 cups lukewarm (90 degrees) water
Canola oil, for brushing

1. IN A SMALL BOWL, sprinkle the yeast over the warm water and set aside to proof until foamy, about 5 minutes. In a large bowl, combine 5 cups of the flour, the salt, and sugar. Make a well in the center of the dry ingredients, pour in the yeast mixture and the lukewarm water and stir with a wooden spoon until the dough forms a ball.

2. TURN THE DOUGH OUT onto a floured surface and knead for 5 to 8 minutes, adding more flour as necessary, until smooth and elastic. Place the dough in a large oiled bowl and turn to coat. Cover with plastic wrap and let rise in a warm place until doubled in bulk, 1½ to 2 hours.

3. GREASE TWO BAKING SHEETS and set aside. Punch down the dough and turn it out onto a floured surface. Cut the dough in half and divide each half into 8 equal pieces. Roll each piece into a ball. Brush each ball of dough with canola oil, dust with flour, and flatten it with your hand into a 4-inch oblong or football shape. Place about 1 inch apart on the prepared baking sheets and cover with damp kitchen towels. Let rise in a warm place until almost doubled in bulk, about 1 hour.

4. PREHEAT THE OVEN to 375 degrees. With a serrated knife or a razor blade, cut a 1-inch-deep slash down the center of each roll. Brush the rolls again with canola oil. Bake the bolillos for 25 to 30 minutes, or until they are golden brown. Transfer to wire racks to cool.

MOCHOS

Mexican bakeries throughout the Heartland make these rich and savory elongated hard rolls, based on bolillo dough. They are a delicious accompaniment to grilled beef, chicken, or pork. I fill mochos with chopped, smoked brisket and spicy tomato barbecue sauce for a hearty sandwich. Traditional recipes use lard in place of canola oil or shortening, but I have adapted them to make a lighter, more contemporary version.

MAKES 1 DOZEN ROLLS

1 large onion, coarsely chopped
3 large garlic cloves, minced
1/2 cup canola oil, plus more for brushing
3/4 teaspoon freshly ground black pepper
1/4 teaspoon ground allspice, preferably freshly ground
1/2 cup sugar
3/4 cup shortening
2 large eggs
1 recipe Bolillo dough (page 130), prepared through Step 2

1. IN A LARGE SAUCEPAN, sauté the onion and garlic in the canola oil until soft, about 5 minutes. Transfer the mixture to a blender or food processor and puree. Add the pepper, allspice, sugar, shortening, and eggs and process to blend. Set aside.

2. GREASE A LARGE BAKING SHEET and set aside. Punch down the dough and turn it out onto a floured surface. Knead in the pureed mixture and continue to knead until the dough is elastic, adding more flour if necessary. Divide the dough into 12 equal pieces. Roll each piece into a ball and shape into a 6-inch-long loaf. With a serrated knife or a razor blade, make two 1-inch-deep diagonal slashes across the top of each roll. Place the rolls on the prepared baking sheet, cover with tea towels, and let rise in a warm place for 1 hour, or until doubled in bulk.

3. PREHEAT THE OVEN to 350 degrees. Bake the rolls for 20 to 25 minutes, or until the tops are golden brown. Transfer to wire racks to cool.

HEART-OF-THE-PRAIRIE PARMESAN ROLLS

Chip and Rosemary Bartlett, former Chicago attorneys, gave up the bright lights of the big city for their own Heart of the Prairie Bakery in West Des Moines, Iowa, in 1992. When the Bartletts traded in their pin-striped suits for baker's smocks, they also traded in an 8-to-5 workday for one that now stretches from 4 A.M. to 4 P.M. Their breads, coffee cakes, rolls, and sweet treats are made, as much as possible, from regional ingredients—eggs from nearby Winterset, honey from Sulla, and corn-

meal and wheat flour from prairie farms. These savory Parmesan Rolls are halfway between a popover and a yeast roll in texture. I like to serve them with a daube and a green salad or with grilled chicken and vegetables.

MAKES 1 DOZEN ROLLS

1 (1/4-ounce) package (2 1/4 teaspoons)
    active dry yeast
1/3 cup warm (110 degrees) water
8 tablespoons (1 stick) unsalted butter,
    softened
2 tablespoons sugar
1/4 teaspoon salt
2 1/3 cups bread flour
3 large eggs
1 cup freshly grated Parmesan cheese
1 large egg, beaten with 1 tablespoon
    water, for egg glaze

1. IN A SMALL BOWL, sprinkle the yeast over the warm water and set aside to proof until foamy, about 5 minutes.

2. IN A LARGE BOWL, beat the butter, sugar, and salt together with an electric mixer. Beat in the flour, the 3 eggs, and the yeast mixture, then beat at medium speed for 2 minutes. With a wooden spoon, stir in the Parmesan. Cover with plastic wrap and refrigerate for 4 to 6 hours.

3. GREASE A 12-CUP MUFFIN TIN and set aside. Punch down the dough and turn it out onto a floured surface. With a serrated knife, cut the dough in half, then cut each half into 6 pieces. Shape each piece into a roll and place in a prepared muffin cup. Cover with plastic wrap and let rise in a warm place until doubled in bulk, 40 to 50 minutes.

4. PREHEAT THE OVEN to 375 degrees. Brush the tops of the rolls with the egg glaze. Bake for 15 minutes, or until the rolls have risen and browned. Serve warm.

DILLED SAFFRON DINNER ROLLS

When Bill Penzey founded the Milwaukee mail-order spice emporium that bears his name, he resolved to make it friendly in the best Midwestern tradition. In every issue of the company's catalog, you'll find Penzey family recipes—especially those from Grandma Moog. It's no wonder that Milwaukee has become an herb and spice capital. More than thirty different immigrant groups—among them Welsh, Danish, Belgian, Swiss, French Canadian, Irish, German, Italian, Polish, Czech, and Dutch—sailed across Lake Michigan to the Wisconsin shore, then trekked farther inland to settle.

These dinner rolls, adapted from a Penzey recipe, echo the baking tradition of saffron breads brought by Cornish lead miners and their families to Mineral Point and Dodgeville, Wisconsin. The dill complements the saffron, making these the perfect rolls to serve with freshly caught lake perch or walleye pike. The rolls are also delicious as luncheon or appetizer bites with a filling of cooked shrimp or lobster blended with mayonnaise, on crisp lettuce leaves. Leftovers make great crumbs to top a fish pie.

MAKES 2 DOZEN ROLLS

1 cup milk
1 (¹/4-ounce) package (2¹/4 teaspoons) active dry yeast
5 tablespoons sugar
4 tablespoons (¹/2 stick) unsalted butter
2 teaspoons saffron threads
1 large egg, beaten
1 teaspoon dillweed
¹/2 teaspoon salt
4 to 4¹/2 cups all-purpose flour
1 large egg white, beaten with 1 tablespoon water, for egg glaze

1. IN A SMALL SAUCEPAN, heat the milk until warm (110 degrees); remove from the heat. Pour ¹/2 cup of the milk into the bowl of an electric mixer or another large bowl and sprinkle 1 tablespoon of the sugar and the yeast over it; set aside to proof until foamy, about 5 minutes. Add the remaining ¹/4 cup sugar, the butter, and saffron to the milk remaining in the saucepan; cover and let steep for several minutes.

2. ADD THE SAFFRON MILK to the yeast mixture. With the paddle attachment or a wooden spoon, beat in the egg, salt, and dillweed. Beat in 4 cups of the flour, 1 cup at a time, until you have a soft dough.

SHAPING DINNER ROLLS

.... ❦ ....

Dinner rolls, hot from the oven and fragrant with yeast, can take on a variety of flavors and colors—pale orange from pureed squash, golden yellow from saffron steeped in milk, flecked green from fresh basil and garlic, speckled red from roasted red pepper or sun-dried tomato. They can also take on a variety of delectable shapes that show off the bread baker's artistry. These rolls may be impossible to resist, but they're easy to make. Try one or more of these fanciful shapes the next time you make yeast rolls, using a bread or roll recipe calling for 3 to 4 cups of flour: that amount of flour will produce a dough that makes a dozen dinner rolls.

Form the rolls into the desired shape and place them on a greased baking sheet, about 2 inches apart, or in greased muffin cups. Cover and let rise in a warm spot until doubled in bulk, about 45 minutes. Bake the rolls at the temperature given in the dough recipe you used. Rolls usually bake in half the time of a loaf; check them after 15 minutes of baking to make sure. Rolls are done when they have risen and browned.

BOWKNOT Divide the dough in half. Cut each half into 6 portions. With your hands, roll each portion into a 6-inch-long rope. Tie each rope into a loose single knot and place on a greased baking sheet.

CLOVERLEAF Pinch off about a tablespoon of dough and roll into a ball about 1 inch in diameter. Dip the ball in melted butter (using 4 tablespoons [1/2 stick] unsalted butter in all) and place in a muffin pan. Repeat the process, placing 3 balls of dough in each muffin cup to form a cloverleaf.

3. SWITCH TO THE DOUGH HOOK and knead the dough for 5 to 8 minutes, adding more flour if necessary, until smooth and elastic. Or turn the dough out onto a floured surface and knead by hand. Place the dough in a large oiled bowl and turn to coat. Cover with plastic wrap and let rise until doubled in bulk, about 1 hour.

4. BUTTER TWO 12-CUP MUFFIN TINS and set aside. Punch down the dough and turn it out onto a floured surface. Divide the dough in half.

Divide each half into 12 equal portions, roll each one into a ball, and place in the prepared muffin tins. Cover with tea towels and let rise in a warm place until doubled in bulk, about 1 hour.

5. PREHEAT THE OVEN to 350 degrees. Brush the egg glaze over the tops of the rolls. Bake for 15 minutes, until risen and golden. Transfer to wire racks and cool for 10 minutes before serving warm.

.... ❦ ....

CRESCENT Roll out the dough to a 12-inch circle. Beat 4 tablespoons (1/2 stick) softened unsalted butter with an electric mixer, or process in a food processor, until creamy. Spread the butter over the surface of the dough. Cut the circle into 12 wedges. Starting at the base of each wedge, roll it up toward the point. Place seam side down on a greased baking sheet and curve into a crescent shape.

FANTAN Roll the dough out to a 12-inch square. Brush the surface with 4 tablespoons (1/2 stick) melted unsalted butter. Cut the dough into twelve 1-inch-wide strips. Stack 6 strips on top of one another, then stack the remaining strips so that you have 2 stacks. Cut each stack crosswise into 2-inch pieces. Press each piece, cut side up, into a greased muffin cup.

PULL-APARTS Divide the dough in half. Divide each half into 6 portions. Roll each portion into a ball. Dip the balls in 4 tablespoons (1/2 stick) melted unsalted butter and arrange in a greased 9-inch round cake pan so that they are touching one another.

SPIRALS Roll the dough out to a 12-by-10-inch rectangle. Brush the surface with 4 tablespoons (1/2 stick) melted unsalted butter and sprinkle with fresh or dried herbs, or spread with a filling of your choice. Starting from a long side, roll up the dough jelly-roll fashion into a 12-inch-long cylinder. Cut the dough into twelve 1-inch-wide slices and place cut side up on a greased baking sheet.

TWISTS Divide the dough in half. Cut each half into 6 portions. With your hands, roll each portion into a 6-inch-long rope. Twist each rope into a spiral and place on a greased baking sheet. Brush the spirals with 4 tablespoons (1/2 stick) melted unsalted butter and sprinkle with herbs, chopped garlic, poppy seeds, sesame seeds, or coarse salt.

APRICOT-FILLED ITALIAN CRESCENTS

Italian bakeries such as the Missouri Baking Company on the Hill in St. Louis, Missouri, or Peter Sciortino's in Milwaukee, Wisconsin, sometimes offer sweet yeast crescent rolls like these, filled with luscious fruit. More tender than the French croissant, these pastries have a brioche-like quality. Serve these as part of an Italian summer brunch, complete with Bellinis made with fresh Summer Pearl or Summer Haven peaches, a frittata of garden vegetables and Italian sausage, chilled melon, and frothy lattes. These pastries can be frozen and then reheated, wrapped in aluminum foil, in a 300-degree oven.

MAKES 2 DOZEN CRESCENTS

2 (¹/4-ounce) packages (1¹/2 tablespoons)
   active dry yeast
¹/2 cup warm (110 degrees) water
³/4 cup milk
³/4 cup granulated sugar
1 teaspoon salt
1 teaspoon vanilla extract
8 tablespoons (1 stick) unsalted butter,
   softened
5¹/2 to 6 cups all-purpose flour
1 large egg
2 large eggs, separated
1 cup best-quality apricot preserves
   (or other fruit preserves)
2 teaspoons water
Coarsely crushed sugar cubes or pearl
   sugar, for sprinkling
Confectioners' sugar, optional,
   for dusting

1. SPRINKLE THE YEAST over the warm water in the bowl of an electric mixer or another large bowl and set aside to proof until foamy, about 5 minutes. Meanwhile, in a small saucepan, heat the milk until warm (110 degrees); remove from the heat.

2. ADD THE MILK to the yeast mixture, then stir in the granulated sugar, salt, vanilla, and butter, stirring until the butter melts. With the paddle attachment or a wooden spoon, beat in 3 cups of the flour, 1 cup at a time. Beat in the egg and egg yolks until well combined, then beat in enough of the remaining flour so you have a soft dough.

3. SWITCH TO THE DOUGH HOOK and knead the dough for 8 to 10 minutes, until smooth and elastic. Or turn the dough out onto a floured surface and knead by hand. Place the dough in a large oiled bowl and turn to coat. Cover with

plastic wrap and let rise in a warm place until doubled in bulk, about 1¹/2 hours.

4. PUNCH DOWN THE DOUGH and turn it out onto a floured surface. Divide the dough in half, cover, and let rest for 10 minutes.

5. GREASE A LARGE BAKING SHEET and set aside. Roll each portion of dough into an 18-inch round. Cut each circle into 12 triangles. Place 2 teaspoons of the preserves near the wide end of each triangle. With your fingers, stretch the wide end of each triangle slightly, then roll it up jelly-roll fashion. Place seam side down on the prepared baking sheet and curve the dough to form a crescent. Cover the crescents with plastic wrap and let rise in a warm place until slightly puffy, about 30 minutes.

6. PREHEAT THE OVEN to 375 degrees. In a small bowl, beat the egg whites with the 2 teaspoons water until just frothy. Brush the crescents with this egg glaze. Sprinkle with crushed or pearl sugar and bake for 15 to 18 minutes, or until the rolls are puffed and browned. Dust with confectioners' sugar, if desired. Cool on wire racks.

SAFFRON BUNS
FOR ST. LUCIA DAY

~꙳~

These sweet buns are served on December 13, St. Lucia's Day, in prairie communities with Swedish heritage. The recipe can also be used to make two tea rings—see the Variation below. Or use half the dough for buns, the other half for a tea ring.

MAKES 40 BUNS

*1 (1/4-ounce) package (2 1/4 teaspoons)
   active dry yeast
1/4 cup warm (110 degrees) water
8 tablespoons (1 stick) unsalted butter
1 cup half-and-half
1/2 cup granulated sugar
1/2 teaspoon saffron threads
1/2 teaspoon salt
1 large egg, beaten
4 cups sifted all-purpose flour
1 large egg, beaten with 1 tablespoon
   water, for egg glaze
Coarse or pearl sugar, for sprinkling
1/4 cup raisins*

1. IN A LARGE BOWL, sprinkle the yeast over the warm water; set aside to proof until foamy, about 5 minutes. Melt the butter in a small saucepan and add the half-and-half. Remove from the heat.

2. POUR THE BUTTER MIXTURE over the yeast mixture, then stir in the granulated sugar, saffron, salt, and egg. Gradually stir in the flour, mixing well, until the dough is smooth and sponge-like (do not knead). Transfer the dough to a large oiled bowl and turn to coat. Cover with plastic wrap and let rise in a warm spot for 30 minutes, or until doubled in bulk.

3. GREASE TWO OR THREE BAKING SHEETS or line with parchment paper; set aside. Turn the dough out onto a lightly floured surface and knead until smooth and shiny, about 5 minutes. With a serrated knife, cut the dough in half. One at a time, roll each portion of dough out into a 10-by-5-inch rectangle. With a serrated knife, cut the dough into twenty 5-by-1/2-inch strips. Roll each strip under your palms into a rope about 6 inches long and shape it into a backwards S shape (known as the Christmas Pig), tightly coiling the ends, or into the shape of your choice (see page 138). Place well apart on the prepared baking sheets, cover with plastic wrap, and let rise until doubled in bulk, about 1 hour.

4. PREHEAT THE OVEN to 375 degrees. Brush the buns with the egg wash, sprinkle with coarse sugar, and place a raisin in each coil of the S shapes. Tighten the coils of each shape if necessary. Bake for 10 to 12 minutes, or until lightly browned.

VARIATION: For Saffron Tea Rings, in Step 3, grease two large baking sheets or line with parchment paper. Roll one portion of dough out into a 12-inch circle and cut the circle into 16 wedges. Invert a 2 1/2-inch-diameter heatproof glass tumbler in the middle of one of the prepared baking sheets and arrange the dough wedges in a circle around the glass. Repeat with the remaining dough. Cover the tea rings with plastic wrap and let rise until doubled in bulk, about 1 hour. Preheat the oven to 375 degrees. Brush the tea rings with the egg glaze, sprinkle with coarse sugar, and decorate with the raisins. Bake for 15 to 20 minutes, or until golden brown. Makes 2 tea rings.

Fun with Saffron Buns

...........🌾........

Saffron Buns for St. Lucia Day show a wonderful variety of folk art patterns. They all start with the basic 5-by-¹/2-inch strip that is coiled at both ends. Raisins decorate the center of the coil or loop at each end, or are sometimes placed in the middle of shapes made by joining two strips. Have some fun experimenting with these traditional shapes.

LILY Lay a strip out lengthwise and coil each end to form the strip into a flattened C. Turn the strip so that it is horizontal, with the coiled ends facing downward. Press your finger into the middle of the strip and draw up the ends to form a V, or lily. Place a raisin in the center of each coil.

PASTOR'S HAIR This fanciful shape resembles the ornate triple-layered powdered wig that an eighteenth-century pastor or judge might have worn. Lay 3 strips out lengthwise and coil the ends of each strip to form the strip into a flattened C. Turn each strip so that it is horizontal, with the coiled ends facing downward. Press your finger in the middle of one strip and draw up the ends to form a V, or lily. Turn it upside down so that it makes a hill with the coiled ends turned upward. Place the second strip on top of the hill so that the coiled ends turn upward, pressing the strips gently together. Place the third strip on top of the second so that the coiled ends turn upward, pressing the strips gently together. Place a raisin in the center of each coil.

LUCIA CAT Lay 2 strips out lengthwise and coil the ends of each strip to form the strip into a flattened C. Place the strips with their backs next to each other, and press them gently together. Place a raisin in the center, at the point where the strips join.

CHRISTMAS WAGON Lay 2 strips out lengthwise and coil the ends of each strip to form the strip into a flattened C. Place the strips with their backs next to each other, and press them gently together. Form a third strip into a circle and place it on the center of the joined strips. Place a raisin in the center of the circle.

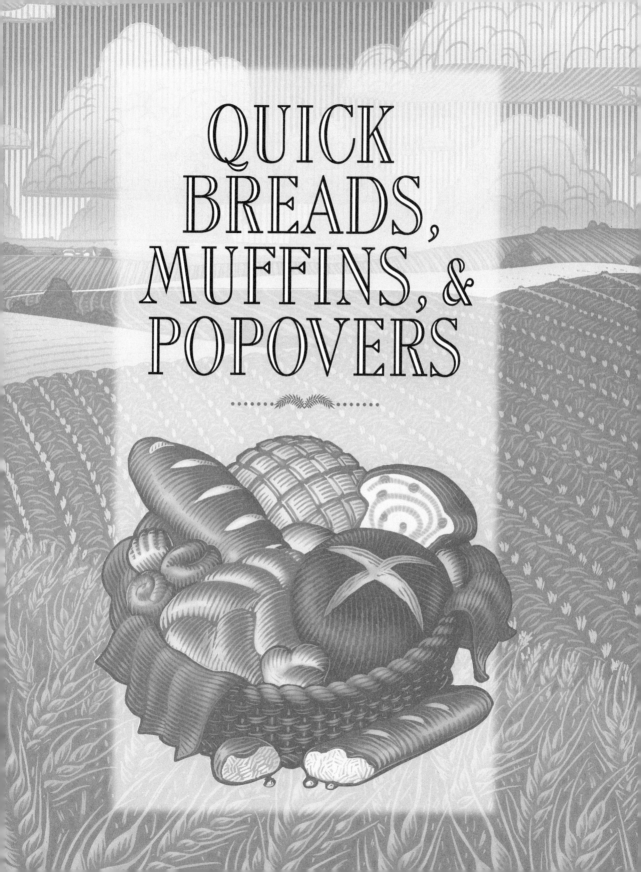

QUICK BREADS, MUFFINS, & POPOVERS

LEMON-SCENTED HERB TEA BREAD

Zionsville, Indiana, is one of those early nineteenth-century eastern prairie settlements of old Georgian brick homes and framed-over log cabins that make us nostalgic for what we think were simpler, less hurried times. Although the urban sprawl of Indianapolis is not far away, Zionsville seems to breathe easier. Starting on Saturdays in June, you can stroll through the farmers' market and enjoy the sensory pleasure of Jean Keneipp's market stall full of fresh kitchen garden herbs, herb-infused local honey, homemade herbal oils and vinegars, and bread dippers. If you're lucky, she'll also have loaves of her delicious glazed tea bread, which I have adapted for this recipe. Use fresh lemon-scented herbs such as lemon verbena, lemon balm, lemon geranium, lemon thyme, or bee balm. (Make sure you use only unsprayed, organic leaves.) Serve slices of the tea bread on thin china plates with dollops of whipped cream and sprigs of fresh herbs or blossoms from the garden.

MAKES 1 LOAF

3/4 cup milk
1 tablespoon finely chopped fresh lemon balm
1 tablespoon finely chopped fresh lemon thyme or lemon geranium leaves
8 fresh lemon verbena leaves, optional
2 cups all-purpose flour
1 1/2 teaspoons baking powder
1/4 teaspoon salt
6 tablespoons (3/4 stick) unsalted butter, softened

1 cup granulated sugar
2 large eggs, beaten
1 tablespoon grated lemon zest

FOR THE GLAZE:
Juice of 1/2 lemon
3/4 cup confectioners' sugar
1/2 teaspoon vanilla extract

1. IN A SMALL SAUCEPAN, scald the milk (heat it just until small bubbles appear around the edges) with the chopped herbs. Remove from the heat, cover, and let steep for 20 minutes.

2. MEANWHILE, preheat the oven to 325 degrees. Butter a 9-by-5-by-3-inch loaf pan. Press the lemon verbena leaves, if using, into the butter on the bottom and sides of the pan to make a pleasing pattern; set aside. Sift the flour, baking powder, and salt together; set aside.

3. IN A LARGE BOWL, with a hand-held electic mixer, cream the butter and granulated sugar until light and fluffy. Beat in the eggs and lemon zest, then beat in the flour mixture, 1 cup at a time. Strain the milk into the bowl and beat until you have a smooth batter.

4. POUR THE BATTER into the prepared pan and bake for 50 minutes, or until a toothpick inserted in the center comes out clean. Turn the bread out onto a wire rack.

5. IN A SMALL BOWL, whisk the glaze ingredients together. Drizzle or spread over the warm bread.

PRAIRIE HONEY PUMPKIN BREAD

Rich, moist, and delicious, this autumn tea bread is wonderful slathered with cream cheese or apple butter. It can be frozen for up to three months, so you can keep one on hand in the freezer for unexpected company.

MAKES 2 (9-BY-5-BY-3-INCH) LOAVES OR 3 (7-BY-4-BY-2-INCH) LOAVES

3¹/2 cups all-purpose flour
2 teaspoons baking soda
1¹/2 teaspoons salt
1 tablespoon ground cinnamon
1 tablespoon freshly grated nutmeg
2 cups sugar

³/4 cup wildflower or other pale amber honey
¹/2 cup water
1 cup vegetable oil
²/3 cup canned or freshly cooked and pureed pumpkin
4 large eggs, beaten
1 cup chopped pecans, optional
¹/2 cup golden raisins, optional
¹/2 cup dried sour cherries, optional

1. PREHEAT THE OVEN to 325 degrees. Grease two 9-by-5-by-3-inch or three 7-by-4-by-2-inch loaf pans and set aside. Sift the flour, baking soda, salt, cinnamon, nutmeg, and sugar together into a large bowl. With a wooden spoon, stir in the honey, water, oil, pumpkin, and eggs until you have a smooth batter. Fold in the pecans, raisins, and/or dried sour cherries, if desired.

2. POUR THE BATTER into the prepared pans and bake for 50 to 60 minutes, or until a toothpick inserted in the center of a loaf comes out clean. Cool in the pans on a wire rack.

HIGH PLAINS LEMONY RHUBARB BREAD

On the high plains, rhubarb is one of the most reliable garden crops and a welcome harbinger of spring. I love the combination of lemon and rhubarb in this crumb-topped quick bread, which is delicious warm from the oven or toasted. It also freezes well.

MAKES 2 LOAVES

1 3/4 cups sugar
2/3 cup canola oil
1 large egg
1 cup buttermilk
1 teaspoon salt
1 teaspoon baking soda
1 tablespoon grated lemon zest
1 teaspoon vanilla extract
2 1/2 cups all-purpose flour
1 1/2 cups diced rhubarb stalks

FOR THE CRUMB TOPPING:
1/2 cup all-purpose flour
1 tablespoon sugar
1 teaspoon grated lemon zest
4 tablespoons (1/2 stick) unsalted butter

1. PREHEAT THE OVEN to 375 degrees. Grease and flour two 9-by-5-by-3-inch loaf pans and set aside. In a medium bowl, combine 1 1/2 cups of the sugar, the oil, egg, buttermilk, salt, soda, lemon zest, vanilla, and flour. Using a hand-held electric mixer, beat to make a smooth batter.

2. IN A SMALL BOWL, combine the rhubarb with the remaining 1/4 cup sugar, tossing to coat.

With a rubber spatula, fold the rhubarb into the batter. Spoon the batter into the prepared pans.

3. MAKE THE TOPPING: In a small bowl, combine the sugar, lemon zest, and flour. Add the butter and work it in with your fingers until the mixture forms large crumbs. Sprinkle the crumbs on top of the loaves.

4. BAKE FOR 50 TO 60 MINUTES, or until a toothpick inserted in the center of a loaf comes out clean. Cool in the pans on a wire rack.

PICKIN' UP PAWPAWS BREAD

On family vacations in the 1950s, when my sister and I were little girls, we headed to lake resorts like the Dunes on the shores of Lake Michigan in northern Indiana or to the lakeside Shady Shores in southern Michigan. We stayed in spartan tourist cabins, swam in the lake, ate dinner in the communal dining room, and then lingered for entertainment afterward. In the days before VCRs and color television, entertainment usually meant games for the kids and dancing for everyone. Actually, the games blended into the dancing, as the kids would make a huge circle to do the "hokey-pokey" and act out "a tisket, a tasket, a green and yellow basket." Another folk song, about "pickin' up pawpaws, put[tin]' em in yer pocket, way down yonder in the pawpaw patch," also required accompanying actions.

So years later, when I received a basket of pale green, stubby, banana-shaped, wild pawpaws in my biweekly bag of subscription produce from a local organic farm, I laughed out loud. I let them ripen on the kitchen counter until they were soft, then I peeled them and, with my fingers, worked the smooth, shiny seeds free of the pawpaw pulp to make this pink-tinted bread, adapted from a recipe in *Reliable Recipes from Reliable People* by the Ladies of the Third Division Presbyterian Church, PawPaw, Michigan. If you don't have any pawpaws, though, ripe bananas also work well in this recipe.

MAKES 1 LOAF

2 cups all-purpose flour
1 teaspoon salt
1 teaspoon baking powder
1/2 teaspoon baking soda
8 tablespoons (1 stick) unsalted butter, softened
1 cup sugar
2 large eggs, beaten
1 tablespoon buttermilk
1 cup mashed ripe pawpaw pulp (from 4 to 5 large pawpaws) or bananas (from 3 medium bananas)
1 cup chopped pecans, black walnuts, or hickory nuts

1. PREHEAT THE OVEN to 350 degrees. Grease a 9-by-5-by-3-inch loaf pan and set aside. Sift the flour, salt, baking powder, and baking soda together into a bowl; set aside.

2. IN A LARGE BOWL, cream the butter and sugar with a hand-held electric mixer or a wooden spoon. Beat in the eggs. Beat in the dry ingredients, 1 cup at a time. Beat in the mashed pawpaws or bananas and the nuts.

3. POUR THE BATTER into the prepared pan and bake for 40 minutes, or until a toothpick inserted in the center of the loaf comes out clean. Cool in the pan or on a wire rack for 10 minutes, then invert onto the rack, turn right side up, and let cool.

FROSTED CARROT, CORIANDER, AND GINGER BREAD

With ingredients from the Midwinter prairie larder, this sweet and spicy bread, warm from the oven, revives flagging spirits. Frosted with spiced cream cheese, it's an even better treat. Serve it on your best china, make a fresh pot of aromatic tea, and invite friends over so you can catch up with one another's lives. Festively wrapped, the bread also makes a delicious hostess gift.

MAKES 2 LOAVES

3/4 cup plus 2 tablespoons corn or canola oil
2 cups sugar
4 large eggs, beaten
2 cups finely grated carrots
2 cups all-purpose flour
2 teaspoons baking soda
1 teaspoon salt
1 tablespoon peeled and grated fresh ginger
1 tablespoon ground coriander

FOR THE FROSTING:
1 (8-ounce) package cream cheese,
   softened
¼ cup sugar
1 teaspoon ground ginger
2 tablespoons milk
1 teaspoon vanilla extract

1. PREHEAT THE OVEN to 350 degrees. Grease two 9-by-5-by-3-inch loaf pans and set aside. In a large bowl, with a wooden spoon or a hand-held electric mixer, beat together the oil, sugar, eggs, and carrots. Beat in the flour, baking soda, salt, ginger, and coriander.

2. POUR THE BATTER into the prepared pans. Bake for 45 minutes, or until a toothpick inserted in the center comes out clean. Cool in the pans on a wire rack, then invert onto the rack and turn right side up.

3. MAKE THE FROSTING: Combine the cream cheese, sugar, ginger, milk, and vanilla in a medium bowl and beat with a wooden spoon until smooth and spreadable. Frost the tops of the cooled loaves.

LEMON-GLAZED NATIVE PERSIMMON MUFFINS

In Mitchell, Indiana, September means the annual Persimmon Festival, when the orange-colored native fruit ripens. That's the perfect time to enjoy these fragrant, moist muffins, lingering over a steaming pot of tea before heading outdoors to rake leaves or plant bulbs for the spring. Enjoy them warm from the oven, but be sure to freeze some to microwave for breakfast on busy weekday mornings. Canned native persimmon pulp is available through mail-order (see Source Guide, page 215) and can be found in many Indiana grocery stores. The more fibrous pulp of Asian Fuyu persimmons, available at produce markets and many supermarkets in the fall, also works well.

MAKES 1 DOZEN MUFFINS

1¾ cups unbleached all-purpose flour
1 teaspoon baking powder
1 teaspoon baking soda
½ teaspoon salt
8 tablespoons (1 stick) unsalted butter,
   softened
½ cup granulated sugar
¼ cup wildflower or other pale amber
   honey
2 large eggs
1½ cups persimmon pulp (from 3 to 4
   persimmons)
1 teaspoon grated lemon zest
Juice of 1 lemon
½ cup chopped walnuts

FOR THE GLAZE:
Juice of ¹/2 lemon
³/4 cup confectioners' sugar
¹/2 teaspoon vanilla extract

1. PREHEAT THE OVEN to 325 degrees. Grease a 12-cup muffin tin or line it with paper liners and set aside. Sift the flour, baking powder, baking soda, and salt together; set aside.

2. IN A LARGE BOWL, with a hand-held electric mixer, cream the butter and granulated sugar together. Beat in the honey, then beat in the eggs, beating until well incorporated. Beat in the persimmon pulp until just combined. Beat in the lemon zest and juice, then beat in the dry ingredients, ¹/2 cup at a time, until you have a fairly smooth batter. Stir in the walnuts.

3. SPOON THE BATTER into the muffin cups, filling them three-quarters full. Bake for 30 minutes, or until a toothpick inserted in the center of a muffin comes out clean. Let the muffins cool in the muffin tins for a few minutes, then turn out onto a rack.

4. MEANWHILE, MAKE THE GLAZE: In a small bowl, whisk all the ingredients together until smooth and spreadable. Spread a little glaze over the top of each warm muffin and allow to cool.

THE FARMHOUSE PANTRY

In The Midwestern Country Cookbook, *Marilyn Kluger remembers her 1930s childhood in southern Indiana, before electricity eventually reached rural communities after World War II and the era she described came to an end. Here she recalls the farmhouse pantry.*

The pantry next to our kitchen in the farmhouse had a look of delicious plenty. Its pine-sheathed walls were lined with sturdy shelves that sagged gently under the weight of sparkling jars of garden vegetables, fruits, and jellies, the overflow from the cellar. Deep covered bins for pastry flour, bread flour, sugar, and cornmeal stood along one wall. On the table under the window were flat pans filled with fresh tomatoes from the garden or potatoes from the cellar, baskets of brown-shelled eggs, shiny tin pails of leaf lard, and earthenware crocks brimming with cream-topped milk. On the windowsill bloomed rose geraniums with their scented leaves, and blue-flowered chives.

GINGERBREAD MUFFINS

A dapted from *Good Things to Eat*, a cookbook published in 1938 by the Gleaners of First Christian Church in New Castle, Indiana, this recipe evokes the time of the Depression, when Midwesterners learned to make the most of what they had on hand. That usually meant garden produce, fresh eggs, lard, pantry staples, and whatever else could be gathered, bartered, or somehow acquired. These muffins are also an example of convenience foods, 1930s-style: the batter takes only a few seconds to mix, and it keeps for weeks in the refrigerator, ready to be spooned into tins and popped into the oven at a moment's notice. So you can make as many muffins as you like, whenever you like. Their spicy, robust flavor helps dispel the blahs of a weekday morning when Saturday seems too far away. Leftovers are delicious in a bread pudding made with fresh apples or pears.

MAKES ABOUT 3 DOZEN MUFFINS

3 large eggs
1 cup molasses
1 cup packed brown sugar
3 1/2 cups all-purpose flour
1 tablespoon baking soda
1 tablespoon ground cloves
1 tablespoon ground ginger
1/2 pound (2 sticks) unsalted butter, melted
1 cup hot water

1. IN A LARGE BOWL, combine all the ingredients and mix together with a wooden spoon. Cover and refrigerate until ready to use.

2. WHEN READY TO BAKE, preheat the oven to 350 degrees. Grease one or more muffin tins and set aside. Spoon the batter into the muffin cups, filing each one two-thirds full.

3. BAKE FOR 20 TO 25 MINUTES, or until a toothpick inserted in the center of a muffin comes out clean. Let cool in the pan on a rack for a few minutes, then serve warm.

OLD-FASHIONED GRAHAM GEMS

I n Midwestern antique shops, you'll often see heavy iron "gem pans." During the late nineteenth century, gems were the Heartland cook's answer to ready-to-eat breakfast cereal and a way to get the benefit of whole grains without making hot oatmeal, cracked wheat cereal, or cornmeal mush. In the 1877 edition of *Buckeye Cookery and Practical Housekeeping*, graham gems were a menu suggestion for winter breakfasts, along with turkey hash, potatoes boiled in their jackets, and sliced oranges. They're best eaten hot, just the thing on a cold day when you'll be doing something active outdoors.

MAKES 2 DOZEN MINIATURE MUFFINS

1 cup milk
1 tablespoon cider vinegar
³/4 cup graham or stone-ground whole
    wheat flour
³/4 cup unbleached all-purpose flour
¹/2 teaspoon baking soda
2 large eggs
¹/4 cup sugar
2 tablespoons unsalted butter, softened

FOR THE TOPPING:
2 tablespoons sugar
2 teaspoons ground cinnamon

1. PREHEAT THE OVEN to 400 degrees. Grease two mini-muffin tins and set aside. In a small bowl, combine the milk and cider vinegar; set aside to sour for a few minutes. Sift the dry ingredients together and set aside.

2. IN A LARGE BOWL, whisk the eggs to blend, then whisk in the sugar and butter. Whisk in the soured milk. Stir in the dry ingredients, ¹/2 cup at a time, until you have a stiff batter. Spoon the batter into the prepared muffin cups, filling them two-thirds full.

3. IN A SMALL BOWL, combine the topping ingredients. Sprinkle about ¹/4 teaspoon of the topping on each muffin. Bake for 10 minutes, or until the muffins have risen and pulled away from the sides of the pan. Serve warm.

PRAIRIE PANTRY WINTER FRUIT CONSERVE

During the long winters on the northern prairie, the taste of something sweet and fruity was a welcome change from root vegetables, soups, and potatoes. When supplies of summer preserves ran low, this conserve could be made from the dried fruits in the pantry. Many households had their own version of this recipe. In Willa Cather's short story "The Bohemian Girl," the absence of a pantry conserve at the breakfast table prompts a quick trip to town: "He asked for prune preserves at breakfast, and I told him I was out of them, and to bring some prunes and honey and cloves from town." Today, this conserve means a delicious, homemade holiday hostess gift that does not require expensive out-of-season fruit. When I make this, of course, I also keep enough for our household. The conserve is wonderful spooned over cream cheese on a slice of fresh bread, but it also makes a nice accompaniment to a slice of roast turkey or an unexpectedly good cake filling.

MAKES 5 HALF-PINT JARS

¹/2 cup dried apples
¹/2 cup pitted prunes
¹/2 cup chopped dates
¹/2 cup dried tart cherries
¹/2 cup golden raisins
¹/2 cup dried apricots
3 cups hot water
Juice of 2 lemons
1³/4 cups sugar

1. USING KITCHEN SHEARS, snip any large pieces of dried fruit into smaller bits. Combine all the fruits in a bowl and pour the hot water over them. Cover and let sit for several hours, or overnight, until the fruits have softened.

2. POUR THE SOFTENED FRUITS and their liquid into a medium saucepan, stir in the lemon juice, and heat over medium-high heat. While the mixture is heating, warm the sugar in a pan in a 350-degree oven for 15 minutes, or until warmed through. (This helps the conserve cook faster.)

3. STIR THE WARM SUGAR into the fruit mixture and bring to a boil. Cook for 30 to 35 minutes, or until the mixture reaches 220 degrees on a candy thermometer. You can also test for jelling by placing a spoonful of the liquid on a cold plate; if it holds its shape, without running, it is done.

4. MEANWHILE, sterilize 5 half-pint canning jars and lids; keep the jars hot.

5. SPOON OR LADLE the conserve into the hot sterilized jars, leaving ¼ inch of headspace. Let cool, then seal the jars. The conserve will keep indefinitely in the refrigerator.

PRAIRIE PANTRY BREAKFAST MUFFINS

I am not the kind of person who gets up before the sun and putters in the kitchen. I'm lucky if I make toast on weekday mornings, much less muffins. But I decided to give these a go when I came across two muffin recipes, an ocean apart. One was a British breakfast muffin with marmalade in the center, the other was the Raspberry-Almond Muffin (page 150) recipe from Wisconsin. With the Prairie Pantry Winter Fruit Conserve in mind, I created these muffins. And even I will get up a little earlier to make them, to be served warm with a little butter. Marmalade, Crabapple Jelly (page 175), Old-Fashioned Quince Preserves (page 12), or other good-quality preserves can also be used in place of these preserves.

MAKES 15 MUFFINS

2¼ cups all-purpose flour
¾ cup sugar
12 tablespoons (1½ sticks) unsalted
    butter, softened
½ teaspoon grated lemon zest
½ teaspoon baking powder
½ teaspoon baking soda
¼ teaspoon salt
¾ cup sour cream
1 large egg, beaten
About ⅔ cup Prairie Pantry Winter
    Fruit Conserve (page 148) or other
    tart preserves

1. PREHEAT THE OVEN to 350 degrees. Grease 15 muffin cups and set aside. In a large bowl, or the bowl of a food processor, combine the flour and sugar. Cut in the butter with a pastry cutter, or by pulsing the food processor, until the mixture resembles coarse crumbs. Transfer 1 cup of the mixture to a small bowl, stir in the lemon zest, and set aside.

2. ADD THE BAKING POWDER, baking soda, salt, sour cream, and egg to the remaining mixture and beat with a wooden spoon, or process, until you have a smooth batter. Spoon half the batter into the prepared muffin tins. Spoon 1 heaping teaspoon of preserves on top of the batter in each muffin cup, then spoon the remaining batter over the preserves. Sprinkle the reserved crumb mixture evenly over the muffins.

3. BAKE THE MUFFINS for 20 minutes, or until risen and puffed. Cool in the pans on wire racks, then remove from the pans.

PRAIRIE PANTRY COFFEE CAKE: Preheat the oven to 350 degrees and grease a Bundt pan. Prepare the batter and crumb mixture as directed. Spoon half of the batter into the prepared Bundt pan and spoon ²/3 cup preserves evenly over the batter. Spoon the remaining batter over the preserves. Bake for 55 to 60 minutes, or until a toothpick inserted in the center of the coffee cake comes out clean. Cool in the pan on a wire rack, then invert onto a serving plate.

RASPBERRY-ALMOND MUFFINS

Midwestern weekend sybarites take their breakfasts seriously. They may work hard during the week, racing out the door in the morning with barely a cup of coffee, before putting in countless hours at work. But when the weekend comes and they get away to a favorite retreat, breakfast is one meal they don't want to rush—especially when it's a multi-course meal. At bed-and-breakfast inns all across the Heartland—like the Thorpe House Inn in Fish Creek, Wisconsin—breakfast might start with a homemade granola and fresh-from-the-oven muffins like these, followed by a fruit dish. And then comes the egg, pancake, or quiche entrée—all washed down with plenty of freshly brewed coffee or tea. These muffins, however, could be the high point of any breakfast. Use the best-quality raspberry preserves you can find—and, if you are buying the almond filling, do the same.

MAKES 15 MUFFINS

2¹/4 cups all-purpose flour
³/4 cup sugar
12 tablespoons (1¹/2 sticks) unsalted
  butter, softened
¹/2 teaspoon baking powder
¹/2 teaspoon baking soda
¹/4 teaspoon salt
³/4 cup sour cream
1 large egg, beaten
1 cup Danish Almond Filling (page 185),
  almond paste, or marzipan
¹/2 cup raspberry preserves
¹/2 cup flaked almonds

1. PREHEAT THE OVEN to 350 degrees. Grease 15 muffin cups and set aside. In a large bowl, or the bowl of a food processor, combine the flour and sugar. Cut in the butter with a pastry cutter, or by pulsing the food processor, until the mixture resembles coarse crumbs. Transfer 1 cup of the mixture to a small bowl and set it aside.

2. ADD THE BAKING POWDER, baking soda, salt, sour cream, and egg to the remaining crumb mixture and beat with a wooden spoon, or process, until you have a smooth batter. Spoon the batter into the prepared muffin tins. Spoon the filling on top of the batter, dividing it evenly, and spoon the preserves on top of the almond filling.

3. ADD THE ALMONDS to the reserved crumb mixture and mix well. Sprinkle this mixture evenly over the muffins. Bake the muffins for 20 minutes, or until risen and puffed. Serve warm.

RASPBERRY-ALMOND COFFEE CAKE: Preheat the oven to 350 degrees and grease a Bundt pan. Prepare the batter and crumb mixture as directed. Spoon the batter into the prepared pan, spoon the filling on top of the batter, and spoon the preserves on top of the filling. Sprinkle the almond-crumb mixture over the top. Bake for 55 to 60 minutes, or until a toothpick inserted in the center comes out clean. Let cool slightly, then invert onto a wire rack. Serve warm.

BLUEBERRY CORNMEAL MUFFINS

The French Loaf in Columbus, Ohio, is justly famous for its moist, flavorful muffins. There's just enough cornmeal in them to add a little texture. In my version, I've included a touch of lemon, which heightens the blueberry flavor and adds sparkle to the taste.

MAKES 1 DOZEN MUFFINS

1 cup yellow cornmeal
1 cup all-purpose flour
3 tablespoons sugar
1 tablespoon baking powder
$1/2$ teaspoon salt
1 large egg, beaten
1 cup milk
Grated zest and juice of 1 large lemon
$1/4$ cup canola or corn oil
$1^1/2$ cups fresh or frozen blueberries

1. PREHEAT THE OVEN to 400 degrees. Grease a 12-cup muffin tin or line with paper liners and set aside. In a medium bowl, combine the cornmeal, flour, sugar, baking powder, and salt. Make a well in the center of the dry ingredients and add the eggs, milk, lemon zest and juice, and oil to the well. With a wooden spoon, mix the wet ingredients into the cornmeal mixture just until the dry ingredients are evenly moistened. With a rubber spatula, fold in the blueberries.

2. SPOON THE BATTER into the prepared muffin cups, filling each one two-thirds full. Bake for 20 to 25 minutes, or until a toothpick inserted in the center of a muffin comes out clean. Cool in the pans on wire racks.

PUMPKIN APPLE STREUSEL MUFFINS

These mellow and delicious American-style muffins are great to have in the freezer to warm and serve houseguests on busy fall weekends or at Thanksgiving. Muffins such as these also lure women with a sweet tooth and yen for adventure from the Iowa State University Women's Club: according to Ames, Iowa, food writer Linda Hodges, there are two special-interest groups in the club—Tea For You and Me, and Tea Room Adventures—devoted to exploring tea rooms and shops. These groups hit the road in search of the perfect muffin, stopping at small-town tea rooms along the scenic backroads of western and central Iowa. If you can't go tearoom trekking in your area, you can at least make these muffins, invite friends over, and plan your own adventure.

MAKES 2 DOZEN MUFFINS

2¹/2 cups all-purpose flour
2 cups sugar
1 teaspoon baking soda
¹/2 teaspoon ground cinnamon
¹/2 teaspoon freshly grated nutmeg
¹/2 teaspoon salt
2 large eggs
1 cup canned pumpkin (not pumpkin pie filling)
¹/2 cup canola or corn oil
2 cups peeled, cored, and finely chopped apples

FOR THE STREUSEL TOPPING:
2 tablespoons all-purpose flour
¹/4 cup sugar
¹/2 teaspoon ground cinnamon
4 tablespoons (¹/2 stick) unsalted butter, softened

1. PREHEAT THE OVEN to 350 degrees. Grease two 12-cup muffin tins or line with paper liners: set aside. In a large bowl, whisk together the flour, sugar, baking soda, cinnamon, nutmeg, and salt; set aside.

2. IN A MEDIUM BOWL, using a hand-held electric mixer, beat the eggs until blended. Beat in the pumpkin and oil until smooth. Add the pumpkin mixture to the flour mixture, beating until smooth. Stir in the apples. Spoon the batter into the prepared tins, filling each cup three-quarters full.

3. IN A SMALL BOWL, combine the topping ingredients and mix with your fingers until crumbly. Sprinkle a little of the streusel topping over the top of each muffin.

4. BAKE FOR 35 TO 40 MINUTES, or until a toothpick inserted in the center of a muffin comes out clean. Let cool slightly in the pans on wire racks, then turn out of the pans and serve warm, or let cool completely on the racks.

FRESH PEACH AND PEACH LEAF MUFFINS

The first ripe peaches of summer are meant to be eaten fresh, with the juice running down your arm. After the first dozen or so, though, you're ready for peaches in some other form, like the peach preserves in these muffins. Although I use my Summer Peach Jam (from *Prairie Home Cooking*, page 76), any wonderful thick peach preserves will do. There's nothing that complements the sugar-crisp flavor of fresh peaches better than a little touch of almond. You can get that by infusing fresh peach leaves in milk, as prairie farm wives did, or by adding a little almond extract to the batter. (Make sure you use unsprayed, organic peach leaves.)

MAKES 15 MUFFINS

12 tablespoons (1¹/₂ sticks) unsalted
  butter, softened
1 teaspoon almond extract or 12 peach
  leaves
2¹/₄ cups all-purpose flour
³/₄ cup sugar
¹/₂ teaspoon baking powder
¹/₂ teaspoon baking soda
¹/₄ teaspoon salt
³/₄ cup sour cream
1 large egg, beaten
About ²/₃ cup good-quality peach preserves

1. MELT THE BUTTER in a medium saucepan over low heat. Stir in ¹/₂ teaspoon of the almond extract or the peach leaves and set aside to infuse for 30 minutes. Remove the peach leaves, if you used them, and refrigerate the butter until it is solid, about 1 hour.

2. PREHEAT THE OVEN to 350 degrees. Grease 15 muffin cups and set aside. In a large bowl, or the bowl of a food processor, combine the flour and sugar. Cut in the butter with a pastry cutter, or by pulsing the food processor, until the mixture resembles coarse crumbs. Transfer 1 cup of the crumb mixture to a small bowl and set aside.

3. ADD THE BAKING POWDER, baking soda, salt, sour cream, egg, and the remaining ¹/₂ teaspoon almond extract, if using, to the remaining crumb mixture and beat with a wooden spoon, or process, until you have a smooth batter. Spoon half the batter into the prepared muffin tins. Spoon a heaped teaspoon of the peach preserves on top of the batter, then spoon the remaining batter over the preserves. Sprinkle the reserved crumb mixture on top of the muffins.

4. BAKE THE MUFFINS for 20 minutes, or until risen and puffed. Serve warm.

FRESH PEACH AND PEACH LEAF COFFEE CAKE: Preheat the oven to 350 degrees and grease a Bundt pan. Prepare the batter and crumb mixture as directed. Spoon half the batter into the Bundt pan and spoon the preserves evenly over the batter. Spoon the remaining batter over the preserves. Bake for 55 to 60 minutes, or until a toothpick inserted in the center of the cake comes out clean. Let cool slightly, then invert the coffee cake onto a wire rack.

SAVORY CHEESE PUFFS

Classic French choux pastry from the Canadian Great Lakes area and fine cheese from the upper Midwest combine in these savory bites, which are perfect cocktail nibbles or accompaniments to a hearty soup. Use Midwestern Gruyère or Leelanau raclette from Michigan and La Paysanne aged pecorino from Minnesota, if possible. Pair these appetizers with a dry red wine such as Norton or Schoolhouse Red from Missouri or a California Cabernet Sauvignon or Merlot.

MAKES 2 DOZEN PUFFS

1 cup milk
8 tablespoons (1 stick) unsalted butter
1/2 teaspoon salt
1/2 teaspoon white pepper
1 cup sifted all-purpose flour
5 large eggs
1 1/4 cups grated La Paysanne or other aged pecorino cheese
3/4 cup grated Gruyère or Leelanau raclette cheese

1. PREHEAT THE OVEN to 350 degrees. Line a large baking sheet with parchment paper; set aside. In a large saucepan, combine the milk, butter, salt, and white pepper and bring to a boil. Remove from the heat, add the flour all at once, and whisk vigorously until smooth.

2. RETURN THE PAN TO THE HEAT and cook, stirring constantly, until the batter has thickened and pulls away from the sides of the pan.

Remove the pan from the heat and beat in 4 of the eggs, one at a time, mixing thoroughly after each addition. Beat in 3/4 cup each of the pecorino and the Gruyère.

3. DROP THE BATTER by the tablespoonful onto the prepared baking sheet, placing the puffs 1 inch apart. Beat the remaining egg in a small bowl. Brush the tops of each puff with the beaten egg and sprinkle with the remaining 1/2 cup pecorino.

4. BAKE FOR 17 TO 20 MINUTES, or until puffed, golden brown, and crackled. Serve warm.

COUNTRY HERB POPOVERS

Feather-light and fragrant with the taste of fresh herbs, these popovers are delicious served with a delicate egg dish for a weekend breakfast or with grilled fish, asparagus, and a red pepper beurre blanc for an elegant dinner.

Make sure you grease the popover pans well so the popovers release easily after baking, and be sure the oven is hot, so the popovers rise properly. These are best eaten right from the oven.

MAKES 2 DOZEN MINIATURE
OR 8 LARGE POPOVERS

2 large eggs
1 cup minus 1 tablespoon milk
1 tablespoon canola oil
1 cup unbleached all-purpose flour
1 teaspoon salt
$1/2$ teaspoon white pepper
$1/4$ cup finely chopped fresh tarragon
$1/4$ cup finely chopped fresh chives
$1/4$ cup finely chopped fresh basil
$1/4$ cup finely chopped fresh Italian parsley
1 tablespoon fresh lemon juice

1. PREHEAT THE OVEN to 450 degrees. Generously grease two 12-cup miniature muffin pans or 8 regular muffin cups and set aside. In a large bowl, whisk together the eggs, milk, and oil. Whisk in the flour, salt, white pepper, herbs, and lemon juice until well blended and smooth. Ladle the batter into the muffin cups, filling them two-thirds full.

2. BAKE MINIATURE POPOVERS for 5 minutes, then turn down the oven temperature to 350 degrees and bake for 10 to 12 minutes more, or until puffed and golden. Or bake large popovers for 10 minutes, then turn down the oven temperature to 350 degrees and bake for 10 to 12 minutes more, or until puffed and golden. Serve hot.

WILD RICE POPOVERS

Wild rice is the only grain native to North America, a staple food of the Sioux and Chippewa tribes. True wild rice still grows in the lakes and rivers of Minnesota, upper Michigan, northern Wisconsin, and lower Canada, but much of the "wild rice" we see today is cultivated in cold water paddies. Wild rice, which can be stored indefinitely in tightly sealed containers, is a Midwestern pantry staple. Because the cooking process takes about 45 minutes, I keep frozen cooked wild rice in the freezer as a convenience food (1 cup raw wild rice makes 3 to 4 cups cooked). Then the rice can easily be transformed into these savory popovers and served as an appetizer or an accompaniment to a main course. Or fill larger popovers with herbed scrambled eggs for breakfast or creamed chicken or braised beef for dinner. You can prepare the batter up to an hour ahead of time.

MAKES 2 DOZEN MINIATURE OR 8 LARGE POPOVERS

2 large eggs
1 cup milk
1 tablespoon canola oil
1 cup unbleached all-purpose flour
$1/2$ teaspoon salt
1 teaspoon white pepper
1 teaspoon bottled Maggi seasoning
$1/2$ cup cooked wild rice
2 tablespoons snipped fresh chives

1. PREHEAT THE OVEN to 475 degrees. Lightly oil two 12-cup miniature muffin pans or 8 regular muffin cups and set aside. In a large bowl, whisk together the eggs, milk, and oil until well

blended and smooth. Whisk in the salt, white pepper, Maggi seasoning, wild rice, and chives. Ladle the batter into the muffin cups, filling them two-thirds full.

2. BAKE MINIATURE POPOVERS for 5 minutes, then turn down the oven temperature to 350 degrees and bake for 10 minutes more, or until puffed and golden. Or bake large popovers for 15 minutes, then turn down the oven temperature to 350 degrees and bake for 20 to 25 minutes more, until puffed and golden. Serve hot.

SCONES, BISCUITS, CRACKERS, AND A SODA BREAD

IRISH BUTTERMILK SODA BREAD

On April 1, 1873, a steamship left Glasgow, Scotland, bound for the shores of America, with the decks full of young aristocrats ready for a prairie adventure. They arrived on May 17 at their new settlement named Victoria, in Ellis County, Kansas, with trunks full of ball gowns, family silver, linens, fine wines, and fox-hunting regalia. What they didn't have was any practical knowledge about life on the frontier. But the English ladies were soon taught to make bread by "a kind, motherly Irish-woman, Mrs. Norton, who will never be forgotten by these women, many of whom never did their own house-work and had no idea how to rough it on the prairie," recalled Jane Hardie Phillip in 1873. Mrs. Norton's bread-making lesson probably involved soda bread. At its simplest, Irish Soda Bread is a round cottage loaf baked in an iron skillet from an easy dough that's a cousin to the scone. This moist version in-cludes a hint of sweetness from the golden raisins. Meant to be enjoyed for breakfast or with tea, traditional soda bread is best eaten the day it's made.

MAKES 1 ROUND LOAF

3 cups all-purpose flour
2/3 cup sugar
1 teaspoon baking powder
1 teaspoon baking soda
1 teaspoon salt
1 1/2 cups golden raisins, plumped in warm water and drained
2 large eggs, beaten
1 3/4 cups buttermilk
2 tablespoons unsalted butter, melted

1. PREHEAT THE OVEN to 350 degrees. Grease and flour a 10-inch cast-iron skillet and set aside. Sift the dry ingredients together into a large bowl, and stir in the raisins.

2. IN A MEDIUM BOWL, beat the eggs, buttermilk, and butter together with a wooden spoon, then stir into the dry ingredients.

3. SPOON THE DOUGH into the prepared pan and bake for 55 to 60 minutes, or until puffed and browned. Carefully transfer the bread to a wire rack to cool.

BUTTERMILK, OLIVE, AND RED PEPPER SCONES

Prairie home bakers of Welsh and Irish descent sometimes "tart up" up basic quick bread or scones with cheese, herbs, or spices. In this recipe, cream cheese, Kalamata olives, and roasted red pepper produce a scone that is savory, delicious, and easy to prepare. Make this to serve with the first ripe tomatoes of the summer for a match made in heaven. It would also be a welcome addition to a fireside meal of hearty soup in the winter.

MAKES 8 SCONES

1 large red bell pepper (see Note)
1 tablespoon olive oil
Coarse sea or kosher salt
2 cups all-purpose flour
1/2 cup yellow cornmeal
2 teaspoons baking powder
1/4 teaspoon cream of tartar
1/4 teaspoon salt
2 teaspoons chopped fresh thyme or
  1 teaspoon dried thyme
4 ounces cream cheese, cut into 1/2-inch
  cubes
1/2 cup oil-cured Kalamata olives, pitted
  and cut in half
1 large egg, beaten
1 teaspoon brown sugar
1 cup buttermilk, plus more if needed
1 large egg white, beaten, for egg glaze

1. PREHEAT THE OVEN to 350 degrees. Place the pepper in a shallow baking dish, drizzle with the oil, and sprinkle with coarse salt. Cover the pan with foil and roast for 40 to 50 minutes, or until the pepper is soft. Set aside to cool. Increase the oven temperature to 425 degrees.

2. GREASE A LARGE BAKING SHEET and set aside. Remove the core, seeds, and skin from the roasted pepper and finely chop the pepper. In a large bowl, with a wooden spoon, stir together the flour, cornmeal, baking powder, cream of tartar, salt, thyme, cream cheese, olives, and roasted pepper.

3. IN A SMALL BOWL, beat the egg with the brown sugar. Make a well in the center of the flour mixture and add the egg mixture and buttermilk. With a fork, blend the liquid ingredients into the flour mixture until you have a soft but not sticky dough; add a little more buttermilk if the dough is too stiff.

4. TURN THE DOUGH OUT onto a floured surface and gently form it into a round loaf about 8 inches in diameter. Place the dough on the prepared baking sheet, lightly score the dough into 8 equal wedges, and brush the top with the egg glaze.

5. BAKE THE BREAD for 5 minutes, then turn the oven temperature down to 375 degrees and bake for 35 to 40 minutes more, or until the loaf has risen and browned. Transfer to a wire rack to cool; for a softer crust, wrap the warm loaf in a tea towel. (This is best served the day it is made.)

NOTE: You can substitute 1/2 cup jarred roasted red peppers in oil, drained, for the roasted bell pepper.

FRENCH VALLEY PEAR SCONES

~

Eighteenth-century French prairie settlers paddled the inland waters of the St. Lawrence Seaway to the Great Lakes, then traveled down the rivers to the rolling prairie of Illinois. Bordered on two sides by the Mississippi and Ohio Rivers, this land was once a major wheat-producing area before the Russian Mennonites established the more successful winter wheat on the western prairie in the 1870s. Fruit trees, however, continue to thrive here due to generally ample rainfall and moist, humid summers. At one time, in fact, the largest pear tree in America was at Fort Cahokia, the French outpost near what is now East St. Louis. This recipe evolved from the traditional French *pain d'epices au miel*, or gingerbread with honey, to the more modern scone—wonderful for breakfast or tea.

MAKES 8 LARGE SCONES

2 cups all-purpose flour
2 teaspoons baking powder
1/4 teaspoon cream of tartar
1/4 teaspoon salt
2 teaspoons ground ginger
1 teaspoon ground cinnamon
1/2 teaspoon ground anise seeds
6 tablespoons (3/4 stick) unsalted butter, softened
1/2 cup buttermilk
2 tablespoons wildflower or other pale amber honey
2 large eggs, beaten
3 large ripe pears, peeled, cored, and finely chopped (about 1 1/2 cups)
1 large egg white, beaten, for egg glaze

1. PREHEAT THE OVEN to 425 degrees. Grease a large baking sheet and set aside. In a large bowl, combine the flour, baking powder, cream of tartar, salt, ginger, cinnamon, and anise seeds. With a pastry blender or two knives, cut in the butter until the mixture resembles coarse crumbs. With a fork, mix in the buttermilk, honey, and eggs until a soft dough forms. With a rubber spatula, fold in the pears.

2. TURN THE DOUGH OUT onto a floured surface and knead gently 6 times. Roll the dough out into a 9-inch round. Place on the prepared baking sheet, lightly score the dough into 8 equal wedges, and brush the top with the egg glaze.

3. BAKE THE LOAF for 30 to 35 minutes, or until golden brown. Transfer to a wire rack to cool. Serve with whipped cream or crème fraîche.

HONEYMOM'S RICH, BUTTERY SCONES

~

One bite of these and you will be in scone heaven. With a great cup of latte and fresh fruit, this is the ultimate indulgent breakfast treat for me. The recipe was developed by Susan Welling, formerly a pastry assistant at Square One in San Francisco. Now they're breakfast stars at her own Kansas City eatery, named Honeymom's after her bee-keeping grandmother. The secret to their buttery goodness is to freeze the scones before baking them. I keep several unbaked scones in my freezer, ready to pop into the oven on a weekend morning.

MAKES 10 TO 12 SCONES

4 cups all-purpose flour
1/2 cup sugar
5 teaspoons baking powder
2 teaspoons salt
1 pound (4 sticks) unsalted butter, cubed
    and chilled
3/4 cup currants or raisins
2 large eggs, beaten
13/4 cups heavy cream

1. IN A LARGE BOWL, mix the flour, sugar, baking powder, and salt together. With a pastry blender or two knives, cut in the butter until the mixture resembles coarse crumbs. With a fork, stir in the currants, eggs, and heavy cream.

2. TURN THE DOUGH OUT onto a floured surface and roll out to a thickness of 2 inches. With a 3-inch biscuit cutter, cut out rounds and place about 1 inch apart on an ungreased baking sheet. Put the baking sheet in the freezer for 1 hour, or until the scones are frozen.

3. PREHEAT THE OVEN to 325 degrees. Bake the scones for 25 to 35 minutes, or until golden. Serve warm or at room temperature.

STRAWBERRY, RHUBARB, AND ROSE PETAL JAM

In late May in Kansas, my roses begin blooming in the small garden on the side of my house. At the first farmers' markets of the season, I can buy ruby-colored rhubarb and luscious, tiny strawberries—or pick them myself at U-Pick farms not far from where I live. So when a friend gave me this recipe from a nineteenth-century British relative who lived on the Canadian prairie, I knew the time was right to make it. The rose enhances the fruity flavor of the strawberries and tones down the sharpness of the rhubarb. (The natural pectin from the lemon seeds helps set the jam.)

The elusive flavor of this jam goes well with fresh butter or mascarpone cheese, on top of Honeymom's Rich, Buttery Scones (page 161) or toasted Old-Fashioned Buttermilk Bread (page 41), or as a filling for homemade donuts, Latticed Rhubarb Sheets (page 201), or Danish Pastry (page 182).

MAKES 6 TO 7 HALF-PINTS

2 pounds rhubarb, trimmed, and stalks
    cut into 1-inch pieces
1 pound slightly underripe small straw-
    berries, hulled and halved lengthwise
63/4 cups sugar
4 lemons, halved
3 cups very fragrant (unsprayed) rose
    petals, preferably dark red, or
    1 teaspoon rose water (available
    at Asian markets and some better
    grocery stores)

1. PLACE THE RHUBARB and strawberries in a large bowl and pour the sugar over them. Squeeze the juice of the lemons over the sugar. Stir to mix. Cover with plastic wrap and let sit overnight at room temperature. Meanwhile, remove the seeds from the lemons. Place the seeds in a plastic bag and refrigerate overnight.

2. THE NEXT MORNING, transfer the rhubarb and strawberry mixture to a large saucepan. Put the lemon seeds in a small muslin bag, or wrap them in a square of cheesecloth and tie the corners together, and place the bag in the saucepan. Bring the mixture to a boil over medium-low heat. Boil for 2 minutes, then transfer the mixture back to the bowl. Cover with plastic wrap and refrigerate overnight.

3. THE NEXT MORNING, sterilize 7 half-pint jars and lids; keep the jars warm.

4. IF USING ROSE PETALS, pinch or cut out the bitter white part at the base of each petal. Put the rhubarb and strawberry mixture into a large saucepan and stir in the rose petals or rose water. Bring to a boil over medium-high heat and boil until the mixture coats the back of a spoon and reaches 220 degrees on a candy thermometer, about 8 minutes. Remove the muslin or cheesecloth bag.

5. FUNNEL THE JAM into the hot sterilized jars, leaving about a 1/4-inch headspace. Remove any air bubbles with a sterilized plastic spatula, then cap the jars according to the manufacturer's directions. Process the jars for 10 minutes in a boiling-water bath. Let the jars cool and test for a seal. Store in a cool, dark place; refrigerate after opening.

CAMPFIRE SKILLET SCONES

My first experience with campfire cooking was during Girl Scout weekends at Camp Butterworth in Loveland, Ohio. Along with the revelations of how cold it actually gets when you sleep outside in a tent, how wonderful it is to sit around a campfire under the night sky, and the wisdom of signing up for the first shift of latrine duty, I gained a new appreciation for wood-fired cooking. These scones, adapted from a griddle-baked scone recipe from Irish immigrants to the Midwest, are perfect for campfire cooking. If you're camping, simply combine all the dry ingredients in a zippered plastic bag, then mix up the recipe right before you bake it. The key is a well-seasoned large cast-iron skillet.

MAKES 8 SCONES

2 cups all-purpose flour
2 tablespoons sugar
2 1/2 teaspoons baking powder
1 teaspoon salt
2 teaspoons cream of tartar
3 tablespoons instant nonfat dry milk
6 tablespoons (3/4 stick) unsalted butter, cut into small pieces
3/4 cup water
1 large egg, beaten

1. PREPARE A MEDIUM-HOT CAMPFIRE or grill fire. Grease a well-seasoned 12-inch cast-iron skillet and set aside. In a medium bowl, combine the dry ingredients. With your fingertips, work in the butter until the mixture resembles coarse crumbs. Stir in the water and egg until a dough forms.

2. TURN THE DOUGH OUT onto a floured surface. Flour your hands and pat or press the dough into an 8-inch round, about ¹/2 inch thick. Cut the round into 8 wedges and arrange the wedges about ¹/2 inch apart in the skillet.

3. PLACE THE PAN over the campfire or grill fire and cook for 10 to 15 minutes, or until the scones have risen and are browned on top. Serve hot.

blender or two knives until the mixture resembles coarse meal. With a fork, quickly blend in the sour cream.

2. DROP THE DOUGH by rounded tablespoonfuls about 2 inches apart onto the prepared baking sheet. Bake for 20 minutes, or until the biscuits are firm to the touch and lightly browned. Serve hot.

············ 〰 ············

SOUR CREAM DROP BISCUITS

〰

A favorite in Fort Scott, Kansas, these are among the simplest of all biscuits, made with only three ingredients and dropped by the tablespoonful onto a baking sheet. My favorite way of enjoying this dough is as a topping for savory Biscuit-Topped Duck, Turnip, and Pear Pie (page 165).

MAKES ABOUT 1 DOZEN BISCUITS

1 cup self-rising flour
8 tablespoons (1 stick) unsalted butter,
  softened
¹/2 cup sour cream

1. PREHEAT THE OVEN to 350 degrees. Grease a baking sheet and set aside. Put the flour in a medium bowl and cut in the butter with a pastry

BISCUIT-TOPPED DUCK, TURNIP, AND PEAR PIE

꧁꧂

One clear, mild day in early November, I took the long way from Columbus to Wooster, Ohio, traveling through Coshocton and up into Amish country around Kidron. I was in no particular hurry, and when I found myself driving behind a horse-drawn black buggy, it gave me a chance to enjoy the rolling farmland. Cornstalks were gathered into shocks standing in the field, a common farm practice a century ago. Weathered signs advertised farm-raised ducks, chickens, and eggs. And farm stands offered gigantic dark green cabbages, lavender and cream-colored turnips, and pearly white cauliflower fresh from the fields. When I got home, I decided to capture my visual experience in this savory deep-dish pie celebrating the Ohio Amish heritage and the bounty of fall.

SERVES 4 TO 6

3 medium turnips, peeled and diced
1/4 cup wildflower, clover, or other pale
    amber honey
1 large ripe pear, peeled, cored, and
    chopped
2 tablespoons unsalted butter or canola oil
1 leek, white part only, rinsed, and thinly
    sliced
2 cups shredded cooked duck or dark
    chicken meat
1/2 teaspoon white pepper
1/2 cup chicken or duck stock or canned
    low-sodium chicken broth
1 recipe Sour Cream Drop Biscuits dough
    (page 164)

1. PREHEAT THE OVEN to 350 degrees. Spread the turnips in a 1-quart casserole and drizzle with the honey. Cover and bake for 5 minutes. Add the pear and bake for 15 minutes more, or until the turnips and pear are tender.

2. MEANWHILE, melt the butter or heat the oil in a small skillet. Add the leek and sauté over medium-high heat until translucent, about 5 minutes. Remove from the heat and set aside.

3. STIR THE LEEK, duck, white pepper, and stock into the turnip mixture. Drop the biscuit dough by the tablespoonful over the top. Bake for 20 minutes longer, or until the filling is bubbling and the biscuit topping is firm. Serve hot.

PORCH SUPPER CHEDDAR BISCUITS

꧁꧂

When you get home from work and just want to relax, yet still would like to eat something good and homemade for dinner, put these biscuits on your menu. With a pot of herbed chicken soup in the spring, a spoonful or two of Garden Tomato Chutney (page 166) in the summer, or a bowl of hearty chili when the weather turns brisk, these golden biscuits can be taken to a table on the porch in a napkin-lined basket. Feel the fresh breeze, put your feet on the furniture if you feel like it, and ignore the news on television. Any leftovers can be frozen, then wrapped in foil to reheat in the oven, even months later. Try a biscuit split in half and topped with good smoked turkey and a dollop of Prairie Pantry Winter Fruit Conserve (page 148).

(page 148)

MAKES ABOUT 1 1/2 DOZEN BISCUITS

4 ounces aged Cheddar cheese, preferably
    from Wisconsin, grated
8 tablespoons (1 stick) unsalted butter,
    softened
1/2 teaspoon salt
1/2 teaspoon paprika
1/2 teaspoon cayenne pepper
4 cups unsifted self-rising flour
1 cup buttermilk
1 cup heavy cream

1. PREHEAT THE OVEN to 375 degrees. Line a baking sheet with parchment paper and set aside. In a large bowl, using a hand-held electric mixer, beat the Cheddar, butter, salt, paprika, and ground red pepper together until smooth and fluffy. On low speed, beat in the flour, 1/4 cup at a time, alternating with the buttermilk and heavy cream, until a somewhat crumbly dough forms.

2. TURN THE DOUGH OUT onto a floured surface and roll it out to a 1-inch thickness. With a 2-inch biscuit cutter, cut out biscuits and place them about 1 inch apart on the prepared baking sheet.

3. BAKE FOR 20 MINUTES or until the tops are golden brown. Serve hot or warm.

GARDEN TOMATO CHUTNEY

The pleasures of the Heartland porch supper are coming back into vogue as new home communities begin to feature this neighborly, friendly architectural feature once again. In summer, there's nothing better than to eat this cold sweet/sour chutney with hot Porch Supper Cheddar Biscuits (page 165) and sliced good smoked turkey or ham, all washed down with freshly brewed iced tea, out on the porch. Make up a batch of this chutney and have it ready in the refrigerator for the perfect appetite pick-me-up when the hot weather makes you wilt.

(page 165)

MAKES ABOUT 6 HALF-PINTS

2 cups cherry tomatoes
2 cups yellow pear tomatoes
1 cup golden raisins
1 red bell pepper, cored, seeded, and diced
1 green bell pepper, cored, seeded, and
    diced
1 cup cooked fresh corn kernels
1 cup sugar
1 cup white vinegar
6 garlic cloves, minced
1 (2-inch) piece fresh ginger, peeled and
    shredded
4 jalapeño peppers, seeded and diced
2 sprigs fresh thyme
1 teaspoon celery seeds
1 teaspoon mustard seeds
1 teaspoon black peppercorns
1 teaspoon allspice berries
1 cinnamon stick

1. PLACE THE TOMATOES, raisins, bell peppers, and corn in a bowl and toss together; set aside.

2. IN A LARGE POT, combine the sugar, vinegar, garlic, ginger, jalapeños, thyme, and spices and bring to a boil over high heat. Boil until the liquid has reduced by half and is syrupy, about 7 minutes. Remove from the heat, cover, and let steep for 10 minutes.

3. BRING THE SYRUP TO THE BOIL AGAIN, then strain it through a sieve into the bowl of tomatoes; discard the spices and seasonings. Gently stir the chutney, mixing well. Cover and refrigerate until ready to serve. The chutney will become juicier over time; it keeps for up to 1 week.

GREAT PLAINS SOURDOUGH CHIVE BISCUITS

In *By the Shores of Silver Lake*, which takes place in the Dakota Territory, Laura Ingalls Wilder describes how her mother made the sourdough starter that produced light and flaky biscuits by putting some flour and warm water in a jar and letting it stand until it soured. The yeasts naturally occurring in the air would help the process along. From this, she would make a sponge for bread, biscuits, and pancakes. From time to time, when she wanted to vary the flavor of the sourdough biscuits, Ma would likely have turned to what was available near the homestead—native plants like wild onions

(*Allium canadense*), which come up in late winter and continue on through the fall. Many Native American tribes also valued the wild onion for eating raw and cooking. Today, we can turn to chives grown in a pot on a sunny windowsill or in the garden, or picked up at the grocery store.

MAKES ABOUT 1 DOZEN BISCUITS

1 cup Great Plains Sourdough Starter (page 51) or other sourdough starter
1 cup unbleached all-purpose flour
2 teaspoons baking powder
1/4 teaspoon baking soda
1/4 teaspoon salt
5 1/3 tablespoons (1/3 cup) unsalted butter, melted
1/4 cup snipped fresh chives

1. GREASE A BAKING SHEET and set aside. In a medium bowl, combine all the ingredients and mix together with a wooden spoon until a dough forms. Turn the dough out onto a floured surface and knead until smooth, about 2 minutes.

2. ROLL THE DOUGH OUT to a thickness of 1/2 inch. With a 2-inch biscuit cutter, cut out biscuits and place 1 inch apart on the prepared baking sheet. Cover with a tea towel and let rise in a warm place for 30 minutes.

3. PREHEAT THE OVEN to 400 degrees. Bake the biscuits for 12 to 15 minutes, or until they have browned and risen. Serve warm.

Biscuit-Topped Pheasant, Morel, and Corn Potpies

Birds, dogs, autumn on the Great Plains, and home cooking—that's what lures city folks to ranches in Iowa, the Dakotas, Nebraska, and Kansas for long weekends of pheasant hunting. In many areas, pheasant season begins in mid-November, when deep blue prairie skies are clear, and the corn and wheat harvests are in, leaving plenty of cover for the game birds. Vans of hunters arrive at these ranches for the experience that once was part of grandpa's farm life. After a day out in the crisp air, hunters work up an appetite. Often the menu includes a homemade pheasant potpie. Whether you use wild pheasant (usually skinned), or farm-raised pheasant from the market (usually plucked, with the skin intact), this recipe will make the most of the game bird. You can roast the pheasant a day ahead, if it's more convenient, and the potpies can be assembled in advance and refrigerated, then baked right before serving. (Any extra potpies can be frozen unbaked, then baked, without thawing, at 375 degrees for about 30 minutes.) You will need four to six 8-ounce individual ovenproof casseroles or twelve 4-ounce ramekins for the potpies.

MAKES 4 TO 6 MAIN-DISH OR
12 LUNCHEON OR APPETIZER POTPIES

1 (3- to 4-pound) pheasant
Salt and freshly ground black pepper
1 tablespoon unsalted butter, softened

4 slices bacon
3 cups chicken stock or canned low-sodium broth
2 leeks, white part only, rinsed, and finely chopped
2 garlic cloves, minced
3 tablespoons canola or corn oil
2 tablespoons all-purpose flour
1 cup chopped carrots or whole baby carrots
2 tablespoons (about 1 ounce) dried morels or other wild mushrooms, rinsed
2 sprigs fresh thyme or 1 teaspoon dried thyme
1 cup frozen shoepeg corn
1 cup frozen baby peas
1 recipe Great Plains Sourdough Chive Biscuits dough (page 167)
1 large egg, beaten, for egg glaze

1. EARLY IN THE DAY (or the day before), roast the pheasant: Preheat the oven to 375 degrees. Season the pheasant with salt and pepper and rub the butter all over the skin. Place the bird breast side up in a roasting pan and drape the bacon over the breast. Roast for 45 to 60 minutes, or until the pheasant has browned all over.

2. ADD 2 CUPS of the chicken stock to the roasting pan, cover, and continue roasting for another 30 minutes, or until the juices run clear when the thigh is pierced at its thickest part. Remove from the oven and let cool slightly.

3. WHEN THE PHEASANT is cool enough to handle, remove it from the roasting pan and set the pan aside, reserving the cooking juices. Remove the meat from the bones, discarding the skin, and set aside in a bowl. Place the pheasant carcass back in the roasting pan, add the remaining 1 cup chicken stock, and bring to a boil over medium-high heat. Boil the stock for 7 to 10 minutes, or until it has thickened and deepened in color. Remove from the heat and set aside.

4. IN A LARGE SKILLET, sauté the leeks and garlic in the oil over medium heat until soft and lightly browned, about 5 minutes. Whisk in the flour and cook for 3 to 4 minutes, whisking constantly, until the sauce is smooth and slightly browned. Whisk in the reserved pheasant stock. Add the carrots, morels, and thyme and simmer for about 15 minutes, stirring occasionally, until the sauce has thickened and the morels have softened. Taste for seasoning, then stir in the reserved pheasant meat, the corn, and peas. Remove from the heat.

5. INVERT AN 8-OUNCE ovenproof casserole or a 4-ounce ramekin, depending on which you are using, on a piece of parchment paper and trace its opening. Cut out this circular template and set aside. Spoon the pheasant mixture into four to six 8-ounce ovenproof casseroles or twelve 4-ounce ovenproof ramekins and set aside.

6. PREHEAT THE OVEN to 400 degrees. On a floured surface, roll out the biscuit dough. Using the circular template and a paring knife, cut out a dough lid for each potpie and place on top of the filling. With the paring knife, cut steam vents in each lid, and brush with the egg glaze. If you wish, using small cookie or canapé cutters, cut out decorations from the dough scraps, brush with egg glaze, and apply to the potpie lids.

7. BAKE FOR 10 TO 15 MINUTES, or until the pastry has browned and the filling is heated through. Serve hot.

NORTH WOODS CABIN ROLLS

On the northern prairies, grassland gives way to woodland, and the hunting changes from game birds like pheasant and quail to deer and elk. Cold northern lakes teem with walleye pike and muskie. For hunters or fishermen bunked into a cabin, this simple recipe produces a high-rising, moist, light, and tender roll with surprisingly good flavor. This would also be a good recipe for getting kids involved in preparing dinner or to make yourself to accompany a slow-cooker entrée on a weekday evening.

MAKES 6 ROLLS

1 cup self-rising flour
³/4 cup milk
3 tablespoons mayonnaise

1. PREHEAT THE OVEN to 350 degrees. Grease 6 muffin cups and set aside. In a medium bowl, whisk all ingredients together. Spoon the dough into the muffin cups, filling them two-thirds full.

2. BAKE THE ROLLS for 20 to 25 minutes, or until risen and lightly browned. Serve warm.

SPOON ROLLS

Spongy-textured spoon rolls, which get a double lift from yeast and self-rising flour, helped busy people in the 1930s and '40s put dinner on the table. Today, they're still a welcome accompaniment to a last-minute soup or a slow-cooker stew. This dough can be covered and kept in the refrigerator for up to a week, ready to be baked at the last minute.

MAKES 2 DOZEN ROLLS

1 ($^{1}/4$-ounce) package ($2^{1}/4$ teaspoons)
    active dry yeast
2 cups warm (110 degrees) water
12 tablespoons ($1^{1}/2$ sticks) unsalted
    butter, melted
$^{1}/4$ cup sugar
1 large egg, beaten
4 cups self-rising flour

1. PREHEAT THE OVEN to 400 degrees. Grease two 12-cup muffin pans and set aside. In a large bowl, sprinkle the yeast over the warm water and set aside to proof until foamy, about 5 minutes. With a wooden spoon, stir in the butter, sugar, and egg until well blended. Beat in the flour, 1 cup at a time, until thoroughly blended.

2. SPOON THE BATTER into the prepared muffin cups, filling them about half-full. Bake for about 15 minutes, or until the rolls have risen and browned. Serve hot.

THYME BISCUITS

These delicate, savory biscuits are easy to make. Their secret ingredient is cake flour, a soft flour with a lower protein content than all-purpose or bread flour, milled from wheat grown on the eastern prairie. This makes a soft dough that will toughen if handled too much. I adapted this recipe from one created by Chef Richard Perry during his tenure at the Hotel Majestic in St. Louis, where he specialized in the more lavish food of riverboats and private homes of nineteenth-century Mississippi River country. Chef Perry likes to serve these alongside a hearty mushroom ragout with bacon and pearl onions.

MAKES ABOUT $1^{1}/2$ DOZEN BISCUITS

6 cups cake flour
2 tablespoons baking powder
$1^{1}/2$ teaspoons salt
3 tablespoons sugar
6 tablespoons chopped fresh thyme
$^{3}/4$ cup shortening, chilled
$2^{1}/4$ cups milk

1. PREHEAT THE OVEN to 350 degrees. Grease a baking sheet and set aside. In the bowl of an electric mixer, using the whip attachment, blend the flour, baking powder, salt, sugar, and thyme on low speed. Beat in the chilled shortening until the mixture resembles coarse crumbs. Switch to the paddle attachment and beat in the milk, $^{1}/4$ cup at a time, until a soft dough has formed.

2. TURN THE DOUGH OUT onto a floured surface and roll out to a 1-inch thickness. With a

2-inch biscuit cutter, cut out biscuits and place 1 inch apart on the prepared baking sheet.

3. BAKE FOR 15 TO 18 MINUTES, or until the biscuits are golden brown. Serve hot.

HOOSIER HAM AND CHEESE BISCUITS

A basic biscuit dough can be transformed with just three ingredients: smoked ham or prosciutto, grated Cheddar or Asiago, and dry mustard. I like to make these biscuits, adapted from a recipe from St. Joseph County, Indiana, in chilly weather, cut them into stick or leaf shapes, and serve them warm in a basket to accompany a homemade soup or chili.

MAKES ABOUT 2 DOZEN BISCUITS

*³/4 cup finely chopped smoked ham or
    prosciutto*
*³/4 cup finely grated Cheddar or Asiago
    cheese*
2 cups self-rising flour
1 teaspoon dry mustard
²/3 cup milk
*8 tablespoons (1 stick) unsalted butter,
    melted*

1. PREHEAT THE OVEN to 450 degrees. In a large bowl, with a wooden spoon, stir together the ham, cheese, flour, mustard, and milk until you have a soft dough.

2. POUR HALF OF THE MELTED BUTTER into the bottom of a 13-by-9-inch baking pan; set aside. Turn the dough out onto a floured surface and roll out or pat into a 10-by-6-inch rectangle. Using a serrated knife or a pizza wheel, cut the rectangle of dough lengthwise in half, then cut crosswise into 3-by-³/4-inch strips (or use canapé or cookie cutters to cut out the shapes of your choice).

3. PLACE THE STRIPS (or shapes) into the prepared pan. Drizzle the dough with the remaining melted butter.

4. BAKE FOR 15 MINUTES, or until the biscuits have risen and browned. Serve hot.

PLAINS INDIAN FRY BREAD

During the summer, powwows are held throughout the Heartland, celebrating the dances and foodways of Native American tribes ranging from the Osage, Omaha, and Kiowa to the Sioux and Comanche. Fry bread is usually on the menu, whether cooked and sold by vendors or cooked by locals in the communal kitchen and dining hall. Fry bread is a relatively recent addition to the Native American diet. When the Dakota tribes encountered explorers Pierre Radisson and Medard Chouart in the late 1600s, they gave the men gifts of the grains they grew and gathered—corn and wild rice—meant to be boiled and eaten as gruel, not for bread. But eventually a new word for bread crept into the Dakota language—*aguyap*,

GOOD FRY BREAD
IN THE BADLANDS

············· ❦ ·············

With the scoured and lunar-looking landscape of the Badlands and the desperate poverty in and around the Pine Ridge Reservation, the prospect of good home cooking seems very far away. But that's not so. In the tiny town of Interior, South Dakota, Ansel Woodenknife and his wife, Teresa, have championed the cause of the Lakota Sioux culinary heritage in a dish Ansel learned from his mother.

Before the Europeans came and displaced the Sioux from their hunting grounds, the Sioux did not make bread. When the buffalo were gone from the prairies and the starving Sioux were confined to reservations, they were given "commodities" by the government—flour, salt, baking powder, and lard. From these they fashioned quick breads like bannock and fry bread, because they had very little else to eat.

The ingenious Woodenknife family, however, made the bread Sioux by adding prairie turnip, which Lewis and Clark called the "white apple" and French voyageurs called *pomme blanche*. Today, Ansel still collects, buys, and barters for the prairie turnip from foragers who know just where to look.

Growing up on the Rosebud Reservation in southwestern South Dakota, Woodenknife and his twelve brothers and sisters never tasted store-bought bread. Their late mother, Mary Woodenknife, always made homemade bread, including the powwow circuit staple, Indian fry bread. Her secret ingredient: a pinch of *tinpsila*, the sacred prairie turnip, which was dried and ground. Growing up, Ansel and his siblings would have fry bread with stew or *wojapi*, a fruit pudding. In 1979, Ansel's mother-in-law, La Vonne Green, built the tiny Woodenknife Drive-In to serve burgers and fries to Badlands tourists. Mary Woodenknife's fry bread, however, became the favorite menu item. When Mary made up the dough, she'd stretch it thin, so when it fried, the inside would be fluffy and the outside crispy.

Today, if you visit the Woodenknife Drive-In, you can order an Indian taco, a piece of fry bread topped with taco-seasoned meat, shredded lettuce, chopped tomato and onion, shredded cheese, and a dollop of sour cream. It's a knife-and-fork job, and there won't be room for a milkshake afterward.

If you ask for the recipe, you'll be referred to a bag containing all the "secret" ingredients for great fry bread, courtesy of Ansel and Teresa's Woodenknife Company.

············· ❦ ·············

or "they burn it"—after the flatbreads that were baked by soldiers or voyageurs at camp sites. During the late nineteenth century, when native Americans were confined to reservations, they were given staple foods like flour, baking powder, powdered milk, and lard. At first they made a bannock-like bread that was quickly mixed, then baked in the oven. Later, they rolled the dough out, cut it into squares or shaped it into circles, and fried it.

This recipe is adapted from one by Marion Ironstar in *Our Daily Bread*, a community cookbook from Enemy Swim Lake, Waubay, South Dakota. Serve the fry breads as the basis for savory "Indian tacos," topped with seasoned taco meat, shredded lettuce, and chopped tomato, or drizzle with a wild berry syrup for dessert.

MAKES ABOUT 2 DOZEN FRY BREADS

2 cups all-purpose flour
2 teaspoons baking powder
1/4 cup sugar
1/2 cup instant nonfat dry milk
1/4 teaspoon salt
1 cup water
Vegetable oil, for deep-frying

1. IN A LARGE BOWL, mix the flour, baking powder, sugar, dry milk, and salt together. Stir in the water until you have a sticky dough.

2. TURN THE DOUGH OUT onto a floured surface and sprinkle with flour. Roll out to a 16-by-12-inch rectangle, about 1/2 inch thick. Cut the dough into twenty-four 2-inch squares. Cut a 1/2-inch slit in the middle of each square.

3. ADD ENOUGH OIL to a deep cast-iron skillet or a deep-fat fryer to reach a depth of 1 to 2

inches and heat it to 350 to 365 degrees. (The oil is ready when a piece of dough sizzles as soon as it is placed in the pan.) In batches, fry the squares of dough, turning once, until browned on both sides, about 3 minutes total. Transfer to paper towels to drain. Serve warm, sprinkled with cinnamon sugar or drizzled with wild berry syrup, or topped with taco fixings.

HUNTER'S BISCUITS

This recipe, a cross between a very thin biscuit and a cracker, comes from the 1875 edition of *The Presbyterian Cook Book* from Dayton, Ohio. Its versatility, good keeping qualities, and delicious flavor still appeal. Baked for 10 minutes, the biscuits turn pale ivory and are soft enough to eat with butter and jam. Baked for 25 to 30 minutes, they are pale gold and cracker-like—especially delicious when topped before baking with your favorite dried herb or spice combination, garlic salt, or sesame or poppy seeds. Use your imagination—and your favorite cookie and canapé cutters—to create your own "house" snack crackers to serve to guests.

MAKES 3 DOZEN 3-BY-2-INCH CRACKERS

3 1/3 cups all-purpose flour

1 teaspoon cream of tartar

1/2 teaspoon salt

1/4 teaspoon baking soda

5 1/3 tablespoons (1/3 cup) unsalted butter, melted

2/3 cup milk, plus more for brushing

An herb or spice blend, garlic salt, poppy seeds, or toasted sesame seeds, optional

1. PREHEAT THE OVEN to 300 degrees. Grease a baking sheet or line it with parchment paper and set aside. Combine the flour, cream of tartar, salt, and baking soda in the bowl of a food processor and process until well mixed. With the processor running, pour in the melted butter and milk and process until a dough forms.

2. TURN THE DOUGH OUT onto a floured surface and divide it in half. Roll each half out to a 12-by-9-inch rectangle, about 1/4 inch thick. Prick the dough all over with the tines of a fork, brush with milk, and sprinkle with the topping of your choice, if desired. With a pizza wheel or cookie or canapé cutters, cut the dough into 3-by-2-inch strips or other shapes and place on the prepared baking sheet.

3. BAKE FOR 10 TO 25 MINUTES, according to the desired doneness (see the headnote above). Let cool, then store in an airtight container for up to a week.

CINNAMON-SPICED OAT CRACKERS

From the Amish country around northern Ohio, these are delicious for snacking or as a fun project for kids in the kitchen. They can be cut into rectangles or the shapes of your choice.

MAKES 3 DOZEN 3-BY-2-INCH CRACKERS

1/2 pound (2 sticks) unsalted butter, softened, or 1 cup shortening

1 cup packed light brown sugar

1 teaspoon ground cinnamon

2 large eggs, beaten

1 teaspoon baking soda

1 tablespoon milk

3 cups old-fashioned or quick rolled oats (not instant)

2 1/2 to 3 cups all-purpose flour

1. PREHEAT THE OVEN to 350 degrees. Grease a baking sheet and set aside. In a large bowl, combine the butter, brown sugar, and cinnamon and beat with a hand-held electric mixer until smooth and creamy. Beat in the eggs. Dissolve the baking soda in the milk, then beat into the butter mixture. Beat in the oats, then beat in the flour, 1 cup at a time, until you have a stiff dough.

2. TURN THE DOUGH OUT onto a floured surface and divide it in half. Roll each half out to a 12-by-9-inch rectangle, about 1/2 inch thick. Prick the dough all over with the tines of a fork. With a pizza wheel or cookie or canapé cutters, cut the dough into 3-by-2-inch strips or other

shapes and place about ¼ inch apart on the prepared baking sheet.

3. BAKE FOR 10 MINUTES, or until lightly
browned. Let cool, then store in an airtight container for up to a week.

ZELNIKY

Delicious served with soup or salad, these
unusual sauerkraut crackers are easy to
make and surprisingly tasty. During the Czech
Days Festival in Tabor, South Dakota, zelniky
are consumed in prodigious quantities. Serve
these as cocktail nibbles or to accompany a
good microbrewed beer, spread with hearty
mustard and topped with slices of cooked
Polish or kielbasa sausage. These keep well.

MAKES ABOUT 3 DOZEN CRACKERS

3 cups all-purpose flour
1 teaspoon white pepper
¾ cup shortening
2 cups sauerkraut, drained

1. PREHEAT THE OVEN to 425 degrees. Grease
two baking sheets and set aside. Combine the
flour and white pepper in a food processor, add
the shortening, and pulse until the mixture resembles coarse crumbs. Add the sauerkraut and
pulse until the dough starts to form a ball.

2. TRANSFER THE DOUGH to a floured surface.
Pinch off tablespoon-sized pieces of dough, roll
each piece into a ball, and place about 2 inches
apart on the prepared baking sheets. Flatten the
balls with the bottom of a drinking glass to
about a ¼-inch thickness.

3. BAKE FOR 10 MINUTES, then reduce the oven
temperature to 350 degrees and bake for 10 to
15 minutes more, or until the crackers are
golden brown and crisp. Let cool, then store in
an airtight container.

CRABAPPLE JELLY

Driving across southern Indiana and Illinois,
it's not unusual to see country lanes lined
with hardy crabapple trees, which serve both
as windbreaks across the fields and as a source
of delicious fruit for jellies and preserves.
They're also beautiful frothed into pink blossom in spring and aflame with fruit dappled
with purple, yellow, salmon, and ruby red in
late summer. Popular varieties still include
the Whitney, an heirloom variety from 1869
Illinois, and the Western. As all crabapples
have differing degrees of tartness, you will need
to taste yours first. Add more lemon juice to
the jelly if necessary. If you have a jelly bag,
get that set up before you start. You can also
improvise one with a fine (not terry cloth) tea
towel clamped over a bowl or with a colander
or strainer lined with a double layer of
cheesecloth.

MAKES 3 TO 4 HALF-PINT JARS

2 pounds crabapples, stemmed and cut in
  half
3 to 4 cups sugar
Juice of 1 lemon, or more to taste

1. PLACE THE CRABAPPLES in a large saucepan, add enough water to barely cover, and bring to a boil over medium heat. Cook for 15 to 20 minutes, or until the skins have cracked and the fruit is soft. Remove from the heat and carefully ladle the juice into a jelly bag set over a bowl (or a tea towel clamped over a bowl, or a colander or sieve lined with a double thickness of cheese-cloth and set over a bowl). Let the juice slowly drain into the bowl. Discard the fruit.

2. MEASURE THE JUICE and pour it into a heavy saucepan. For each cup of juice, add 1 cup sugar. Bring the juice to a boil, stirring to dissolve the sugar. Stir in the lemon juice; taste, and add more if needed. Boil for 10 minutes, or until the mixture coats the back of a spoon and reaches 220 degrees on a candy thermometer.

3. FUNNEL THE JELLY into clean jars and let cool. Seal the jars and store in the refrigerator. The jelly keeps almost indefinitely.

SAVORY WHEAT AND SUNFLOWER CRACKERS

By the time the winter wheat has been harvested, from mid-June in the southern Great Plains and through July in the Prairie Provinces of Canada, the sunflowers are already several feet high. By August, their large heads turn to follow the position of the sun, and soon they are drooping with the heaviness of their seeds. Farmwives had to shell and roast them before using them in recipes like this one, but now they're as convenient as the nearest grocery store salad bar. Vary the flavor of these hearty snack crackers by substituting poppy seeds, dried onions and herbs, or sesame seeds for the sunflower seeds.

MAKES 8 DOZEN CRACKERS

3/4 cup all-purpose flour
1/4 cup graham or whole wheat flour
4 tablespoons (1/2 stick) unsalted butter or
*   margarine, chilled and cut into pieces*
1 teaspoon honey
1/4 teaspoon salt
1 cup small-curd cottage cheese
1/4 cup salted roasted sunflower seed
*   kernels*

1. PREHEAT THE OVEN to 325 degrees. Put both flours into a food processor, add the butter, and pulse until the mixture resembles fine crumbs. Add the honey, salt, and cottage cheese and process until you have a smooth dough.

2. TURN THE DOUGH OUT onto a floured surface and divide it in half. Roll out each half into a 16-by-12-inch rectangle and place on a large ungreased baking sheet. Prick the dough all over with a fork, then cut into 2-inch squares with a pizza wheel and gently separate the squares. Sprinkle with the sunflower seed kernels.

3. BAKE FOR 15 TO 20 MINUTES, or until the crackers are lightly browned. Let cool, then store in an airtight container for up to 2 weeks.

BOHEMIAN CARAWAY STICKS

Adapted from a recipe from the Sykora Bakery in Cedar Rapids, Iowa, these savory sticks would be just the thing served with a creamy dip, a homemade soup, or a frosty mug of microbrewed beer. Or just eat them by the handful!

MAKES 8 DOZEN STICKS

2 cups all-purpose flour, plus more if
     needed
1/2 pound (2 sticks) unsalted butter,
     softened
1 cup unseasoned mashed potatoes, at
     room temperature or slightly warm
1/2 teaspoon salt
1/2 teaspoon white pepper
1 large egg, beaten, for egg glaze
Coarse sea or kosher salt, for sprinkling
1/4 cup caraway seeds

1. IN THE BOWL of a food processor, combine the flour, butter, mashed potatoes, salt, and white pepper and process until a stiff dough forms, adding more flour if necessary. Turn the dough out onto a piece of plastic wrap. Press the dough into a rectangular shape, wrap in the plastic wrap, and refrigerate for 1 hour, or until firm.

2. PREHEAT THE OVEN to 400 degrees. Grease two baking sheets or line with parchment paper and set aside. Transfer the dough to a floured surface and roll out to a 16-by-12-inch rectangle, about 1/4 inch thick. Using a pizza wheel or a chef's knife, cut the pastry into 4-by-1/2-inch strips and place about 1/4 inch apart on the prepared baking sheets. Brush each strip with the egg glaze and sprinkle with coarse salt and the caraway seeds.

3. BAKE FOR 20 MINUTES, or until the sticks are golden brown. Cool on the pans, then store in airtight containers.

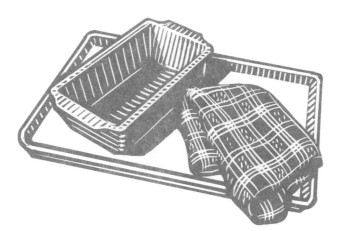

COFFEE CAKES AND PASTRIES

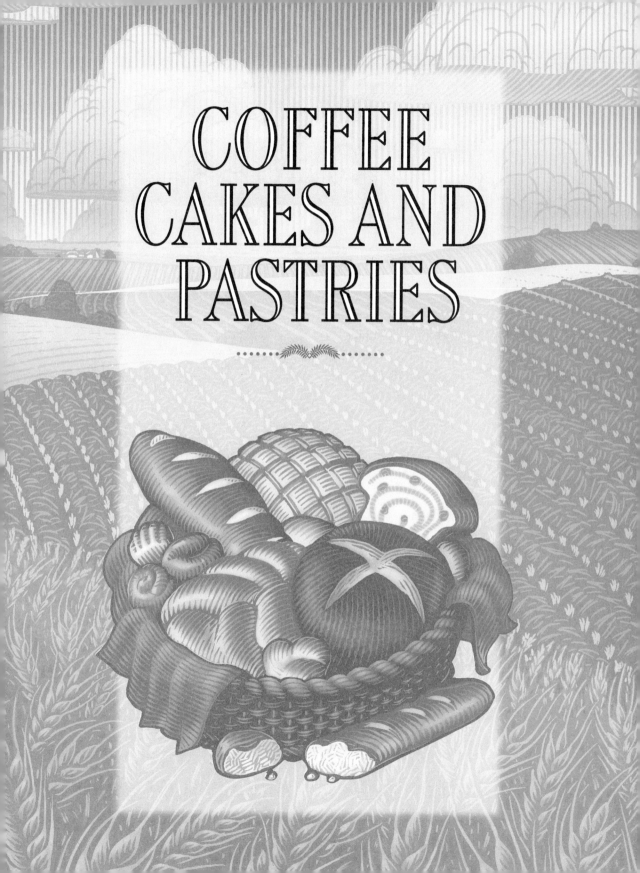

SUMMERY LEMON COFFEE CAKE WITH FRESH BERRIES

On a Saturday morning visit to our local farmers' market in July, I snatched up punnets of blackberries, blueberries, and raspberries, then got home and wondered what I was going to do with them all. Fortunately, I remembered a glorious coffee cake, topped with tiny berries and lightly dusted with confectioners' sugar, that I had seen on a pastry cart. Here is my version, moist from the sour cream in the batter and topped with a variety of fresh berries. Serve with whipped cream or crème fraîche for an indulgent summertime breakfast or brunch. Although the cake itself can be made a day or two in advance, covered and refrigerated, once you've arranged the fresh berries on the top, it's best eaten within several hours.

MAKES 1 COFFEE CAKE

1/2 pound (2 sticks) unsalted butter,
   softened
2 cups granulated sugar
2 large eggs, beaten
1 (8-ounce) container sour cream
2 cups sifted cake flour
1 1/4 teaspoons baking powder
1/4 teaspoon salt
Grated zest and juice of 1 lemon
1 teaspoon vanilla extract
2 cups mixed fresh berries, such as
   raspberries, blueberries, and
   blackberries
Confectioners' sugar, for garnish

1. PREHEAT THE OVEN to 350 degrees. Butter a 9-inch springform pan and set aside. In a large bowl, with a hand-held electric mixer on low speed, cream the butter and granulated sugar. Beat in the eggs and sour cream, then beat in the flour, baking powder, and salt. Beat in the lemon zest, lemon juice, and vanilla.

2. POUR THE BATTER into the prepared pan and bake for 50 to 60 minutes, or until a toothpick inserted in the center comes out clean. Let cool in the pan.

3. REMOVE THE SIDES OF THE PAN and invert the coffee cake onto a serving plate or cake stand lined with a paper doily. Arrange the berries on top of the cake and dust with confectioners' sugar.

HUCKLEBERRY BUCKLE

In late fall, when garden huckleberries ripen on their forty-acre farm near Belleville in southwestern Illinois, Elsie and Ralph Press pick enough to turn into pies, breads, jellies, desserts, and coffee cakes like this one. Garden huckleberries are fat purple fruits with a taste similar to blueberries; wild huckleberries are smaller and more tart. Although huckleberries used to grow all over the Midwest, farmers pulled them up as weeds, forcing aficionados like the Presses to plant them from seed every few years.

SERVES 8

2¹/4 cups unbleached all-purpose flour
2 teaspoons baking powder
¹/2 teaspoon salt
¹/2 teaspoon baking soda
12 tablespoons (1¹/2 sticks) unsalted
   butter, softened
³/4 cup granulated sugar
2 large eggs
1 teaspoon vanilla extract
1 (8-ounce) container sour cream

FOR THE STREUSEL TOPPING:
8 tablespoons (1 stick) unsalted butter
¹/4 cup all-purpose flour
1 teaspoon ground cinnamon
²/3 cup packed light brown sugar
²/3 cup chopped pecans or walnuts

2 cups fresh or thawed frozen huckleberries
   or blueberries

1. PREHEAT THE OVEN to 350 degrees. Butter a 13-by-9-inch baking pan and set aside. Sift the dry ingredients together into a medium bowl and set aside.

2. IN A MEDIUM BOWL, using a hand-held electric mixer, cream the butter and granulated sugar. Beat in the eggs one at a time, then beat in the vanilla. Add the dry ingredients, alternating with the sour cream, and blend well.

3. MAKE THE TOPPING: Combine all the ingredients in a small bowl and mix together with your fingers until clumps form. Pour half the batter into the prepared baking pan. Scatter the huckleberries or blueberries over the batter, then carefully spread the remaining batter on top of the fruit and sprinkle the topping over it.

4. BAKE FOR 45 MINUTES, or until a toothpick inserted in the center comes out clean. Serve warm or at room temperature, directly from the pan.

YEAST-AND-BUTTER DANISH PASTRY

Danish bakeries in the Racine, Wisconsin, area offer more than just great kringle (page 187). Their true yeast-and-butter Danish pastry is almost indescribably good—buttery, flaky, soft, and yeasty. Real Danish pastry tastes nothing like what you get in those cellophane packages at the airport. But even bakeries can take shortcuts with ingredients, so making your own ensures the highest quality. Because this is a time-consuming process, it's best to plan on making Danish pastry over a weekend. The fillings can be prepared before you make the dough. On the first day, mix and chill the dough, roll out the butter layer, fold the dough and butter layer together, and let the pastry rise. The next day, roll, cut, shape, and bake the dough. This makes a large batch; you can freeze the dough as well as some of the buttery treats.

Then you'll have the true luxury of sinfully good Danish pastry on hand to warm in the oven for a midwinter breakfast.

MAKES 3¹/₂ POUNDS DOUGH;
ENOUGH FOR 4 TEA RINGS OR
ABOUT 4 DOZEN PASTRIES

¹/₂ cup plus 1 teaspoon sugar
2 (¹/₄-ounce) packages (1¹/₂ tablespoons) active dry yeast
¹/₂ cup warm (110 degrees) water
1 cup milk
2 large eggs, beaten
5¹/₄ cups all-purpose flour, plus more for dusting and rolling
1³/₄ teaspoons salt
³/₄ pound (3 sticks) unsalted butter, chilled
Danish Almond Filling (page 185), Cream Cheese Filling (page 186), and/or good-quality fruit preserves of your choice
1 large egg, beaten with 1 tablespoon water, for egg glaze
White Icing (page 186)

1. MIX THE DOUGH: In the bowl of an electric mixer, sprinkle 1 teaspoon of the sugar and the yeast over the warm water and set aside to proof until foamy, about 5 minutes. Add the remaining ¹/₂ cup sugar, the milk, and eggs to the yeast mixture. Using the paddle attachment or a spoon, gradually beat in 4 cups of the flour, ¹/₂ cup at a time, add the salt, and then beat the dough for about 3 minutes. Gradually beat in the remaining 1¹/₄ cups flour.

2. KNEAD THE DOUGH: Switch to the dough hook, turn the mixer to medium-high, and knead the dough for 5 minutes. Or turn the dough out onto a floured surface and knead by hand. Place the dough in an oiled bowl and turn to coat. Cover with plastic wrap and refrigerate for 30 minutes.

3. MAKE THE BUTTER LAYER: Place the sticks of butter a few inches apart on a piece of waxed or parchment paper. On a second piece of waxed or parchment paper, draw a 12-by-10-inch rectangle with a pencil. Lay the second piece of paper (penciled side up) on top of the butter. Press hard with a rolling pin and then roll back and forth to flatten the butter into the rectangle outlined on the top sheet of paper. Remove the top sheet and cut the butter rectangle in half, all the way through the paper, to form two 10-by-6-inch rectangles. Replace the top sheet and refrigerate the butter.

4. ROLL OUT THE DOUGH: Punch down the dough and turn it out onto a floured surface. Roll it into a 18-by-12-inch rectangle. Turn the dough if necessary so one of the short sides is facing you. Peel off the top sheet of paper from one of the butter rectangles and place it on the lower third of the dough, leaving a 1¹/₂-inch border along the right and left sides; peel off the remaining paper and fold the bottom third of the dough, with the butter, over (like the first fold of a business letter); make sure the edges of the butter layer and the dough are evenly aligned. Peel the top sheet of paper off the second butter rectangle and place it on top of the dough-and-butter layer. Peel off the remaining paper and fold the top third of the dough over to enclose the butter layer. You should have a 12-by-6-inch rectangle of folded dough and butter.

5. ROLL AND "TURN" THE DOUGH: Position the dough so that the fold is to your left and the dough can be opened like a book. Roll the dough into a 24-by-12-inch rectangle, dusting

CUTTING AND FILLING DANISH PASTRIES

Yeast-and-Butter Danish Pastry dough can be cut and filled in many different ways. Many shapes are traditional, based on centuries-old patterns brought to the prairie by Scandinavian home bakers. Here are four basic shapes from which to choose—or make all four!

To shape and bake the pastries, preheat the oven to 400 degrees. Grease four baking sheets or line with parchment paper. Remove the chilled dough from the refrigerator and cut it into quarters. Work with one quarter at a time, keeping the remaining dough in the refrigerator. Have the filling(s) and the icing prepared. In a small bowl, beat 1 large egg with 2 tablespoons water for an egg glaze; set aside.

TEA RING On a floured surface, roll one-quarter of the dough into a 16-by-10-inch rectangle. Spread the dough evenly with $1/3$ cup of the filling of your choice, leaving a 1-inch margin all around. Starting at a long side, roll up the dough jelly-roll fashion, using both hands to gently coax it into shape. Place the roll of dough on a prepared baking sheet and connect the ends to form a ring, pinching the ends to seal. With kitchen shears, cut 12 diagonal slashes three-quarters of the way into the dough, about $1^1/4$ inches apart, around the outside of the ring. Turn each slice of dough on its side to show the filling. Cover with a tea towel and let rise in a warm place for 30 minutes.

Preheat the oven to 400 degrees. If desired, with a floured thumb, press an indentation into each spiral, and place a candied cherry or teaspoon of jam in each indentation. Brush the dough with the egg glaze and bake for 20 to 25 minutes, or until risen and browned. Transfer to a wire rack set over a baking sheet and let cool for 5 minutes, then drizzle with the icing.

CRESCENTS On a floured surface, roll one-quarter of the dough into a 15-by-6-inch rectangle. Starting at a narrow end of the dough, make a diagonal cut to form a long triangle with a 3-inch base, then make a crosswise cut to form another triangle, and then another diagonal cut;

it with flour when necessary. Fold the dough in thirds again, like a business letter, to complete the first "turn." Cover and refrigerate for 15 minutes, then repeat the process twice to make two more turns. Cover the dough with plastic wrap and chill in the refrigerator for at least several hours, or overnight.

6. CUT AND FILL THE DOUGH: Preheat the oven to 400 degrees. Cut the dough into quarters and make a tea ring or pinwheels, crescents, bear claws, or other pastry shapes from each quarter (see sidebar). Brush with the egg glaze and bake as directed until browned. Drizzle the warm pastries with the icing.

repeat the process to form a total of 10 triangles. Mound 2 teaspoons of the filling of your choice or jam (a total of about ¹/2 cup) about 1 inch from each triangle's base. Starting at the base, roll up each triangle. Arrange the pastries about 2 inches apart on a prepared baking sheet, tucking the tip of each triangle under the pastry and shaping the pastry into a crescent. Cover with a tea towel and let rise in a warm place for 30 minutes.

Preheat the oven to 400 degrees. Brush the crescents with the egg glaze and bake for 20 to 25 minutes, or until risen and browned. Transfer to a wire rack set over a baking sheet and let cool for 5 minutes, then drizzle with the icing.

BEAR CLAWS On a floured surface, roll one-quarter of the dough into a 16-by-8-inch rectangle. Cut the dough into eight 4-inch squares. Spread 1 tablespoon of the filling of your choice or jam (a total of ¹/2 cup) in the middle of each square, leaving a ¹/2-inch margin all around. Brush one side of each dough square with egg glaze, fold the dough over, and press the edges together to seal. Make 3 cuts in the folded side, almost but not all the way through to the seam side. Arrange the bear claws about 2 inches apart on a prepared baking sheet, gently fanning out the "toes" slightly. Cover with a tea towel and let rise in a warm place for 30 minutes.

Preheat the oven to 400 degrees. Brush the bear claws with egg glaze and bake for 20 to 25 minutes, or until risen and browned. Transfer to a wire rack set over a baking sheet and let cool for 5 minutes, then drizzle with the icing.

PINWHEELS OR SNAILS On a floured surface, roll one-quarter of the dough into a 16-by-10-inch rectangle. Spread ¹/2 cup Cream Cheese Filling or jam or 1 cup Danish Almond Filling over the dough, leaving a 1-inch margin all around. Starting at a long end, roll up jelly-roll fashion, using your hands to gently coax the dough into a coil. Turn the roll seam side down and cut into sixteen 1-inch slices. Place the slices 2 inches apart on a prepared baking sheet. Cover with a tea towel and let rise in a warm place for 30 minutes.

Preheat the oven to 400 degrees. Brush the pastries with egg glaze and bake for 20 to 25 minutes, or until risen and browned. Transfer to a wire rack set over a baking sheet and let cool for 5 minutes, then drizzle with the icing.

NOTE: Cooled pastries can be placed in plastic freezer bags and frozen for up to 3 months. To reheat, bake the still-frozen pastries at 375 degrees for 10 to 15 minutes, or until warmed through.

DANISH ALMOND FILLING

Midwesterners of Scandinavian descent love a vanilla-scented almond filling. If you prefer a stronger almond flavoring, substitute almond extract for the vanilla. This filling tastes best if made several days ahead so the flavors have a chance to mature.

MAKES 1²/₃ CUPS

8 ounces (about 1¹/₂ cups) whole almonds
1 cup sugar
1 teaspoon vanilla extract
1 large egg white

1. PREHEAT THE OVEN to 300 degrees. Place the almonds in a large bowl, pour boiling water to cover over them, and let stand for about 3 minutes to loosen the skins; drain. Slip the almonds' skins off with your fingers or by rubbing them between two tea towels.

2. SPREAD THE ALMONDS in a single layer on a baking sheet and toast them in the oven for 10 to 15 minutes, just until golden; do not let brown, or they will be unusable for this recipe. Let cool.

3. TRANSFER THE COOLED ALMONDS to a food processor or blender and grind to a fine paste. Add the sugar and process until the mixture resembles coarse flour. Add the vanilla extract and egg white and process for 2 to 3 minutes, until a stiff paste forms. Wrap in plastic wrap and store in the refrigerator until ready to use. (The filling will keep for up to 1 week.)

CREAM CHEESE FILLING

Delicious in Danish pastries or German kuchen.

MAKES 1¹/₃ CUPS

1 (8-ounce) package cream cheese, softened
1 large egg yolk
¹/₄ cup sugar
1 teaspoon vanilla extract
2 tablespoons all-purpose flour

IN A FOOD PROCESSOR, combine all ingredients and process until smooth. Cover and refrigerate until ready to use. (The filling will keep for 2 days.)

WHITE ICING

Drizzle warm Danish pastries with this quick icing.

MAKES ABOUT 1 CUP

1¹/₂ cups confectioners' sugar
1 large egg white
1 teaspoon vanilla extract

PUT THE CONFECTIONERS' SUGAR in a medium bowl and whisk in the egg white and vanilla until smooth and glossy. Cover and set aside until ready to use; use the same day.

CRANBERRY KRINGLE

Danish settlers on the prairie brought their holiday tradition of *smorekringle*, a filled yeast-and-butter pastry formed in the shape of a large pretzel, symbolizing *hygge*, or "the good life." Old Midwestern cookbooks offer up versions of kringle with all kinds of fillings. *Good Things to Eat*, published in 1929, includes kringles filled with sugared prunes or sugared almonds. The 1941 *From Danish Kitchens*, published in Iowa City, features kringles with almond and walnut fillings. But today, the most renowned kringles come from Racine, Wisconsin, based on recipes brought to the shores of Lake Michigan by Danish immigrants in the 1880s. Over the years, the pretzel shape has evolved into an oval, the better to keep the filling from escaping from the dough.

Traditionally served at weddings, Easter, and Christmas, kringle also comforts the bereaved at Wilson's Funeral Home in Racine. Like stollen, Danish pastry, or povitica (see page 208), making kringle is a real labor of love, but the delectable results are worth it. Instead of the cranberry filling, you can use 1^1/$_2$ cups of Danish Almond Filling (page 185) or the filling for Prairie Stollen (page 188), Cheese Pocket Coffee Cake (page 198), or Croatian Walnut Bread (page 207).

MAKES 4 KRINGLES, EACH SERVING 8

FOR THE BUTTERSCOTCH FILLING:
1 cup packed brown sugar
5^1/$_3$ tablespoons (^{1}/$_3$ cup) unsalted butter, softened
^{1}/$_4$ teaspoon salt
^{1}/$_4$ teaspoon ground cinnamon
1 small egg white

FOR THE CRANBERRY FILLING:
2 cups canned whole-berry cranberry sauce
2 tablespoons granulated sugar
2 teaspoons Instant ClearJel or cornstarch
1 tablespoon warm water

1 recipe Yeast-and-Butter Danish Pastry (page 182), prepared through Step 5
1 recipe White Icing (page 186)

1. MAKE THE BUTTERSCOTCH FILLING: Combine all ingredients in a small bowl, stirring until smooth.

2. MAKE THE CRANBERRY FILLING: Place the cranberry sauce in a small saucepan over medium heat. In a small cup, mix the granulated sugar and ClearJel or cornstarch together. Stir the warm water into the sugar mixture, then stir the sugar mixture into the cranberry sauce. Heat, stirring, until the sugar dissolves and the sauce thickens. Remove from the heat and set aside to cool to lukewarm (90 degrees).

3. LINE TWO BAKING SHEETS with parchment paper or aluminum foil and set aside. Transfer the chilled dough to a floured surface and cut it into quarters. Work with one quarter at a time, keeping the rest covered and refrigerated. Roll each piece of dough out to a 20-by-6-inch rectangle. Spread one-quarter of the Butterscotch Filling down the middle third of the rectangle, leaving a 1^1/$_2$-inch margin all around. Spread one-quarter of the Cranberry Filling over the Butterscotch Filling. Fold the right side of the dough over to the center of the filling. Brush the edge of the dough with a little water. Fold the left side of the dough over so that it overlaps the folded dough. Press the seam down with your fingers to seal the dough. Place seam side down on one of the prepared baking sheets and form the rectangle into an oval, pinching the ends of the dough together. Repeat with the remaining dough quarters. Cover the kringles with plastic wrap and let rise in a warm place until doubled in bulk, about 1 hour.

4. PREHEAT THE OVEN to 350 degrees. Bake the kringles for 20 to 35 minutes, or until puffed and golden. Cool for 5 minutes on the baking sheet, then transfer to a rack (set over a baking sheet if you are using the icing) and drizzle with the White Icing.

PRAIRIE STOLLEN

At Christmastime, German-style bakeries throughout the Midwest work nonstop to serve the onslaught of holiday customers wanting special ethnic breads and baked goods such as stollen. Traditional stollen features dried fruits like citron and currants and nuts like almonds encased in a rich bread dough. The stollen from the New Glarus Bakery in New Glarus, Wisconsin, adds another level of flavor with nuggets of marzipan enriching the dough. The holiday stollen from Zingerman's Bakehouse in Ann Arbor, Michigan, is flavored with white rum, glacéed and dried fruits, lemon and orange zest, almonds, and vanilla. But in early frontier communities, expensive dried fruits and almonds were not available. Home cooks had to substitute foods they had on hand, such as spices, native pecans or hickory nuts, and home-dried fruits.

In this version of traditional stollen, dried sour cherries and/or cranberries take the place of the more exotic dried currants from warmer climes, and the filling is made with pecans. Make the filling a day ahead to allow the flavors to mellow. This will keep, wrapped well and in a cool place, all throughout the holidays—if you and your family can resist it. It can also be frozen for up to three months and then reheated, so you can bake one for now, one for later. A slice of stollen dunked in a steaming cup of homemade hot chocolate will dispel any post-holiday blues when the credit card bills arrive.

MAKES 2 LARGE STOLLEN

FOR THE FILLING:

8 ounces (about 2 cups) pecans
3/4 cup granulated sugar
1/4 cup corn syrup
2 teaspoons vanilla extract
1 large egg white

1/4 cup French Valley Spiced Pear Cordial
    (from Prairie Home Cooking, page
    112), rum, or brandy
2 cups dried sour cherries or cranberries
2 cups golden raisins
1/4 cup warm (110 degrees) water
1/3 cup plus 2 tablespoons granulated sugar
2 (1/4-ounce) packages (1 1/2 tablespoons)
    active dry yeast
1 cup milk
10 tablespoons (1 1/4 sticks) unsalted butter
Grated zest and juice of 1 lemon
2 large eggs, beaten
4 1/2 cups bread flour, sifted, plus 2 to 3
    teaspoons (unsifted) flour
1 tablespoon ground cinnamon
1 teaspoon freshly grated nutmeg

FOR THE ICING:

3 tablespoons unsalted butter, melted
1 teaspoon vanilla extract
1/2 cup confectioners' sugar

1. MAKE THE FILLING: Preheat the oven to 300 degrees. Spread the pecans in a single layer on a baking sheet and bake for 10 to 15 minutes, until lightly toasted. Transfer the pecans to a blender or food processor, add the remaining filling ingredients, and blend for 2 minutes, or until the nuts are very finely chopped and the mixture holds together.

2. DIVIDE THE FILLING IN HALF and place on two pieces of waxed paper. With your hands, form each portion into an 8-inch-long log. Wrap well and refrigerate overnight.

3. A FEW HOURS BEFORE making the stollen (or the night before), warm the pear cordial, rum, or brandy in a small saucepan. Place the dried cherries or cranberries and raisins in a bowl and pour the liquor over them. Cover and let steep until the fruit has softened; drain and set aside.

4. IN THE BOWL OF AN ELECTRIC MIXER or another large bowl, combine the warm water and 2 tablespoons of the sugar. Sprinkle the yeast over the water and set aside to proof until foamy, about 5 minutes. In a medium saucepan, scald the milk (heat it until small bubbles form around the edges). Remove from the heat and add the butter, the remaining 1/3 cup sugar, and the lemon zest and juice. Stir to melt the butter, then set aside to cool to lukewarm (90 degrees).

5. ADD THE COOLED MILK MIXTURE to the yeast mixture. With a wooden spoon, beat in the eggs. Add 2 1/4 cups of the flour, the cinnamon, and nutmeg and mix well to form a thick batter.

6. USING THE PADDLE ATTACHMENT or the wooden spoon, beat in 2 1/4 cups more flour until you have a stiff but manageable dough. Switch to the dough hook and knead the dough for several minutes, or until smooth and shiny. Or turn the dough out onto a floured surface and knead by hand. Place the dough in a large buttered bowl and turn to coat. Cover with plastic wrap and let rise in a warm place until doubled in bulk, 1 1/2 hours.

7. TOSS THE DRIED CHERRIES or cranberries and raisins with a few teaspoons of flour to coat them. Turn the dough out onto a floured surface and knead in the dried fruit, a little at a time. The stollen can be finished and baked now, but for best results, cover the dough and refrigerate overnight; bring to room temperature before proceeding.

8. GREASE A LARGE BAKING SHEET or line with parchment paper and set aside. Divide the dough in half. On a floured surface, roll out half the dough into a large oval about 12 inches long. Place one of the logs of pecan filling down the center of the oval. Fold one long side over to enclose the filling, pinch the edges of the dough together to seal, and place the stollen on one side of the prepared baking sheet. Repeat with the remaining dough and filling, placing the second stollen at least 3 inches away from the first one. Cover with tea towels and let rise in a warm place until doubled in bulk, about 45 minutes.

9. PREHEAT THE OVEN to 350 degrees. Bake the stollen for 45 to 50 minutes, or until a cake tester inserted in the center comes out clean; an instant-read thermometer inserted in the center should register 180 degrees. After the first 15 minutes of baking, loosely cover the stollen with a sheet of aluminum foil to prevent overbrowning.

10. MEANWHILE, MAKE THE ICING: In a small bowl, whisk all ingredients together. Drizzle the icing over the warm stollen.

CARDAMOM-AND-CINNAMON-SCENTED SWEDISH TEA RING

Tea rings like this one are the glory of bake sales in Swedish communities like Lindsborg, Kansas, and Bishop Hill, Illinois. The soft, rich dough needs gentle coaxing into shape, using both hands at times, but the opulent results are worth it. Cardamom scents the dough and the glaze; cinnamon flavors the filling. For greater flavor intensity, use the seeds from whole cardamom pods rather than ground cardamom, and if possible, ground Chinese cassia cinnamon (see Source Guide, page 215). This recipe also makes wonderful cinnamon rolls; see the Variation below.

MAKES 2 LARGE TEA RINGS

2¹/2 cups milk
1 cup granulated sugar
1 tablespoon packed brown sugar
4 large eggs, beaten
8 tablespoons (1 stick) unsalted butter, melted
Seeds from 24 cardamom pods, crushed, or 2 teaspoons ground cardamom
1¹/2 teaspoons salt
2 (¹/4-ounce) packages (1¹/2 tablespoons) active dry yeast
1 cup warm (110 degrees) water
8 to 9 cups all-purpose flour, plus more if needed

FOR THE FILLING:
6 tablespoons granulated sugar
¹/4 cup ground cinnamon

SWEDE TOOTH

············ ✦ ············

When people argue that Swedish pastry is "to die for," they have more proof than they may realize. In 1771, Swedish King Adolf Fredrik gorged himself to death on *semla*, a particularly rich yeast-raised cardamom-and-cinnamon-scented bun, scooped out and filled with almond paste, then topped with whipped cream. Although a favorite with King Fredrik, *semla* was a little too decadent for the Swedish country folk who left the homeland for the Heartland in the 1860s.

By the nineteenth century, even the middle classes and farm households could afford sugar, and there was an explosion in Swedish home baking. The Swedish love affair with breads and yeast-raised pastries crossed the Atlantic, then made its way to the prairie with the first Swedish settlers to places like Bishop Hill, Illinois, and Lindsborg, Kansas. Breads, rolls, and pastries came to represent hearth and heart, and the image of the flour-dusted Swedish grandmother became a comforting reminder of home for the settlers.

Cardamom, cinnamon, saffron, and almond are the primary flavorings these Swedish home bakers transported to the Heartland. Yeast-raised *kanelbullar* are the plump and tender forerunners of the Midwesterner's classic cinnamon roll. *Skorpor*, the twice-baked cardamom-scented sweet toasts like the Russian Mennonite zwieback or the Italian biscotti, were meant to be dunked in coffee, the requisite beverage to accompany breads and pastries. Sweet, densely textured *limpa*, or Swedish rye bread flavored with molasses and sometimes fennel or orange peel, is a unique and mysterious twist on peasant rye bread. *Kaffebullar*, sweet yeasty coffee buns, are like individual coffee cakes, sometimes flavored with cardamom or almond. *Lussekatter*, "Luciacats," are shaped yeast-raised buns made at Christmas, flavored with saffron. These buns might also be formed into shapes such as *Julvagn*, "Christmas wagon;" or *Prastens har*, "pastor's hair" (like an ornate eighteenth-century wig).

12 tablespoons (1 1/2 sticks) unsalted
   butter, softened

FOR THE GLAZE:
2 cups confectioners' sugar
1/4 cup milk
1/2 teaspoon almond extract

1 cup green candied cherries, optional
1 cup red candied cherries, optional

1. IN A SMALL SAUCEPAN, heat the milk until lukewarm (90 degrees). Transfer to the bowl of an electric mixer or another large bowl and stir in the sugar, eggs, butter, cardamom, and salt. In a small bowl, sprinkle the yeast over the warm water; set aside to proof until foamy, about 5 minutes.

2. STIR THE YEAST MIXTURE into the milk mixture. Using the paddle attachment or a wooden spoon, gradually beat in the flour, adding additional flour if necessary to make a soft dough. Transfer the dough to a large oiled bowl and turn to coat. Cover with plastic wrap and let rise in a warm place until doubled in bulk, 45 minutes to 1 hour.

3. MAKE THE FILLING: In a medium bowl, combine the granulated sugar and 2 tablespoons of the cinnamon. Beat in the butter until smooth and well blended.

4. GREASE TWO BAKING SHEETS or line with parchment paper and set aside. Punch down the dough, turn it out onto a floured surface, and divide it in half. One at a time, roll each piece of dough into an 18- by-12-inch rectangle. Spread half of the filling over each rectangle, leaving a 1-inch margin all around, and sprinkle 1½ teaspoons of the remaining cinnamon over the filling. Starting at a long side, roll up the dough jelly-roll fashion, using both hands to gently coax the dough along. Pinch the long edges together to seal. Place seam side down on one of the prepared baking sheets and shape the roll into a ring, pinching the ends together to seal. With kitchen shears, on a diagonal, cut slashes in each tea ring, three-quarters of the way through the dough, at 2-inch intervals all around the ring. Gently fan the slices so the filling shows. Cover the tea rings with tea towels and let rise until doubled in bulk, about 30 minutes.

5. PREHEAT THE OVEN to 375 degrees. Bake the tea rings for 20 minutes, or until golden brown. Cool on the baking sheets.

6. MAKE THE GLAZE: Combine all the ingredients in a medium bowl and beat until smooth.

Drizzle the glaze over the cooled tea rings. Garnish with the candied cherries, if desired.

VARIATION: For Cardamom-and-Cinnamon-Scented Rolls, in Step 4, cut each roll of filled dough into 12 pieces. Lay the pieces on the prepared baking sheet, cover, and let rise for 30 minutes, or until doubled in bulk. Bake as directed for 15 minutes, or until golden brown. Let cool, then drizzle with the glaze. Makes 24 rolls.

SCHNECKEN

W illie Little is a rare Cincinnatian. His knees don't weaken, his resolve doesn't crumble, and his mouth doesn't water at the mere mention of schnecken—that quintessential German confection that is a cross between a homemade cinnamon roll and the upside-down buttery goodness of a tarte Tatin. Little is somewhat immune to schnecken because, he says, "I'm around it all the time." At the Virginia Bakery, owned by fourth-generation bakers Tom and Maureen Thie, Little makes three batches of schnecken a day, a process that takes several hours. *Schnecken* is the German word for snails, referring to their spiral shape. A loaf of schnecken is composed of three coils of cinnamon-brown sugar-and-raisin-filled yeast dough baked on a thick bed of softened butter sprinkled with sugar. (Don't even think about the calories or fat grams.) This recipe is adapted from recipes from the 1964 edition of *The Joy of Cooking*, by Cincinnatian and schnecken fan

Marion Rombauer Becker, and the 1903 *Settlement Cook Book*, which was published in Milwaukee. This recipe makes two loaves, but schnecken freeze well.

MAKES 2 LOAVES

FOR THE DOUGH:

¹/2 cup milk
1 (¹/4-ounce) package (2¹/4 teaspoons) active dry yeast
3 tablespoons plus 1 teaspoon granulated sugar
3 tablespoons unsalted butter, softened
2 large eggs, beaten
¹/2 teaspoon salt
3 cups sifted all-purpose flour, plus more if needed

8 tablespoons (1 stick) unsalted butter, softened
¹/2 cup granulated sugar

FOR THE FILLING:

4 tablespoons (¹/2 stick) unsalted butter, melted
³/4 cup packed brown sugar
1¹/2 teaspoons ground cinnamon
1 cup dark raisins

1. MAKE THE DOUGH: In a small saucepan, heat the milk until lukewarm (90 degrees); transfer to a small bowl. Sprinkle the yeast and 1 teaspoon of the granulated sugar over the warm milk and set aside to proof until foamy, about 5 minutes.

2. IN THE BOWL OF AN ELECTRIC MIXER or another large bowl, beat the butter, the remaining 3 tablespoons granulated sugar, the eggs, and salt together with the paddle attachment or a wooden spoon. Beat in the yeast mixture, then beat in the flour, 1 cup at a time, until you have a soft dough.

3. SWITCH TO THE DOUGH HOOK and knead the dough for 5 minutes, adding a little more flour if necessary, until the dough is smooth and elastic. Or turn the dough out onto a floured surface and knead by hand. Place the dough in a large oiled bowl and turn to coat. Cover with plastic wrap and let rise in a warm place until doubled in bulk, 1¹/2 to 2 hours.

4. WITH A RUBBER SPATULA or your hands, spread 4 tablespoons of the softened butter into the bottom of each of two 9-by-5-by-3-inch loaf pans, making sure to cover the bottom entirely, or the schnecken will stick. Sprinkle ¹/4 cup of the granulated sugar over the butter in each pan; set aside. Punch down the dough and transfer to a floured surface. Roll it out to a 12-inch square. Brush the melted butter over the dough, then sprinkle with the brown sugar, cinnamon, and raisins. Roll up the dough jelly-roll fashion. With a sharp knife, cut the dough into six 2-inch-wide slices.

5. LAY 3 SLICES in the bottom of each prepared pan, so the coils show. Cover the pans with a damp tea towel and let rise in a warm place to rise until doubled in bulk, about 45 minutes.

6. PREHEAT THE OVEN to 350 degrees. Bake the schnecken for 15 to 20 minutes, or until risen and slightly browned. Let cool briefly, then turn out onto a rack or serving platter and serve warm.

CIDER-GLAZED FRENCH CANADIAN SAVARIN

A sweet, egg-rich yeast bread baked in a ring mold, savarin, which has its roots in country French cuisine, was brought to the Prairie Provinces of Canada and the upper Midwest by the westward migration of French Canadian settlers. In more formal French cuisine, a savarin is glazed with a rum syrup or apricot jelly, but in the early days of prairie settlements in Alberta, Manitoba, and Saskatchewan, rum and apricots were hard to come by. In households set up enough to do fancier baking, a maple syrup or cider glaze, as in this recipe, might finish off the dish. The 1903 *Settlement Cook Book* (from Milwaukee), includes a recipe for a lemon-scented savarin drizzled with a sugar syrup flavored with maraschino, an almond liqueur.

Savarin dough is very light and delicate, so it needs to be handled gently. The center of the savarin can be filled with whipped cream, fresh fruit, sautéed apples, or fresh flowers for a brunch offering, a centerpiece on a tea table, or a dessert.

SERVES 8

1 (¼-ounce) package (2¼ teaspoons)
  active dry yeast
¼ cup warm (110 degrees) water
4 tablespoons (½ stick) unsalted butter,
  softened
1 tablespoon sugar
1¼ cups unbleached all-purpose flour
2 large eggs, beaten

For the Glaze:
2 cups apple cider
½ cup sugar
¼ cup dark rum, optional

1. IN A SMALL BOWL, sprinkle the yeast over the warm water and set aside to proof until foamy, about 5 minutes. In a medium bowl, with a hand-held electric mixer, cream the butter and sugar. Sift the flour into a large bowl and make a well in the center. Add the yeast mixture, butter mixture, and eggs to the well and mix together with your hands. Scrape down the sides of the bowl. Cover with plastic wrap and let the dough rise in a warm place until doubled in bulk, about 30 minutes.

2. GREASE A SAVARIN MOLD or a 1-quart ring mold and set aside. Punch down the dough and knead it in the bowl until smooth and elastic. Spread the dough in the prepared mold, cover with a tea towel, and set aside in a warm place to rise until doubled in bulk, about 30 minutes.

3. PREHEAT THE OVEN to 400 degrees. Bake the savarin for 5 minutes, then turn the heat down to 350 degrees and bake for 15 minutes more, or until the savarin feels firm to the touch.

4. MEANWHILE, MAKE THE GLAZE: Combine the cider and sugar in a small saucepan, bring to the boil, and boil for 15 to 20 minutes, or until reduced by half. Remove from the heat and stir in the rum; keep hot over low heat.

5. WITH A KNIFE OR A SPATULA, loosen the savarin from the sides of the pan. Turn the savarin out onto a wire rack set over a baking sheet. The savarin can be served upside down or right side up, depending on what is the best looking—turn it again now if necessary. Poke holes all over the surface with a cake tester. Gradually brush the savarin all over with the hot glaze, continuing until all the glaze has been absorbed. Serve warm or at room temperature.

·········· ❧❧❧ ··········

RICH SOUR CREAM COFFEE CAKE WITH CREAM CHEESE FILLING

❧❧

Spirals of tender, rich dough enclose an equally rich cream cheese filling in this recipe from the Dairy Belt. Delicious for an Easter breakfast, served with fresh fruit. The recipe makes four coffee cakes, but they freeze and reheat well.

MAKES FOUR 12-INCH-LONG COFFEE CAKES, EACH SERVING 6 TO 8

FOR THE DOUGH:
1 (8-ounce) container sour cream
8 tablespoons (1 stick) unsalted butter
2/3 cup granulated sugar
1 teaspoon salt
2 (1/4-ounce) packages (1 1/2 tablespoons)
    active dry yeast
1/2 cup warm (110 degrees) water
2 large eggs
4 cups all-purpose flour

FOR THE FILLING:
1 (8-ounce) package cream cheese,
    softened

3/4 cup confectioners' sugar
1 large egg, beaten
1 teaspoon vanilla extract

FOR THE GLAZE:
2 cups sifted confectioners' sugar
1/4 cup milk
2 teaspoons vanilla extract

1. MAKE THE DOUGH: In a small saucepan, heat the sour cream just until it begins to simmer. Remove from the heat and add the butter, granulated sugar, and salt, mixing well and stirring until the butter is soft. Let cool to lukewarm (90 degrees). Meanwhile, in a large bowl, sprinkle the yeast over the warm water and set aside to proof until foamy, about 5 minutes.

2. STIR THE LUKEWARM sour cream mixture and the eggs into the yeast mixture. Gradually stir in the flour, 1 cup at a time, until you have a soft dough. Cover the bowl with plastic wrap and let rise at room temperature for 4 hours, or refrigerate overnight.

3. MAKE THE FILLING: In a medium bowl, combine all the ingredients and beat with a handheld electric mixer until smooth. Set aside.

4. GREASE TWO BAKING SHEETS or line them with parchment paper; set aside. Turn the dough out onto a heavily floured surface and divide it into 4 equal portions. One at a time, knead each portion 4 or 5 times, then roll out into a 12-by-8-inch rectangle. (The dough will be very elastic; just keep rolling and pressing it into shape.) Spread one-quarter of the filling over each rectangle, leaving a 1-inch margin all around. Beginning at a long side, carefully roll up jelly-roll fashion and firmly pinch the ends to seal. Carefully place seam side down on one of the prepared baking sheets. Cover the coffee cakes with tea towels and let rise in a warm place until doubled in bulk, about 2 hours.

5. PREHEAT THE OVEN to 375 degrees. Bake the coffee cakes for 15 to 20 minutes, or until risen and browned.

6. MEANWHILE, MAKE THE GLAZE: Combine all the ingredients in a medium bowl and whisk until smooth. Spread the glaze over the warm coffee cakes.

POLISH LEMON–POPPY SEED COFFEE CAKE

The windows of Polish bakeries along Chicago's Milwaukee Avenue seem to blossom with pastries at Easter. Babkas of every sort, *mazurek* (Polish cake decorated with dried fruit icing), and coffee cakes like this one displayed elegantly in the windows will be the stars at Easter celebrations in neighborhood homes, along with homemade breads, butter molded into the shape of a lamb, and eggs, ham, and cheese. In small mom-and-pop grocery stores in this area, you can buy a butter lamb as well as bags of ground poppy seeds, saving a step in making this coffee cake. I can't buy ground poppy seeds locally, so I grind them in a clean electric coffee grinder.

MAKES 1 COFFEE CAKE

FOR THE FILLING:
1 cup ground poppy seeds (about ¹/₂ cup whole poppy seeds)
³/₄ cup milk
¹/₂ cup granulated sugar
1¹/₂ teaspoons grated lemon zest
1 teaspoon vanilla extract
1 large egg, beaten

FOR THE DOUGH:
¹/₂ cup milk
2 tablespoons unsalted butter, softened
¹/₄ cup sugar
¹/₂ teaspoon salt
1 (¹/₄-ounce) package (2¹/₄ teaspoons) active dry yeast
1 tablespoon warm water
2 large egg yolks
¹/₂ teaspoon ground cardamom
2 cups all-purpose flour

FOR THE ICING:
1 cup confectioners' sugar
2 tablespoons fresh lemon juice

1. MAKE THE FILLING: In a medium saucepan, combine the ground poppy seeds, milk, granulated sugar, and lemon zest and bring to a boil over medium-high heat. Cook for 5 minutes, stirring occasionally, until the poppy seeds soften and the filling thickens. Remove from the heat, stir in the vanilla and egg, and set aside.

2. MAKE THE DOUGH: In a small saucepan, scald the milk (heat it until small bubbles form around the edges). Remove from the heat and whisk in the butter, granulated sugar, and salt until the butter melts; set aside to cool to lukewarm (90 degrees). In the bowl of an electric mixer or another large bowl, sprinkle the yeast over the warm water and set aside to proof until foamy, about 5 minutes.

3. WITH THE PADDLE ATTACHMENT or a wooden spoon, beat the egg yolks into the yeast mixture, then beat in the milk mixture. Beat in the cardamom and then the flour, 1 cup at a time, until you have a soft dough.

4. SWITCH TO THE DOUGH HOOK and knead the dough for 5 minutes, or until smooth and elastic. Or turn the dough out onto a floured surface and knead by hand. Place the dough in a large oiled bowl and turn to coat. Cover with plastic wrap and let rise in a warm place until doubled in bulk, 1½ to 2 hours.

5. PUNCH THE DOUGH DOWN, cover, and let rise again until doubled in bulk, about 1 hour.

6. LINE A BAKING SHEET with parchment paper. Turn the dough out onto a floured surface and roll or pat into a 10-by-8-inch rectangle. Spread the filling over the dough, leaving a 1-inch margin all around. Starting at a long end, roll up the dough jelly-roll fashion, and place seam side down on the prepared baking sheet. Cover with a tea towel and let rise until doubled in bulk, about 1 hour.

7. PREHEAT THE OVEN to 350 degrees. Bake the coffee cake for 45 minutes, or until risen and browned.

8. MEANWHILE, MAKE THE ICING: Whisk all the ingredients together in a small bowl until smooth. Transfer the coffee cake to a wire rack set over a baking sheet. Drizzle the icing over the warm coffee cake. Serve warm or at room temperature.

Born, raised, and educated in the Bay Area of California, I knew little of the Midwest. I imagined flat, boring plains and cornfields, the bright lights and the lust of Chicago's glamorous Rush Street lying somewhere near the end. Job-searching in Iowa and Illinois, both sprinkled with small liberal arts colleges, I was not ready for my first February evening in rural northwestern Illinois, broad snowflakes spinning down and round an avenue of immense black elms, the branches piled high with glistening snow, the streets impassable, drifted over four feet high with snow. Looming, solid white, the wooded hills at the northwest edge of town seemed to block the village off from the rest of the world. Somehow, I was at home.

—ROBERT SCHULER, "PUTTING MYSELF IN MY PLACE"

Kuchen Dough

꧁꧂

This sweet yeast dough is the basis for coffee cakes of all kinds, from the German *schmierkuchen,* or Cheese Pocket Coffee Cake (this page), to the Swiss *bienenstohn* (page 200), with its honeyed flavor, to the Bavarian Apple Custard Kuchen (page 199) to other fruit-topped kuchen. This dough can be made up to three days ahead, then rolled out like a piecrust and topped with a mixture of your choice. Deliciously easy.

MAKES ENOUGH FOR 2 COFFEE CAKES

1/2 cup milk
1/4 cup sugar
1 teaspoon salt
2 tablespoons unsalted butter
1 (1/4-ounce) package (2 1/4 teaspoons)
  active dry yeast
1/4 cup lukewarm (90 degrees) water
1 large egg, beaten
2 cups all-purpose flour

1. IN A SMALL SAUCEPAN, combine the milk, sugar, salt, and butter and scald the milk (heat just until small bubbles form around the edges). Remove from the heat and stir until the butter melts, then set aside to cool to lukewarm (90 degrees). In a large bowl, sprinkle the yeast over the lukewarm water and set aside to proof until foamy, about 5 minutes.

2. STIR THE MILK MIXTURE and egg into the yeast mixture, then stir in the flour, 1 cup at a time, until you have a soft dough. Place the dough in a large oiled bowl and turn to coat. Cover with

plastic wrap and place in the refrigerator to rise for at least 3 hours, or for up to 3 days.

Cheese Pocket Coffee Cake

꧁꧂

When I lived in Cincinnati, one of my favorite treats was to buy a Cheese Pocket Coffee Cake from Servatii's Bakery in Hyde Park for a special weekend breakfast. When I moved to Kansas City, I often longed for the taste of that coffee cake, known in German as *schmierkuchen.* Now I make a very satisfying, and delicious, similar coffee cake from scratch.

MAKES 2 COFFEE CAKES

FOR THE FILLING:
1 1/2 cups small-curd cottage cheese
1/4 cup heavy cream
1/2 cup sugar
1 tablespoon all-purpose flour
1/2 teaspoon salt
2 large eggs, beaten
1 teaspoon vanilla extract

1 recipe Kuchen Dough (this page)

1. PREHEAT THE OVEN to 350 degrees. Grease two 9-inch square baking pans and set aside. Make the filling: Combine the cottage cheese, cream, sugar, flour, salt, eggs, and vanilla extract in the bowl of a food processor or blender and process until smooth. Set aside.

2. TURN THE DOUGH OUT onto a floured surface and divide it in half. One at a time, roll each piece of dough into an 11-inch square. Fold 1 inch of the dough over all around the perimeter to form a raised edge and place the dough in one of the prepared baking pans, pressing it against the sides of the pan to help shape it. Add half the filling to each pan.

3. BAKE THE KUCHEN for 20 to 25 minutes, until the edges of the coffee cake have browned and risen and the filling does not shake when the pan is lightly tapped. Serve warm or room temperature.

APPLE CUSTARD KUCHEN

Apple orchards, created from seeds brought first by the legendary Johnny Appleseed to Ohio and Indiana, and then by settlers moving westward, dot the Heartland. This homey coffee cake is the pride of the vanishing small-town bakery.

MAKES 2 KUCHEN

FOR THE FILLING:
1 large egg, beaten
1 cup heavy cream
¹/2 cup sugar
1 teaspoon ground cinnamon
1 cup Honeyed Applesauce (page 87) or
*   other chunky homemade applesauce*

1 recipe Kuchen Dough (page 198)

1. PREHEAT THE OVEN to 350 degrees. Grease two 9-inch square baking pans and set aside. Make the filling: In a small bowl, whisk the egg, cream, sugar, and cinnamon together.

2. TURN THE DOUGH OUT onto a floured surface and divide it in half. One at a time, roll each piece into an 11-inch square. Fold 1 inch of the dough over all around the perimeter to form a raised edge and place the dough in one of the prepared baking pans, pressing it against the sides of the pan to help shape it. Spoon half the applesauce into each pan and top with the egg and cream mixture.

3. BAKE THE KUCHEN for 20 to 25 minutes, until the edges of the coffee cake have browned and risen and the filling has browned. Serve warm or at room temperature.

SWISS BEE STING KUCHEN

When I first saw squares of *bienenstohn* ("bee sting") in the tiny New Glarus Bakery in New Glarus, Wisconsin, I just had to have one. Sandwiched between thin layers of sweetened yeast dough and topped with honeyed almonds was a layer of Bavarian cream filling rising several inches high. Totally decadent. And so rich I couldn't finish all of it. Whether you make this as a stand-out brunch coffee cake or as a dessert, make sure you save room for it—or cut small portions. Two baked square kuchen crusts serve as the top and bottom of this coffee cake. One is plain, the other sprinkled with almonds and drizzled with honey. For best results, make both the crusts and the filling a day ahead. Serve fresh fruit as a foil to the richness of the pastry.

SERVES 12

1 recipe Kuchen Dough (page 198)

FOR THE FILLING:
5 large eggs
1/2 cup sugar
1 1/2 tablespoons unflavored gelatin
1/4 cup cold water
2 cups heavy cream
1 tablespoon vanilla extract
1 cup flaked almonds
1/2 cup wildflower or clover honey

1. MAKE THE CRUSTS: Preheat the oven to 350 degrees. Grease two 9-inch square baking pans and set aside. Turn the dough out onto a floured surface and divide it in half. Roll one piece into an 11-inch square. Fold 1 inch of the dough over all around the perimeter to form a raised edge and place the dough in one of the prepared baking pans, pressing it against the sides of the pan to help shape it. Roll out the remaining dough into a 9-inch square and place it in the second baking pan. Sprinkle the almonds over the top and drizzle with the honey.

2. BAKE THE CRUSTS for 15 to 20 minutes, or until risen and browned. Remove from the pans and cool on wire racks.

3. MAKE THE FILLING: Pour 1¹/₂ inches of hot water into the bottom of a double boiler and place over medium-high heat. Set the top of the double boiler over the bottom, add the eggs and ¹/₄ cup of the sugar, and beat with a hand-held electric mixer until pale and thick, about 7 minutes; the mixture should have the consistency of mayonnaise. Beat in the remaining ¹/₄ cup sugar and continue beating for several minutes, until soft peaks form. Transfer the egg mixture to a large bowl and set aside.

4. IN A SMALL HEATPROOF BOWL or cup, sprinkle the gelatin over the cold water. Place the bowl in the hot water remaining in the bottom of the double boiler and let stand for several minutes, until the gelatin has softened and dissolved. Whisk the gelatin mixture into the egg mixture until smooth. Cover with plastic wrap and refrigerate for 30 minutes.

5. IN A MEDIUM BOWL set over a larger bowl of ice, beat the cream until soft peaks form. Add the vanilla and beat until soft peaks form again. With a rubber spatula, fold the egg mixture into the cream.

6. LINE A 9-INCH SQUARE BAKING PAN with plastic wrap, leaving a 5-inch overhang over two opposite sides. Place the plain kuchen crust in the pan. Spoon the filling into the crust. Place the top crust over the filling. Carefully cover with plastic wrap and refrigerate for at least 4 hours to set the filling.

7. TO SERVE, carefully cut into small squares with a serrated knife. Serve chilled.

LATTICED RHUBARB SHEETS

"My mother churned her own butter, rendered her own lard, made her own bread, and canned whatever she could glean out of the summer's parched garden. She always had rhubarb. . . . And, of course, potatoes," recalls Carrie Young in *Nothing to Do But Stay: My Pioneer Mother* of her Dakota childhood. Even folks who live in the milder regions of the prairie enjoy rhubarb in pastries like this one, from prairie painter Lisa Grossman of Kansas. A cross between a pie, a shortcake, and a coffee cake, the pastry also tastes wonderful made with 1 cup of Old-Fashioned Quince Preserves (page 12) or Strawberry, Rhubarb, and Rose Petal Jam (page 162) instead of the rhubarb filling.

SERVES 12

FOR THE FILLING:
¹/₄ cup water
1¹/₂ teaspoons cornstarch
1¹/₂ cups chopped rhubarb stalks
¹/₂ cup sugar

FOR THE DOUGH:
1¹/₂ cups all-purpose flour
¹/₂ cup sugar
1¹/₂ teaspoons baking powder
¹/₂ teaspoon salt
8 tablespoons (1 stick) unsalted butter
1 large egg, beaten
1 teaspoon vanilla extract
2 to 3 tablespoons milk, or more as
  necessary

1. PREHEAT THE OVEN to 350 degrees. Grease a baking sheet or line with parchment paper and set side. Make the filling: Combine the water and cornstarch in a small cup and stir until well blended and smooth. Put the rhubarb and sugar in a medium saucepan, stir in the cornstarch mixture, and cook over medium heat for 10 minutes, or until the rhubarb has softened. Set aside to cool.

2. MAKE THE DOUGH: In a food processor, combine the flour, sugar, baking powder, and salt and pulse to blend. Add the butter and pulse until the mixture resembles coarse crumbs. Add the egg and vanilla and process to blend. Add just enough milk to make a soft, workable dough.

3. DIVIDE THE DOUGH into 2 pieces, one twice as large as the other. On a floured surface, roll out or spread the larger piece of dough into a

PAINTING THE PRAIRIE

The sweeping expanse of wheat-fringed horizon on the western prairie has inspired not only great breads, but also great art. Seen from a distance, small-town grain elevators rise like prairie cathedrals from the surrounding farmland. The mystery in a stalk of wheat, the energy of wheat sheaves waving in the wind, and the contrast of row upon row of wheat against a threatening sky are all images that have captured artists' imaginations.

The Reverend Philip Bentley, in Sinclair Ross's novel *As for Me and My House*, is just such an artist. His wife appreciates how difficult it is to capture, on paper or canvas, the limitations of life in their small prairie town of Horizon, contrasted with the big open spaces. "I turned and looked back at Horizon," she writes in her diary, "the huddled little clutter of houses and stores, the five grain elevators, aloof and imperturbable, like ancient obelisks, and behind, the dust clouds, lapping at the sky. . . . It was like one of Philip's drawings. There was the same tension, the same vivid immobility, and behind it all somewhere the same sense of transience. . . . I walked on, remembering how I used to think that only a great artist could ever paint the prairie—the vacancy and stillness of it, the bare essentials of a landscape, sky and earth, and how I used to look at Philip's work, and think to myself that the world would some day know of him."

The very absence of geographic detail moves prairie landscape painters to consider the mood and the moment—the way the sunlight changes by the hour, the shifts in color and clouds in the sky, the subtle transformations in prairie grasses during the turnings of the year, the stars in the night sky. Although Georgia O'Keeffe was born and raised in Sun Prairie, Wisconsin, she had not experienced the sheer expanse of sky and horizon that confronted her until she became chairwoman of the art department at West Texas Normal (now part of Texas

9-by-7-inch rectangle; trim the edges to even them if necessary. Carefully transfer the rectangle to the prepared baking sheet. Spread the cooled rhubarb filling over the dough, leaving a 1/2-inch margin on all sides. Roll out the smaller piece of dough into a 9-by-7-inch rectangle. With a pizza wheel or a chef's knife, cut it crosswise on the diagonal into twelve 1/2-inch-wide strips. Place the strips over the filling on a diagonal to form a lattice-like crust and trim the ends even with the border of the rectangle. Dip the tines of a fork in water and press the strips into the dough all around the perimeter to make a decorative border.

4. BAKE FOR 20 TO 25 MINUTES, or until the crust has browned. Serve warm or at room temperature, cut into squares.

A & M's West campus) in 1916. "I had nothing but to walk into nowhere and the wide sunset space with the star," she wrote of the series of watercolors called "Evening Star" that she painted at Canyon in 1917.

Thomas Hart Benton, born in Neosho, Missouri, in 1889, spent his life capturing regional scenes, as in his 1938 painting *Cradling Wheat*, depicting farmers harvesting wheat by hand. His elemental painting simply titled *Wheat* shows a foreground of a harvested row of wheat with green shoots already springing up, and row upon row of golden wheat sheaves all the way to the horizon—as far as the eye can see. The viewer is drawn into the mystery of the grain and the vivid generative force of seed and prairie earth.

The past several years have seen a reemergence of interest in the prairie as landscape. Phil Epp portrays majestic technicolor skies like gods on Mt. Olympus, dwarfing the landscape and the people below. Lisa Grossman depicts "slices of life" in small, horizontal canvases that capture the sky, the horizon, the mood, and the moment of a prairie landscape. Judith Mackey depicts the drama of prairie earth and sky, most notably in her painting *Storm over the Flint Hills*, which graced the cover of William Least-Heat Moon's *PrairyErth (A Deep Map)*.

DUTCH LETTERS

Rich, buttery, flaky dough surrounding a homemade almond filling. Who can resist a Dutch Letter? During the Tulip Time Festival in Pella, Iowa, scores of home bakers produce hundreds of these almond-filled pastries to sell at local churches. Visitors from all over the Heartland descend on this small town in early May to view the tulips in bloom and enjoy quilt shows and craft demonstrations, such as wooden shoe making and Dutch cookie baking. Those who want to take a taste of Pella home with them might stop at the Jaarsma Bakery, where these treats are for sale. Leaving the butter in pieces, then rolling and folding it into the dough creates pockets when the butter melts, which expand during baking to make a light, flaky confection. Dutch Letters were originally formed into the initial of the family's surname, but the most common shape is now the letter S.

MAKES 2 DOZEN PASTRIES

4¹/2 cups all-purpose flour, plus more for
    kneading
1 teaspoon salt
1 pound (4 sticks) unsalted butter, cut into
    ¹/2-inch cubes and chilled
2 large eggs, beaten
¹/2 cup water
1 cup Danish Almond Filling (page 185),
    almond paste, or marzipan
Milk, for brushing
Sugar, for sprinkling

1. IN A LARGE BOWL, or in the bowl of a food processor, combine the flour and salt. Add the butter and stir with a wooden spoon, or pulse

the processor, until the butter pieces are coated with flour but still separate. In a small bowl, combine the eggs and water. Add to the flour mixture and stir, or pulse, until you have a lumpy dough.

2. TURN THE DOUGH OUT onto a floured surface. Dust it with a little flour and knead for 3 to 4 minutes, or until it forms a rough ball. Press the dough into a rough rectangle, then roll it out into a 15-by-10-inch rectangle. Fold the short sides over to meet in the center, then fold the dough crosswise in half so you have 4 layers of dough. Roll out the dough to a 15-by-10-inch rectangle again and repeat the folding process. If the dough gets sticky, cover it with plastic wrap and refrigerate it for 20 minutes to firm up. Roll out and fold the dough a total of four times, then cover with plastic wrap and chill for 20 minutes.

3. PREHEAT THE OVEN to 375 degrees. Line two baking sheets with parchment paper. Divide the dough into 4 portions. Place one portion on a floured surface and return the rest of the dough to the refrigerator. Roll the dough out to a 12-by-10-inch rectangle. Cut the dough into six 10-by-2-inch strips. Using one-quarter of the filling in all, spread a heaping teaspoon of filling in a thin line down the center of each strip of dough. Fold the strips of dough over lengthwise to enclose the filling and crimp the edges with your fingers or the tines of a fork to seal. Place the filled strips seam side down on one of the prepared baking sheets. Form the strips into S-shapes (or a letter of your choice). Repeat with the remaining dough and filling.

4. BRUSH EACH LETTER with a little milk and sprinkle with sugar. Bake for 20 to 25 minutes, or until the pastries are puffed and browned. Let cool on the pans.

HUNGARIAN STRUDEL DOUGH

Eastern European immigrants to the Midwest brought a home and village baking tradition of thin layers of yeast-risen dough used to enclose thin pockets of filling, as in the Serbo-Croatian povitica (see Croatian Walnut Bread, page 207) or this Hungarian strudel. Home bakers of Hungarian ancestry in communities surrounding Cleveland, Ohio, and Detroit, Michigan, are still justifiably proud of their strudels, which have a more sumptuous quality than those made from papery-thin packaged phyllo dough.

MAKES ENOUGH FOR 2 STRUDELS

2/3 cup sugar
2 1/2 teaspoons active dry yeast
1/4 cup warm (110 degrees) water
1/2 cup milk
1 large egg
2 large egg yolks
2 tablespoons sour cream
1 tablespoon fresh lemon juice
1 teaspoon vanilla extract
5 cups all-purpose flour
1/2 teaspoon salt
1/4 teaspoon baking powder
1/2 pound (2 sticks) unsalted butter, cut
    into pieces, softened

1. IN A MEDIUM BOWL, sprinkle 1/2 teaspoon of the sugar and the yeast over the warm water; set aside to proof until foamy, about 5 minutes. Meanwhile, in a saucepan, heat the milk until warm (110 degrees); remove from the heat.

2. WITH A WOODEN SPOON, stir the milk, the remaining sugar, the egg, egg yolks, sour cream, lemon juice, and vanilla into the yeast mixture.

3. COMBINE 4 CUPS of the flour, the salt, and baking powder in the bowl of a food processor and pulse to blend. Scatter the butter pieces on top of the flour and pulse until the mixture resembles coarse meal. With the machine running, drizzle in the yeast mixture through the tube and process until you have a thick, batter-like dough.

4. TURN THE DOUGH OUT onto a floured surface and knead for 4 to 5 minutes, gradually adding the remaining 1 cup flour, until smooth and elastic. Shape the dough into a ball, place in a large oiled bowl, and turn to coat. Cover with plastic wrap and let rise in a warm place until doubled in bulk, about 1 1/2 hours.

Savory Sweet Potato Strudel

Midwesterners love their strudel. Dinkel's in Chicago has been making poppy seed and walnut strudels since 1922, and more recently added pecan praline and almond apricot versions to its repertoire. Lucy's Sweet Surrender, on Buckeye Road in Cleveland, Ohio, has also offered enticing fruit strudels made of apple and cherry since 1953, as well as savory versions with spinach or potato fillings. So why not a sweet potato strudel? Serve this as part of a Thanksgiving meal or buffet, as an unusual hors d'oeuvre, or as an accompaniment to a home-made soup. The strudel is also good made with a filling of 2 cups prepared pumpkin butter.

This recipe makes two, but the strudel freezes well, so you can save one for later. After the strudel is baked and cooled, place in a large zippered plastic bag and freeze. To reheat, place on a baking sheet, cover with aluminum foil, and warm in a 350-degree oven for 10 to 15 minutes.

MAKES 2 STRUDELS, EACH SERVING 10 TO 12

FOR THE FILLING:
4 large sweet potatoes
8 tablespoons (1 stick) unsalted butter, softened
1 cup freshly grated Parmesan cheese (about 4 ounces)
1/4 teaspoon freshly grated nutmeg
1/4 teaspoon ground cinnamon
1/4 teaspoon ground allspice
Salt and freshly ground black pepper to taste
1 recipe Hungarian Strudel Dough (page 205)

FOR THE GLAZE:
1 large egg yolk
2 to 3 tablespoons heavy cream

1. MAKE THE FILLING: Preheat the oven to 375 degrees. Prick the sweet potatoes all over and bake for 1 hour, or until soft. (The sweet potatoes can also be cooked in the microwave on High for about 15 minutes.) Let cool.

2. WITH A PARING KNIFE, peel the potatoes. Place the potato pulp in a medium bowl. With a potato masher, mash in the butter, Parmesan, and spices.

3. GREASE A BAKING SHEET and set aside. Divide the dough in half. One at a time, roll each half out on a floured surface to a 16-inch square. Spread half the filling over the dough, leaving a 1-inch margin all around. Fold the uncovered 1 inch of the left and right sides over, then roll up jelly-roll fashion. Place seam side down on the prepared baking sheet and press the strudel down slightly. Cover with a damp tea towel and let rise in a warm place until nearly doubled in bulk, about 45 minutes.

4. PREHEAT THE OVEN to 350 degrees. Make the glaze: In a small bowl, mix the egg yolk and cream together. Brush over the strudels. With a serrated knife, make several shallow diagonal slashes in the top of each strudel.

5. BAKE THE STRUDELS for 35 to 40 minutes, or until well browned. Cool on a wire rack before serving. (Store leftovers at room temperature, covered with plastic wrap.)

SPICED APPLE STRUDEL: Substitute 2 cups Honeyed Applesauce (page 87) for the sweet potato filling. Proceed as directed.

SWEET CHEESE, RAISIN, AND ALMOND STRUDEL

The Sykora Bakery in Cedar Rapids, Iowa, sometimes makes a Czech strudel with a filling of sweetened cheese, raisins, lemon zest, and almonds.

MAKES 2 STRUDELS, EACH SERVING 8 TO 10

FOR THE FILLING:

1 1/2 cups small-curd cottage cheese
1/4 cup heavy cream
1/2 cup sugar
1 tablespoon all-purpose flour
1/2 teaspoon salt
2 large eggs, beaten
1 teaspoon vanilla extract
1 teaspoon grated lemon zest
1/2 cup golden raisins
1/2 cup dried sour cherries or dark raisins
1/2 cup flaked almonds

1 recipe Hungarian Strudel Dough
   (page 205)

FOR THE GLAZE:

1 large egg yolk
2 to 3 tablespoons heavy cream

1. MAKE THE FILLING: In the bowl of an electric mixer or a food processor, blend the cottage cheese, cream, sugar, flour, salt, eggs, vanilla, and lemon zest until smooth; if using the processor, transfer to a bowl. Fold the raisins, dried sour cherries, and flaked almonds into the filling; set aside.

2. GREASE A BAKING SHEET and set aside. Divide the dough in half. One at a time, roll each half out on a floured surface to a 16-inch square. Spread half the filling over the dough, leaving a 1-inch margin all around. Fold the uncovered 1 inch of the left and right sides over, then roll up jelly-roll fashion. Place seam side down on the prepared baking sheet and press the strudel down slightly. Cover with a damp tea towel and let rise in a warm place until nearly doubled in bulk, about 45 minutes.

3. PREHEAT THE OVEN to 350 degrees. Make the glaze: In a small bowl, mix the egg yolk and cream together. Brush over the strudels. With a serrated knife, make several shallow diagonal slashes in the top of each strudel.

4. BAKE THE STRUDELS for 35 to 40 minutes, or until well browned. Cool on a wire rack before serving. (Store leftovers at room temperature, covered with plastic wrap.)

CROATIAN WALNUT BREAD

From 1890 to 1910, thousands of Croatians left Europe for America. In Kansas City, they settled in the West Bottoms area, until a flood forced them to relocate to higher ground in an area where wild strawberries once grew, called Strawberry Hill. The Croatians were known for their tamburitza music, their strong work ethic, and their swirled walnut bread, *povitica*. The name is from a Croatian word meaning "swaddled." This bread is like a soft

strudel. A thin yeast dough is rolled out, covered with an English walnut filling, as in this recipe, or a sweet cheese filling (such as the Cheese Pocket Coffee Cake filling on page 198), and rolled up like a jelly roll. Then it's folded to fit into a loaf pan and baked.

Growing up in Strawberry Hill, Don Wolf remembers his grandmother "working with the huge round of dough. My job was to crack the walnuts," he says. "My mother came from a family of four girls and I remember one of my aunts played piano and someone was always singing while we were baking." Making povitica is very convivial, as stretching the dough is easier when two people work on it at the same time. Today in Kansas City, four ethnic bakeries specialize in povitica. It is also a popular offering at the Sunrise Bakery in Hibbing, Minnesota. Home bakers of Croatian, Slovenian, Serbian, and Slavic descent make this specialty bread for Christmas, New Year's, Easter, and weddings. It's delicious toasted or served with slices of ham.

IN THE POVITICA UNDERWORLD

In the weeks before Christmas, Richard Grosko begins referring to the home he shares with his wife, Donna, as "The Povitica Underworld." There in the basement kitchen, Donna and her sister, Theresa Stimac, are getting ready to bake loaves of the rich Croatian nut bread known as povitica, a symbol of holiday giving. Povitica making, brought to the Heartland by Croatian immigrants during the period from 1890 to 1910, is a culinary art now being revived at Donna Grosko's classes at the Culinary Center of Kansas City, the Strawberry Hill Museum and Cultural Center, and local bakeries such as Eugenia's Bread Shoppe in Kansas City, Kansas, and Kobe House Bakery in Sugar Creek, Missouri.

The huge island in the Grosko's cramped basement has been covered with a clean bedsheet. On top of the vibrating clothes dryer, a big bowl of sweet dough, covered with plastic wrap, is rising to double its size. When the dough is just the right size, the sisters cut it in half, weighing each portion—2 1/2 pounds. They turn one half of the dough out onto the flour-dusted sheet and start rolling it with a rolling pin. And that's when the fun begins.

After removing rings, bracelets, and anything else that might tear the dough, the sisters start moving around the table, tugging and pulling at the dough, stretching it until it eventually it forms a 44-by-50-inch oval. Quickly, they spread the walnut filling over the dough with large offset spatulas. After trimming any uneven edges, they lift the sheet and roll up the dough jelly-roll fashion. Then they cut the huge snake of dough into four equal parts and form each section into a S-shape before putting it into loaf pans. Each loaf is brushed with an egg white glaze, then baked. From start to finish, the povitica takes five hours to make.

To freeze the bread, wrap it in aluminum foil and place in a zippered plastic freezer bag. To reheat, wrap in foil and warm in a 300- to 350-degree oven for about 15 minutes.

MAKES 2 LOAVES

1/2 cup warm (100 degrees) water
3/4 cup plus 2 teaspoons sugar
7 to 8 cups plus 1 teaspoon all-purpose flour
2 (1/4-ounce) packages (1 1/2 tablespoons) active dry yeast
2 cups 2% milk
1 tablespoon salt
1 large egg
3 large egg yolks
8 tablespoons (1 stick) unsalted butter, melted

FOR THE FILLING:
2 pounds English walnuts (about 8 cups)
5 cups sugar
2 cups milk, plus more if needed
1/2 pound (2 sticks) unsalted butter
2 large eggs, beaten

Flour, for dusting
1 large egg white, beaten, for egg glaze

1. IN A LARGE BOWL, combine the warm water, 2 teaspoons of the sugar, and 1 teaspoon of the flour. Sprinkle the yeast over the mixture and set aside to proof until foamy, about 5 minutes. Meanwhile, in a small saucepan, heat the milk until lukewarm (90 degrees); remove from the heat.

2. WITH A HAND-HELD ELECTRIC MIXER or a wooden spoon, blend the milk, the remaining 3/4 cup sugar, the salt, egg, egg yolks, and melted butter into the yeast mixture. Beat in 2 cups of the flour, 1/2 cup at a time, until you have a thin batter. Beat in enough of the remaining flour, 1/2 cup at a time, so the dough starts to pull away from the bowl.

3. TURN THE DOUGH OUT onto a floured surface and knead for 5 to 8 minutes, until smooth and elastic, adding more flour if necessary. Divide the dough in half. Place each half in a large oiled bowl and turn to coat. Cover with plastic wrap and let rise in a warm place until doubled in bulk, about 1 hour.

4. MAKE THE FILLING: Finely grind the walnuts using the grinder attachment of a stand mixer or in a food processor. Transfer to a large bowl and stir in the sugar.

5. COMBINE THE MILK AND BUTTER in a medium saucepan and bring almost to the boil, stirring to melt the butter. Pour over the walnut mixture and stir to blend. Stir in the eggs and blend well. The filling should have the consistency of thick soup; if it is too thick, add a tablespoon or so more milk. Set aside.

6. GREASE TWO 9-BY-5-BY-3-INCH LOAF PANS and set aside. Spread a clean white sheet or old tablecloth over a kitchen table, kitchen island, or other freestanding large work surface. Dust the cloth with about $1/2$ cup flour. Punch down the dough and divide it in half. Place one piece of dough in the center of the cloth and roll out to a 12-inch square. Gently lift an edge of the dough and guide your arm underneath the dough to the center, then gently bring your arm back, pulling and stretching the dough with the back of your hand or your upturned palm. Repeat this motion all around the dough, stretching it out until it is a uniformly thin and opaque rectangle about 20 by 16 inches. (It's easier if two people do this at the same time, at opposite sides of the dough.) With a rolling pin, roll the edges of the dough so they are not thicker than the middle part of the dough.

7. WITH A RUBBER SPATULA or offset metal spatula, thinly spread half the walnut filling evenly over the dough, all the way to the edges. Starting at a long side, roll up the dough jelly-roll fashion, lifting the sheet as you go to help roll the dough into a cylinder. With kitchen shears or a paring knife, cut off any uneven ends off, or tuck them into themselves. Gently fold the cylinder into a horseshoe shape and place it in one of the prepared loaf pans. Brush the top with the egg glaze. Repeat the process with the remaining dough and filling. Cover the loaf pans loosely with plastic wrap and let the dough rise in a warm place until doubled in bulk, about 1 hour.

8. PREHEAT THE OVEN to 325 degrees. Bake the breads for 1 hour and 15 minutes, or until browned on top. If after 30 minutes, the loaves are turning a medium brown, cover them loosely with aluminum foil. Let cool on a wire rack for 20 to 30 minutes before serving.

NEW YEAR'S DAY FRITTERS

Traditional New Year's Day treats in Russian Mennonite homes through the wheat-growing prairie, these fritters, known as *portselkje*, were adapted from the Dutch *oliebollen*, enjoyed during the Mennonites' sojourn in the Netherlands. The sweet, raisin-studded yeasty fritters symbolized affluence and luxury. Cookbook author Norma Jost Voth remembers these treats from when she was growing up in Newton, Kansas: "Crisp on the outside, loaded with raisins on the inside, and buried in a blizzard of sugar—nothing quite matched this treat. In spite of the snowy, cold gray day outside, all was bright and warm in Mom's kitchen. . . for New Year's Day was the only day of the year she made *portselkje*. Warm fritters, cold milk, a steaming pot of coffee—that was lunch. . . . Nothing else. Eating until we fairly burst with satisfaction, we did not even mind the resulting stomachache." At Vern and Janice Demel's Country Kitchen restaurant in tiny Moundridge, Kansas, these fritters are served as part of the Russian Mennonite buffet every weekend.

MAKES ABOUT 2 DOZEN FRITTERS

1 cup milk
4 tablespoons ($1/2$ stick) unsalted butter, softened
1 teaspoon salt
$1/4$ cup plus 1 teaspoon granulated sugar
1 tablespoon active dry yeast
$1/2$ cup lukewarm (90 degrees) water
2 cups all-purpose flour
$1/2$ teaspoon baking powder

3 large eggs
*1 1/2 cups raisins, plumped in hot water
and drained*
Canola oil or shortening, for deep-frying
Confectioners' sugar, for dusting

1. COMBINE THE MILK, butter, and salt in a small saucepan and bring almost to a boil; stir to melt the butter and set aside to cool to lukewarm (90 degrees). In a small bowl, sprinkle 1 teaspoon of the granulated sugar and the yeast over the lukewarm water; set aside to proof until foamy, about 5 minutes. Sift the flour and baking powder together; set aside.

2. IN A LARGE BOWL, with a hand-held electric mixer, beat the eggs until frothy. Gradually beat in the remaining 1/4 cup granulated sugar, a tablespoon at a time, until the mixture is thick and lemon-colored, about 5 minutes. Beat in the milk and yeast mixtures. Beat in the flour mixture, 1 cup at a time, until you have a soft dough. Fold in the raisins. Cover with plastic wrap and let rise in a warm place until doubled in bulk, about 1 hour.

3. STIR THE DOUGH DOWN, cover, and let rise again until doubled in bulk, about 45 minutes.

4. SPREAD THE CONFECTIONERS' SUGAR on a plate. Add enough oil or shortening to a deep-fat fryer, electric skillet, or deep heavy skillet to reach a depth of 2 inches and heat to 375 degrees. In batches, using a teaspoon, drop the batter, without crowding, into the hot oil and fry until the fritters are browned on both sides, about 3 to 4 minutes. Transfer to paper towels to drain. While they are still warm, roll the fritters in confectioners' sugar. These are best eaten warm.

PUMPKIN BUTTER DOUGHNUTS WITH SUGAR 'N' SPICE

Nothing finer with cider. These doughnuts freeze well; refresh them, still frozen, in a microwave on High for about 10 seconds.

MAKES ABOUT 18 DOUGHNUTS
(AND DOUGHNUT HOLES)

FOR THE DOUGHNUTS:
3/4 cup plus 1 1/2 tablespoons sugar
1 cup lukewarm (90 degrees) water
*1 (1/4-ounce) package (2 1/4 teaspoons)
active dry yeast*
3 3/4 to 4 1/2 cups all-purpose flour
3 tablespoons instant nonfat dry milk
1 teaspoon salt
*1 cup prepared pumpkin butter or canned
pumpkin (not pumpkin pie filling)*
2 large eggs, beaten
3 tablespoons canola or corn oil
1/2 cup golden raisins, optional
*Canola or other vegetable oil, for
deep-frying*

FOR THE TOPPING:
1/2 cup sugar
2 tablespoons ground cinnamon
1/2 teaspoon freshly grated nutmeg

1. IN A SMALL BOWL, combine 1 1/2 tablespoons of the sugar and 1/2 cup of the lukewarm water. Sprinkle the yeast over the water and set aside to proof until foamy, about 5 minutes. In a large bowl, combine 3 cups of the flour, the dry milk, and salt. Stir in the yeast mixture, then stir in the remaining $^3/4$ cup sugar, the remaining $^1/2$ cup lukewarm water, the pumpkin butter, eggs, oil, and optional raisins until you have a batter-like dough.

2. TURN THE DOUGH OUT onto a floured surface. Flour your hands and the dough and knead it for 7 to 10 minutes, using a dough scraper to fold the dough over on itself and adding up to $1^1/2$ cups more flour, until the dough is soft and slightly sticky. Place the dough in a large oiled bowl and turn to coat. Cover with plastic wrap and let rise in a warm place until doubled in bulk, 45 minutes to 1 hour.

3. GREASE A BAKING SHEET and set aside. Turn the dough out onto a floured surface and roll out to a 12-by-8-inch rectangle. With a 3-inch

doughnut cutter, cut out doughnuts and place them—and the doughnut holes—on the prepared baking sheet. Gather the scraps of dough together, reroll, and cut out more doughnuts. Cover with tea towels and let rise until doubled in bulk, 1 to $1^1/2$ hours.

4. MAKE THE TOPPING: In a shallow bowl, combine the sugar and spices; set aside. Pour enough vegetable oil into a deep-fat fryer, deep heavy skillet, or electric skillet to reach a depth of 2 inches and heat to 350 to 365 degrees. A few at a time, deep-fry the doughnuts (and doughnut holes), turning once, until browned on both sides, about 1 minute per side. Transfer to paper towels to drain. While they are still warm, dredge the doughnuts in the spiced sugar. Serve warm.

RESOURCES

SOURCE GUIDE

American Spoon Foods, Inc.
411 East Lake Street
Petoskey, MI 49770
(800) 222-5886

Mail-order business brainchild of Chef Larry Forgione and former forager Justin Rashid. Spectacular jams and jellies, dried fruits, hickory nuts and black walnuts, persimmon pulp, smoked whitefish, and morels.

American White Wheat Producers Association
P.O. Box 326
Atchison, KS 66002
(800) 372-4422
Fax: (913) 367-4443

Contact Kent Symns to order white wheat products by mail, telephone, or fax. Natural s'Wheat Whole Wheat Flour, bran, bulgur, cracked wheat, and white wheat berries.

Baker Boulanger Online Magazine
www.betterbaking.com

Cookbook author and baker Marcy Goldman, who also writes for the *Washington Post*, has created this charming Web site that appeals to both readers and bakers. Besides an archive full of bread, muffin, coffee cake, and sweet roll recipes, Goldman also features articles on baking products and techniques, answers to baking questions, and her own take on life in "BB Lifestyle." Grab a latte and a slice of homemade buttered toast and take a virtual visit to her "home" in Montreal.

Bread Baker's Electronic Mailing List
www.bread-bakers.com

Provides a weekly e-mail including bread-making queries, recipes, and answers from subscribers all over the world, who ask questions and/or contribute their knowledge and expertise. A great resource for both novice and experienced bread bakers.

To subscribe, send an e-mail to bread-bakers-request@lists.best.com.

In the body of the message, type only the word "subscribe" (without capitalizing it or indenting it).

Carey's Wheat Berries
19111 W. 56th Ave.
Sterling, KS 67579
(316) 278-3731
e-mail: bccarey@sterlingks.net
www.careyswheatberries.com

Whole wheat berries or kernels for home milling or cooking. Contact Connie Carey if you have questions.

Dandy Pantry
212 Hammonds Drive East
Stockton, MO 65785
(800) 872-6879

Midwestern black walnuts, native pecans, and hickory nuts by mail order.

DYMPLE'S DELIGHT
Route 4, Box 53
Mitchell, IN 47446
(812) 849-3587

Fresh and canned native persimmons.

EARTHY DELIGHTS
4180 Keller
Suite B
Holt, MI 48842
(800) 367-4709
www.earthy.com

Started as a cooperative for wild foods foragers, now a premier mail-order foods business. Prairie specialties include morels, dried tart cherries, wheat berries, wild leeks, farmstead chèvres, and, sometimes, pawpaws.

HEARTLAND MILL
Route 1, Box 2
Marienthal, KS 67863
(800) 232-8533
www.heartlandmill.com

A farmer-owned company specializing in certified organic products from the farm. Some of their organic flour has appeared in the King Arthur catalog. I am very partial to their Golden Buffalo Flour, when they have it. Contact Mark Nightengale by phone to order flour.

HODGSON MILL, INC.
1203 Niccum Ave.
Suite #1
Effingham, IL 62401
(800) 525-0177
e-mail: customerservice@hodgsonmill.com

Originally powered by water from Bryant Creek, with a paddle wheel, Hodgson Mill was established in Missouri in 1837. By the 1880s, Hodgson Mill was grinding grain with imported French buhrstones. Today, the headquarters have shifted to Effingham, Illinois, where Hodgson Mill produces white whole wheat flour as well as eight varieties of organic flour: whole wheat graham flour, yellow cornmeal, soy flour, oat bran flour, whole wheat pastry flour, rye flour, naturally bleached white flour, and spelt flour.

INDIAN HAND GIFTS
Colleen's Gardens
P.O. Box 68
Marvin, SD 57251-0068
(605) 398-6923
www.indiangifts.com

Colleen Heminger-Cordell, a descendant of Sioux Chief Little Crow, keeps her family's traditions alive and encourages others to do so with her mail-order products such as *waskuya*, or Native American sweet corn locally grown, then dried using only the Dakota sunshine and wind. Also wild rice and prairie herbs harvested by hand.

KING ARTHUR FLOUR
P.O. Box 876
Norwich, VT 05055-0876
(800) 827-6838
Bakers' hotline: (802) 649-3717
www.kingarthurflour.com

The King Arthur Flour Baker's Catalogue offers many kinds of flours, including organic bread flours like Golden Buffalo from Heartland Mill in Marienthal, Kansas, on occasion, as well as vital wheat gluten and other ingredients, along with every piece of equipment you might need for baking breads of all kinds. A wonderful retail and knowledge resource for home bakers.

KITCHEN GLAMOR

P.O. Box 876
Norwich, MI 05055-0876
(800) 827-6838

The Kitchen Glamor stores and catalog offer delicious pecan and marzipan fillings for coffee cakes and pastries, jars of Pan-Eze to grease your pans and baking sheets, and all types of bakeware and baking equipment.

MAYTAG DAIRY FARMS

P.O. Box 806
Newton, IA 50208
(800) 247-2458

Since 1941, when the first wheels of Maytag Blue were placed in nearby caves to age, it has been America's premier blue cheese, made from sweet, fresh Holstein milk.

NORTH DAKOTA FLOUR MILL

www.ndmill.com

Founded in 1922 because local farmers had to ship their grain to Minneapolis to be milled and lost money. Each year, the North Dakota Flour Mill makes 325,000 tons of Dakota Maid bread flour from 14 million bushels of grain.

PENZEYS SPICES

P.O. Box 933
Muskego, WI 53150
(414) 679-7207
www.penzeys.com

Colorful and informative catalog of hard-to-find seasonings: China cassia cinnamon (one of four kinds) for the best cinnamon rolls, Holland blue poppy seeds for Eastern European breads, and almost any other spice or herb you can imagine. Bill Penzey's family recipes, which ap-

pear in each catalog, make you want to get right in the kitchen.

THE SECRET GARDEN

P.O. Box 544
Park Rapids, MN 56470
(218) 732-4866
www.secretgardengourmet.com

Anne Morgan and her husband, Dewane, specialize in unusual prairie products such as natural lake wild rice, wild bergamot and giant hyssop teas from Midheaven Farm, wild rice pancake mix, wild fruit syrups, and clover-basswood blossom honey.

SEEDS BLÜM

HC 33 Idaho City Stage
Boise, ID 83706
(800) 742-1423
www.seedsblum.com

Seed catalog featuring heirloom varieties and hard-to-find seeds such as Giant Hyssop for prairie tea, spring and winter wheat for the home garden, Nutmeg melon, garden huckleberries, and many more.

STAFFORD COUNTY FLOUR MILLS COMPANY

P.O. Box 7
Hudson, KS 67545-0007
(316) 458-4121
www.flour.com

In 1882, Gustav Krug migrated from Saxony, Germany and settled on a small farm in Hudson, Kansas. Gustav had a vision and desire to mill not just a good flour, but a great flour. In 1904, his dream became a reality when the original seventy-five-barrel flour mill was built in Hudson. Today, Hudson Cream Flour, milled from hard red winter wheat, is a "cream of the crop" all-purpose flour, whose virtues have been extolled in major food magazines. It's well worth ordering by mail. The company also offers high-gluten or bread flour milled from hard red spring wheat from Prairie Flour Mills, founded by Johann Leitgeb, a farmer from Austria, and Andreas Boeorsch, a farmer from Germany, in Manitoba's Red River Valley in the late nineteenth century.

SUR LA TABLE
Catalog Division
1765 Sixth Avenue South
Seattle, WA 98134-1608
(800) 243-0852
www.surlatable.com

Cookware stores and catalog offering bannetons, an electric grain mill, an automatic bread machine, electric stand mixers, wooden butter molds, and other accoutrements for baking and serving homemade breads.

THE WALL-ROGALSKY MILLING CO.
McPherson, KS 67460

An independent mill in the heart of wheat country, producing self-rising, all-purpose, bread, unbleached, and whole wheat flours. Their pancake and waffle mix makes incredible pancakes.

THE WHEAT BIN
201 West Cole
P.O. Box 797
Moundridge, KS 67107
(620) 345-2611
e-mail: wbin@wheatbin.com
www.wheatbin.com

Locally grown and ground flours including white whole wheat, rye, and soy, some of them stoneground. Their online catalog offers red and white wheat berries and several different types of grain mills for home milling.

Prairie Bakeries

THE BREADBASKET RESTAURANT & BAKERY
219 North Main
Newton, KS 67114
(316) 263-3811

Russian Mennonite regional specialties: the ravioli-like verenicke, breads from locally grown and milled wheat, zwieback (rich yeast rolls with a topknot; also sliced and twice-baked as a snack), yeast-dough coffee cakes, peppernuts.

CORNER BAKERY
2711 West George Street
Chicago, IL 60610
(773) 463-0665

Bakery-café famous for its hearth-style breads, shaped by hand and baked in a European steam-injected oven. Several other locations throughout Chicago.

DINKEL'S
3329 North Lincoln Avenue
Chicago, IL 60657
(773) 281-7300
www.dinkels.com

Strudel heaven: praline pecan, poppy seed, walnut, and almond apricot.

EVERIX BAKERY
120 West Second Street
Fond du Lac, WI 54935
(920) 921-2250

More than 100 years old, a landmark bakery with old hardwood floors where everything is still made from scratch. Semmel (hard) rolls, kolache, fresh peach coffee cake, Danish pastry.

KOBE HOUSE
212 South Sterling
Sugar Creek, MO 64054
(816) 254-3334

Specializes in Croatian baked goods: povitica, egg bread, specialty cookies.

NEW GLARUS BAKERY AND TEA ROOM
534 First Street
New Glarus, WI 53574
(608) 527-2916

Swiss bakery featuring nut horns, spicy pear bread, bee sting kuchen, stollen, hearth breads.

O & H DANISH BAKERY

1841 Douglas Avenue
Racine, WI 53402
(414) 637-8895
(800) 227-6665 for mail order

Third-generation bakery. Throughout most of the year, makes 2,000 kringles a week, just for the mail-order side of their business; during December, produces 15,000 kringles with thirty different fillings.

PETER SCIORTINO'S BAKERY

1101 East Brady Street
Milwaukee, WI 53202
(414) 272-4623

Owned by Peter Sciortino from 1946 to 1997, now owned by Giuseppe Vella, a former employee. Italian bread, panettone, Italian cookies, cannoli.

SYKORA BAKERY

73 Sixteenth Avenue
Cedar Rapids, IA 52404
(319) 364-5271

Czech bakery in the Czech Village area of Cedar Rapids, still making *pernik* (honey bread), bishop's bread, dumplings, caraway sticks, poppy seed strudel.

QUALITY BAKERY

154 North Iowa Street
Dodgeville, WI 53533
(608) 935-3812

Cornish saffron bread and buns, English tea biscuits, Cornish pasties (which have been popular since Cornish miners settled in the area in the early 1800s).

VIRGINIA BAKERY

286 Ludlow Avenue
Cincinnati, OH
(513) 861-0672

Wonderful schnecken—decadent, buttery, sugary, and cinnamony—every weekend.

WHEATFIELDS BAKERY AND CAFÉ

904 Vermont
Lawrence, KS 66044
(785) 841-5553

Artisanal bakery and café featuring breads crafted from a simple starter, fed three times a day with regional organic flours and spring water. Founded by Freestate Brewery owner Chuck Magerl and artisanal baker Thom Leonard of Farm to Market Breads in Kansas City.

ZINGERMAN'S BAKEHOUSE

422 Detroit Street
Ann Arbor, MI 48104
(888) 636-8162
www.zingermans.com

A variety of artisanal breads, Jewish breads such as challah and Chernushka rye, sour cream coffee cake, currant scones, stollen, panettone. In 1982, Zingerman's partners Ari Weinzweig and Mo Frechette started a culinary ripple in the Ann Arbor pool that has since spread across the country.

Index